Java Programming
A Beginner's Course

Noel Kalicharan

Senior Lecturer, Computer Science
The University of the West Indies
St. Augustine, Trinidad

First published September 2007

© Noel Kalicharan, 2007
  noel.kalicharan@sta.uwi.edu
  noelk@hotmail.com

All rights reserved

The text of this publication, or any part thereof, may not be reproduced or transmitted in any form or by any means, electronic or mechanical, including photocopying, recording, storage in an information retrieval system, the Internet, or otherwise, without prior written permission of the author.

Preface

This book attempts to teach computer programming to the complete beginner using the Java language. As such, it assumes you have no knowledge whatsoever about programming. And if you are worried that you are not good at high-school mathematics, don't be. It is a myth that you must be good at mathematics to learn programming. In this book, a knowledge of primary school mathematics is all that is required—basic addition, subtraction, multiplication, division, finding the percentage of some quantity, finding an average or the larger of two quantities.

What will be an asset is the ability to think logically or to follow a logical argument. If you are good at presenting convincing arguments, you will probably be a good programmer. Even if you aren't, programming is the perfect vehicle for teaching logical thinking skills. You should learn programming for these skills even if you never intend to become a serious programmer.

The main goal of this book is to teach fundamental programming principles using Java, one of the most widely used programming languages in the world today. Java is considered a 'modern' language. Today it is used for writing all kinds of programs—wordprocessing programs, spreadsheet programs, database management programs, accounting programs, games, educational software—the list is endless.

However, this book is more about teaching programming basics than it is about teaching Java. We discuss only those features and statements in Java that are necessary to achieve our goal. Once you learn the principles well, they can be applied to any language.

Though Java is an object-oriented programming language, this book does not take the 'object-oriented' approach to teaching basic programming concepts. This is deliberate. When Java came on the scene, many people switched to teaching programming starting out with 'objects'. We did. For the most part, this has not worked well. Direct experience with hundreds of undergraduate students indicated that they learnt about objects but failed to come to terms with very elementary ideas—things like reading character or numeric data and writing functions with a little more than trivial logic. They built the house but the foundation was weak.

We are now convinced that it is best to ground the student in traditional 'procedural' concepts before tackling objects. Our experience over the last few years has shown that this approach is working well. By the time we get to objects, the student seems more comfortable and ready to understand the new ideas. Because of the solid foundation, we can use more meaningful and realistic examples—not just trivial, artificial ones—in working with objects. This book is geared to building the foundation. It ends with an introduction to objects.

Chapter 1 gives an overview of the programming process. Chapter 2 describes the basic building blocks needed to write programs. Chapter 3 explains how to write programs with the simplest kind of logic—sequence logic. Chapter 4 shows how to write programs which can make decisions. Chapter 5 explains the notion of 'looping' and how to use this powerful programming idea to solve more interesting problems. Chapter 6 deals with the oft-neglected, but important, topic of working with characters. Chapter 7 introduces methods—the key concept needed for writing large programs. Chapter 8 tackles the nemesis of many would-be programmers—array processing. Chapter 9 deals with strings in some detail. Chapter 10 gives an introduction to classes and objects.

Before Java 5.0, it was difficult to write programs to do a simple thing like read numbers and strings. Someone, like the author of a book, had to write a 'class' for you to use since Java did not provide such facilities. But Java 5.0 introduced the Scanner class, making life much easier for beginning programmers and authors.

Previously, it was also difficult to print nicely formatted output. Borrowing yet again from C, Java 5.0 provides printf, an almost exact duplicate of the powerful C statement for printing output. With Scanner and printf, the book is self-contained. It does not depend on having someone provide a class to read data and print output.

The first step in becoming a good programmer is learning the syntax rules of the programming language. This is the easy part and many people mistakenly believe that this makes them a programmer. They get carried away by the cosmetics— they learn the features of a language without learning how to use them to solve problems. Of course, you must learn some features. But it is far better to learn a few features and be able to use them to solve many problems rather than learn many features but can't use them to solve anything. For this reason, this book introduces a feature and then discusses many examples to illustrate how the feature can be used to solve different problems.

This book is intended for anyone who is learning programming for the first time, regardless of age or institution. The material has been taught successfully to students preparing for high-school examinations in Computer Studies or Information Technology, students at college, university and other tertiary-level institutions.

While computer programming is essentially a mental activity and you can learn a fair amount of programming from just reading the book, it is important that you "get your hands dirty" by writing and running programs. One of life's thrills is to write your first program and get it to run successfully on a computer. Don't miss out on it.

But do not stop there. The best way to learn programming well is to write programs to solve new problems. The end-of-chapter exercises are a very rich source of problems, a result of the author's more than 30 years in the teaching of programming.

Thank you for taking the time to read this book. We trust that you will enjoy your experience here and will get to the point where you can continue your programming journey in a painless, pleasant and enjoyable way.

Noel Kalicharan

Contents

1 Elementary Programming Concepts 1
   1.1   How a computer solves a problem 3
          1.1.1   Define the problem 3
          1.1.2   Analyze the problem 4
          1.1.3   Develop an algorithm for solving the problem 4
          1.1.4   Write the program for the algorithm 6
          1.1.5   Test and debug the program 8
          1.1.6   Document the program 9
          1.1.7   Maintain the program 10
   1.2   How a computer executes a program 10
   1.3   Data types 11
   1.4   Characters 12
   1.5   Welcome to Java Programming 13
          1.5.1   Running the program 15
          1.5.2   A word on program layout 15
   1.6   Writing output with **printf** 16
          1.6.1   The newline character, **\n** (backslash **n**) 16
          1.6.2   Escape sequences 18
          1.6.3   Printing the value of a variable 18
   1.7   Comments 19
   1.8   Programming with variables 20
   Exercises 1 23

2 Java – the basics 24
   2.1   The Java alphabet 25
   2.2   Java tokens 25
          2.2.1   Reserved words 27
          2.2.2   Identifiers 28
   2.3   Basic data types 29
   2.4   The integer types – **byte, short, int, long** 30
          2.4.1   Declaring variables 31
          2.4.2   Integer expressions 31
          2.4.3   Precedence of operators 32
          2.4.4   Printing an integer using a "field width" 33
   2.5   Floating-point numbers – the types **float** and **double** 35
          2.5.1   Printing the values of **double** and **float** variables 36
          2.5.2   Assignment between **double** and **float** 38
          2.5.3   Floating-point expressions 38
          2.5.4   Expressions with integer and floating-point values 39
          2.5.5   Assigning integer types to **double/float** 40
          2.5.6   Assigning **double/float** to integer types 41
   2.6   The type **char** 42

2.7	The type **boolean**	43
2.8	Strings	44
2.9	The assignment statement	46
2.10	**printf**	47
	Exercises 2	49

3 Writing programs using sequence logic 51

3.1	How to read data supplied by a user	51
3.2	How to read data into a **double/float** variable	55
3.3	How to read strings	57
3.4	Examples	58
	Exercises 3	65

4 Writing programs using selection logic 67

4.1	Boolean expressions	67
4.2	The **if** construct	70
	Example – finding the sum of two lengths	73
4.3	The **if...else** construct	76
	Example – calculating pay	78
4.4	On program testing	81
4.5	Using symbolic constants in Java	82
4.6	More examples	84
	Example – printing a letter grade	84
	Example – classifying a triangle	87
	Exercises 4	88

5 Writing programs using repetition logic 91

5.1	The **while** construct	91
	Example – finding the highest common factor	96
5.2	Keeping a count	98
	Finding the average	99
5.3	Increment and decrement operators	100
5.4	Assignment operators	101
5.5	Finding the largest	102
5.6	Finding the smallest	104
5.7	How to read data from a file	106
5.8	How to send output to a file	110
5.9	Example – payroll	112
5.10	The **for** construct	117
5.11	Producing multiplication tables	123
5.12	Temperature conversion table	127
5.13	The expressive power of **for**	129
	Exercises 5	130

6 Working with characters 133
- 6.1 Character constants and values 133
- 6.2 Characters in arithmetic expressions 134
- 6.3 Reading and printing characters 135
- 6.4 Counting characters 142
- 6.5 Counting blanks in a line of data 143
- 6.6 Comparing characters 144
- 6.7 Reading characters from a file 145
- 6.8 Writing characters to a file 147
- 6.9 Converting digit characters to an integer 150
- Exercises 6 152

7 Methods 154
- 7.1 skipLines 155
- 7.2 A program with a method 156
  - The method header 157
  - How a method gets its data 157
- 7.3 max 159
- 7.4 Print the day 163
- 7.5 Highest Common Factor 165
- 7.6 factorial 167
- 7.7 An example – job charge 174
- 7.8 An example – calculating pay 175
- 7.9 An example – finding the sum of exact divisors 175
  - Classifying numbers as deficient, perfect or abundant 176
- 7.10 Some character functions 177
- 7.11 Example – fetch the next integer 180
- Exercises 7 182

8 Working with arrays 184
- 8.1 Declaring an array 185
- 8.2 Storing values in an array 187
- 8.3 Example – finding average and differences from average 190
- 8.4 Example – letter frequency count 192
- 8.5 Passing an array as an argument to a method/function 195
- 8.6 Finding the largest number in an array 197
- 8.7 Finding the smallest number in an array 199
- 8.8 Example – a voting problem 200
- 8.9 Searching an array - sequential search 204
- 8.10 Sorting an array – selection sort 207
- 8.11 Sorting an array – insertion sort 211
- 8.12 Inserting an element in place 216
- 8.13 Binary search 217
- 8.14 Merging sorted lists 220
- Exercises 8 223

9 Strings 226
9.1 Creating strings 227
9.2 Some useful **String** methods 228
9.3 Example – palindrome 230
9.4 Array of strings – name of the day revisited 234
     The **do...while** statement 235
9.5 Strings and character arrays 236
9.6 A flexible **getString** function 240
9.7 A Geography quiz program 243
9.8 Improving Geography quiz 245
9.9 Passing a **String** as an argument 249
9.10 Searching a **String** array 250
9.11 Sorting a **String** array 250
9.12 Example – word frequency count 252
Exercises 9 255

10 Introduction to objects 258
10.1 Defining classes and creating objects 259
10.2 Constructors 264
10.3 Data encapsulation, accessor and mutator methods 267
10.4 Printing an object's data 272
10.5 The class **Part** 274
10.6 Working with objects 277
10.7 The **null** pointer 281
10.8 Passing an object as an argument 281
10.9 Array of objects 282
10.10 Searching an array of objects 285
10.11 Sorting an array of objects 288
10.12 Word frequency count revisited 290
Exercises 10 292

Appendix A - Keywords in Java 294
Appendix B - The ASCII character set 295
Appendix C - Representation of integers 296
Appendix D - How to get a Java compiler 299

Index 300

1 Elementary programming concepts

In this chapter, we will explain:

- how a computer solves a problem
- the various stages in the development of a computer program: from problem definition to finished program
- how a computer executes a program
- what is a 'data type' and its fundamental role in writing a program
- the role of characters—the basic building blocks of all programs
- the concepts of *constants* and *variables*
- the distinction between syntax and logic errors
- how to produce basic output in Java using the **printf** statement
- what is an escape sequence
- how descriptive or explanatory comments can be included in your program
- what is an *assignment statement* and how to write one in Java

---

We are all familiar with the computer's ability to perform a wide variety of tasks. For instance, we can use it to play games, write a letter or a book, perform accounting functions for a company, learn a foreign language, listen to music on a CD, send a fax or search for information on the Internet. How is this possible, all on the same machine? The answer lies with programming—the creation of a sequence of instructions which the computer can perform (we say "execute") to accomplish each task. This sequence of instructions is called a *program*. Each task requires a different program:

- to play a game, we need a game-playing program;
- to write a letter or a book, we need a word processing program;
- to do accounts, we need an accounting program;
- to learn Spanish, we need a program that teaches Spanish;
- to listen to a CD, we need a music-playing program;
- to send a fax, we need a fax-sending program;
- to use the Internet, we need a program called a *Web browser*;

For every task we want to perform, we need an appropriate program. And in order for the computer to run a program, the program must be stored (we sometimes say *loaded*) in the computer's memory.

But what is the nature of a program? First, we need to know that computers are built to execute instructions written in what is called *machine language*. In machine language, everything is expressed in terms of the binary number system —1's and 0's. Each computer has its own machine language and the computer can execute instructions written *in that language only*.

The instructions themselves are very simple, for example, add or subtract two numbers, compare one number with another or copy a number from one place to another. How, then, can the computer perform such a wide variety of tasks, solving such a wide variety of problems, with such simple instructions?

The answer is that no matter how complex an activity may seem, it can usually be broken down into a series of simple steps. It is the ability to analyze a complex problem and express its solution in terms of simple computer instructions that is one of the hallmarks of a good programmer.

Machine language is considered a *low-level* programming language. In the early days of computing (1940s and 50s) programmers had to write programs in machine language, that is, express all their instructions using 1s and 0s.

To make life a little easier for them, *assembly language* was developed. This was closely related to machine language but it allowed the programmer to use mnemonic[1] instruction codes (such as **ADD**) and names for storage locations (such as **sum**) rather than strings of binary digits (bits). For instance, a programmer could refer to a number by **sum** rather than have to remember that the number was stored in memory location 10000111011010111.

A program called an *assembler* is used to convert an assembly language program into machine language. Still, programming this way had several drawbacks:

- it was very tedious and error prone;
- it forced the programmer to think in terms of the machine rather than in terms of his problem;
- a program written in the machine language of one computer could not be run on a computer with a different machine language. Changing your computer could mean having to rewrite all your programs.

To overcome these problems, *high-level* or *problem-oriented* languages were developed in the late 1950s and 60s. The most popular of these were FORTRAN (FORmula TRANslation) and COBOL (COmmon Business-Oriented Language). FORTRAN was designed for solving scientific and engineering problems which involved a great deal of numerical computation. COBOL was designed to solve the data-processing problems of the business community.

The idea was to allow the programmer to think about a problem in terms familiar to him and relevant to the problem rather than have to worry about the machine. So, for instance, if he wanted to know the larger of two quantities, **A** and **B**, he could write

---

[1] Meant to help to remember; e.g. DIV suggests what it means—divide

> IF A IS GREATER THAN B THEN BIGGER = A ELSE BIGGER = B

rather than have to fiddle with several machine or assembly language instructions to get the same result. Thus high-level languages enabled the programmer to concentrate on solving the problem at hand, without the added burden of worrying about the idiosyncrasies[2] of a particular machine.

However, the computer *still* could only *execute* instructions written in machine language. A program called a *compiler* is used to translate a program written in a high-level language to machine language.

Thus we speak of a FORTRAN compiler or a COBOL compiler for translating FORTRAN and COBOL programs, respectively. But that's not the whole story. Since each computer has its own machine language, we must have, say, a FORTRAN compiler for an Intel Pentium computer and a FORTRAN compiler for a Macintosh G5 computer.

1.1 How a computer solves a problem

Solving a problem on a computer involves the following activities:

(1) Define the problem.
(2) Analyze the problem.
(3) Develop an *algorithm* (a method) for solving the problem.
(4) Write the computer program which *implements* the algorithm.
(5) Test and debug (find the errors in) the program.
(6) Document the program. (Explain how the program works and how to use it).
(7) Maintain the program.

There is normally some overlap of these activities. For example, with a large program, a portion may be written and tested before another portion is written. Also, documentation should be done at the same time as all the other activities; each activity produces its own items of documentation which will be part of the final program documentation.

1.1.1 Define the problem

Suppose we want to help a child work out the areas of squares. This defines a problem to be solved. However, a brief analysis reveals that the definition is not complete or specific enough to proceed with developing a program. Talking with the child might reveal that she needs a program which asks her to enter the length of a side of the square; the program then prints the area of the square.

---

[2] Distinguishing characteristics or features

1.1.2 Analyze the problem

We further analyze the problem to

(a) ensure that we have the clearest possible understanding of it;

(b) determine general requirements such as the main inputs to the program and the main outputs from the program. For more complex programs, we would, for instance, also need to decide on the kinds of *files*[3] which may be needed.

If there are several ways to solve the problem, we should consider the alternatives and choose the best or most appropriate one.

In this example, the input to the program is the length of one side of the square and the output is the area of the square. We only need to know how to calculate the area. If the side is **s**, then the area, **a**, is calculated by:

$$a = s \times s$$

1.1.3 Develop an algorithm for solving the problem

An *algorithm* is a set of instructions which, if faithfully followed, will produce a solution to a given problem or perform some specified task. When an instruction is followed, we say it is *executed*. We can speak of an algorithm for finding a word in a dictionary, for changing a punctured tyre or for playing a video game.

For any problem, there will normally be more than one algorithm to solve it. Each algorithm will have its own advantages and disadvantages. When we are searching for a word in the dictionary, one method would be to start at the beginning and look at each word in turn. A second method would be to start at the end and search backwards. Here, an advantage of the first method is that it would find a word faster if it were at the beginning, while the second method would be faster if the word were towards the end.

Another method for searching for the word would be one which used the fact that the words in a dictionary are in alphabetical order—this is the method we all use when looking up a word in a dictionary. In any situation, a programmer would usually have a choice of algorithms, and it is one of her more important jobs to decide which algorithm is the best, and why this is so.

In our example, we must write the instructions in our algorithm in such a way that they can be easily converted into a form which the computer can follow. Computer instructions fall into three main categories:

(1) *Input* instructions, used for supplying data from the 'outside world' to a program; this is usually done via the keyboard or a file.

---

[3] Think of a file as a place in the computer used for storing things like documents, pictures, programs, even songs and movies

(2) *Processing* instructions, used for manipulating data inside the computer. These instructions allow us to add, subtract, multiply and divide; they also allow us to compare two values, and act according to the result of the comparison. Also, we can move data from one location in the computer's memory to another location.

(3) *Output* instructions, used for getting information out of the computer to the outside world.

Data and variables

All computer programs, except the most trivial, are written to operate on *data*. For example:

- the data for an action game might be keys pressed or the position of the cursor when the mouse is clicked;
- the data for a word processing program are the keys pressed while you are typing a letter;
- the data for an accounting program would include, among other things, expenses and income;
- the data for a program that teaches Spanish could be an English word that you type in response to a question.

Recall that a program must be stored in the computer's memory for it to be run. When data is supplied to a program, that data is also stored in memory. Thus we think of memory as a place for holding programs and data. One of the nice things about programming in a high-level language (as opposed to machine language) is that you don't have to worry about which memory locations are used to store your data. But how do we refer to an item of data, given that there may be many data items in memory?

Think of memory as a set of boxes (or storage locations). Each box can hold one item of data, for example, one number. We can give a name to a box, and we will be able to refer to that box by the given name. In our example, we will need two boxes, one to hold the side of the square and one to hold the area. We will call these boxes **s** and **a**, respectively.

If we wish, we can change the value in a box at any time; since the values can vary, **s** and **a** are called variable names, or simply *variables*. Thus, a variable is a name associated with a particular memory location or, if you wish, it is a *label* for the memory location. We can speak of giving a variable a value, or setting a variable to a specific value, 1, say. Important points to remember are:

- a box can hold only one value at a time; if we put in a new value, the old one is lost;
- we must not assume that a box contains *any* value unless we specifically store a value in the box. In particular, we must not assume that the box contains 0.

Variables are a common feature of computer programs. It is very difficult to imagine what programming would be like without them. In everyday life, we often use variables. For example, we speak of an 'address'. Here, 'address' is a variable whose value depends on the person under consideration. Other common variables are telephone number, name of school, subject, size of population, type of car, television model, etc. (What are some possible values of these variables?)

Example – develop the algorithm

Using the notion of an algorithm and the concept of a variable, we develop the following algorithm for calculating the area of a square, given one side:

Algorithm for calculating area of square, given one side

(1) Ask the user for the length of a side
(2) Store the value in the box **s**
(3) Calculate the area of the square (**s** × **s**)
(4) Store the area in the box **a**
(5) Print the value in box **a**, appropriately labelled
(6) Stop

When an algorithm is developed, it must be checked to make sure that it is doing its intended job correctly. We can test an algorithm by 'playing computer', that is, we execute the instructions by hand, using appropriate data values. This process is called *dry running* or *desk checking* the algorithm. It is used to pinpoint any errors in logic before the computer program is actually written. We should *never* start to write programming code unless we are confident that the algorithm is correct.

1.1.4 Write the program for the algorithm

We have specified the algorithm using English statements. However, these statements are sufficiently 'computer-oriented' for a computer program to be written directly from them. Before we do this, let us see how we expect the program to work from the user's point of view.

First, the program will type the request for the length of a side; we say the program *prompts* the user to supply data. The screen display might look like this:

```
Enter length of side:
```

Elementary programming concepts

The computer will then wait for the user to type the length. Suppose the user types 12. The display will look like this:

```
Enter length of side: 12
```

The program will then accept (we say *read*) the number typed, calculate the area and print the result. The display may look like this:

```
Enter length of side: 12

Area of square is 144
```

Here we have specified what the *output* of the program should look like. For instance, there is a blank line between the prompt line and the line that gives the answer; we have also specified the exact form of the answer. This is a simple example of *output design*. This is necessary since the programmer cannot write the program unless he knows the precise output required.

In order to write the computer program from the algorithm, a suitable *programming language* must be chosen. We can think of a *program* as a set of instructions, *written in a programming language*, which, when executed, will produce a solution to a given problem or perform some specified task.

The major difference between an algorithm and a program is that an algorithm can be written using informal language without having to follow any special rules (though some *conventions*[4] are usually followed) whereas a program is written in a programming language and *must* follow all the rules (the *syntax* rules) of the language. (Similarly, if we wish to write correct English, we must follow the syntax rules of the English language).

In this book, we will be showing you how to write programs in Java, the programming language developed by Sun Microsystems in the 1990s, and one of the most popular and widely used today. ①very recent

The Java program which requests the user to enter the length of a side and prints the area of the square is shown on the next page.

It is not too important that you understand anything about this program at this time. But you can observe that a Java program consists of something called a **class** (named **AreaOfSquare** here) which contains something (a *method*) called **main**. After the name of the class comes a left brace { which indicates the beginning of the class; a matching right brace } (the last one) ends the class. Similarly, there is a left brace to begin **main** and a matching right brace to end it.

---

[4] convention—an agreed-upon way of doing something; it is not *required* that we do it this way

```
import java.util.*;
public class AreaOfSquare {
    public static void main(String[] args) {
        Scanner in = new Scanner(System.in);
        int a, s; //declare the 'boxes' to hold side and area
        System.out.printf("Enter length of side: ");
        s = in.nextInt();    //read and store length in s
        a = s * s;           //calculate area; store in a
        System.out.printf("\nArea of square is %d\n", a);
    } //end main
} //end class AreaOfSquare
```

The statement

    int a, s;

is called a *declaration*. The parts after // are *comments* which help to explain the program to a human being but have no effect when the program is run. And * is used to denote multiplication.

Note also that Java uses **System.in** to refer to the *standard input* (usually the keyboard) and **System.out** to refer to the *standard output* (usually the monitor/screen). In this program, the user will be expected to type the length of the side on the keyboard and the computer will print the result on the monitor (screen).

All of these terms will be explained in detail in due course.

Finally, a program written in a high-level language is usually referred to as a *source program* or *source code*.

1.1.5 Test and debug the program

Having written the program, the next job is to *test* it to find out whether it is doing its intended job. Testing a program involves the following steps:

1. *compile the program*: recall that a computer can execute a program written in *machine language only*. Before the computer can run our Java program, the latter must be converted to machine language. We say that the *source code* must be converted to *object code* or *machine code*[5]. The program which does this job is called a *compiler*. Appendix D tells you how you can acquire a Java compiler for writing and running your programs.

   Among other things, a compiler will check the source code for *syntax errors*—errors which arise from breaking the rules for writing statements in

---

[5] Java, however, does not produce machine code directly. It converts Java source code into something called Java *bytecode*. This bytecode is executed (we say *interpreted*) by another program called the Java interpreter. We will get to details later.

the language. For example, a common syntax error in writing Java programs is to omit a semicolon or to put one where it is not required.

If the program contains syntax errors, these must be corrected before compiling it again. When the program is free from syntax errors, the compiler will convert it to machine language (*bytecode* in Java) and we can go on to the next step.

2. *run the program*: here we request the computer to execute the program and we supply data to the program *for which we know* the *answer*. Such data is called *test data*. Some values we can use for the length of a side are 3, 12 and 20.

If the program does not give us the answers 9, 144 and 400, respectively, then we know that the program contains at least one *logic* error. A logic error is one which causes a program to give incorrect results for valid data. A logic error may also cause a program to *crash* (come to an abrupt halt).

If a program contains logic errors, we must *debug* the program—we must find and correct any errors that are causing the program to produce wrong answers.

To illustrate, suppose the statement which calculates the area was written (incorrectly) as:

```
a = s + s;
```

and when the program is run, 10 is entered for the length. Assume we *know* that the area should be 100. But when we run the program, we get

```
Enter length of side: 10
Area of square is 20
```

Since this is **not** the answer we expect, we know that there is an error (perhaps more than one) in the program. Since the area is wrong, the logical place to start looking for the error is in the statement which calculates the area. If we look closely, we should discover that **+** was typed instead of *****. When this correction is made, the program works fine.

1.1.6 Document the program

The final job is to complete the *documentation* of the program. So far, our documentation includes:

- the statement of the problem;
- the algorithm for solving the problem;
- the program listing;
- test data and the results produced by the program.

These are some of the items that make up the *technical documentation* of the program. This is documentation that is useful to a programmer, perhaps for modifying the program at a later stage.

The other kind of documentation which must be written is *user documentation*. This enables a non-technical person to use the program without needing to know about the internal workings of the program. Among other things, the user needs to know how to load the program in the computer and how to use the various features of the program. If appropriate, the user will also need to know how to handle unusual situations which may arise while the program is being used.

1.1.7 Maintain the program

It's not done!

Except for things like class assignments, programs are normally meant to be used over a long period of time. During this time, errors may be discovered which previously went unnoticed. Errors may also surface because of conditions or data that never arose before. Whatever the reason, such errors must be corrected.

But a program may need to be modified for other reasons. Perhaps the assumptions made when the program was written have now changed due to changed company policy or even due to a change in government regulations (e.g. changes in income tax rates). Perhaps the company is changing its computer system and the program needs to be *migrated* to the new system. We say the program must be *maintained*.

Whether or not this is easy to do depends a lot on how the original program was written. If it was well-designed and properly documented, then the job of the *maintenance programmer* would be made so much easier.

1.2 How a computer executes a program

First, recall that a computer can execute a program written in machine language only. For the computer to execute the instructions of such a program, those instructions must be *loaded* into the computer's *memory* (also called *primary storage*), like this:

memory

| instruction 1 |
| instruction 2 |
| instruction 3 |
| etc. |

You can think of memory as a series of storage locations, numbered consecutively starting at 0. Thus you can speak of memory location 27 or memory location 31548. The number associated with a memory location is called its *address*.

Elementary programming concepts

A computer *runs* a program by executing its first instruction, then the second, then the third, and so on. It is possible that one instruction might say to jump over several instructions to a particular one and continue executing from there. Another might say to go back to a previous instruction and execute it again.

No matter what the instructions are, the computer faithfully executes them exactly as specified. That is why it is so important that programs specify precisely and exactly what must be done. The computer cannot know what you *intend*, it can only execute what you actually *write*. If you give the computer the wrong instruction, it will blindly execute it just as you specify, giving incorrect results.

1.3 Data types

Every day we meet names and numbers—at home, at work, at school or at play. A person's name is a type of data; so is a number. We can thus speak of the two *data types* called 'name' and 'number'. In the statement:

> **Mimi bought 3 dresses for $199.95**

we can find:
- an example of a name: **Mimi**;
- two examples of numbers: 3 and 199.95.

Usually, we find it convenient to divide numbers into two kinds:

(1) whole numbers, or *integers*;
(2) numbers with a decimal point, so-called *real* or *floating-point* numbers.

In the example, 3 is an integer and 199.95 is a real number.

Exercise: Identify the data types—names, integers and real numbers—in the following:

(a) Bill's batting average was 35.25 with a highest score of 75.
(b) Abigail, who lives at 41 Third Ave, worked 36 hours at $11.50 per hour.
(c) In his 8 subjects, Richard's average mark was 68.5.

Generally speaking, programs are written to manipulate data of various types. We use the term *numeric* to refer to numbers (integer or floating-point). We use the term *string* to refer to non-numeric data such as a name, address, job description, title of a song or vehicle number (which is not really a number as far as the computer is concerned—it usually contains letters, e.g. **PBN8652**).

Programming languages in general, and Java in particular, precisely define the various types of data which can be manipulated by programs written in those languages. Integer, real (or floating-point), character (data consisting of a single character such as **'K'** or **'%'**) and string data types are the most common.

Each data type defines *constants* of that type. For example,

- some integer constants are 3, -52, 0 and 9813;
- some real (or floating-point) constants are 3.142, -5.0, 345.21 and 1.16;
- some character constants are 't', '+', '8' and 'R';
- some string constants are "Hi there", "The Art of Computer Programming" and "Java World".

Note that, in Java, a *character* constant is delimited by single quotes and a *string* constant is delimited by double quotes.

When we use a variable in a program, we have to say what type of data (the kind of constants) we intend to store in that variable—we say we must *declare* the variable. It is usually an error if we try to store a type of data in a variable that is different from the type that the variable is declared to hold (we get a *type mismatch* error). For example, it is an error to attempt to store a string constant in an integer variable. Java data types are discussed in detail in Chapter 2.

1.4 Characters

In computer terminology, we use the term *character* to refer to any one of the following:

- a digit from 0 to 9;
- an uppercase letter from **A** to **Z**;
- a lowercase letter from **a** to **z**;
- a special symbol like (,), $, =, <, >, +, -, /, *, etc.

The following are commonly used terms:

letter	–	one of **a** to **z** or **A** to **Z**
lowercase letter	–	one of **a** to **z**
uppercase letter	–	one of **A** to **Z**
digit	–	one of 0,1,2,3,4,5,6,7,8,9
special character	–	any symbol except a letter or a digit e.g. +, <, >, $, &, *, /, =
alphabetic	–	used to refer to a letter
numeric	–	used to refer to a digit
alphanumeric	–	used to refer to a letter or a digit

Characters are the basic building blocks used in writing programs;

we put characters together to form *variables* and *constants*;

we put variables, constants and special characters to form *expressions* such as (a + 2.5) * c;

we add special words such as **if, else** and **while** to form *statements* such as if (a > 0) b = a + 2;

and we put statements together to form *programs*.

1.5 Welcome to Java Programming

We take a quick peek at the Java programming language by writing a program to print, on the screen, the message

Welcome to Trinidad & Tobago

One solution is Program P1.1.

```
Program P1.1
public class Welcome {
    public static void main(String[] args) {
        System.out.printf("Welcome to Trinidad & Tobago");
    }
}
```

A Java program consists of one or more *classes*. Our sample program consists of one class called **Welcome**. A class normally contains two kinds of members—*variables* and *methods*. A *variable* is used to hold data used by the class. *Method* is the Java term for a group of statements which perform a subtask, perhaps one of many, which can be executed to help accomplish the task for which the class is written. (Other languages use the term *function* instead of *method*). Our program contains no variables and one method called **main**.

For now, the programs we will write *must* have a method named **main** which we will write with the following "header":

public static void main(String[] args)

The Java interpreter starts executing a program by executing the statements in **main**. The word **public** makes this possible; it indicates that **main** is 'known' (and can be called from) outside the class in which it is defined. Thus the Java interpreter 'knows' and can 'call' **main**. The other terms in the header of **main** will be explained in due course. For now, just think of them as required.

The *body* of **main** (the part between the left and right braces) contains one statement:

System.out.printf("Welcome to Trinidad & Tobago");

When executed, this statement will print

Welcome to Trinidad & Tobago

on the 'standard output'. For now, take this to mean the monitor (screen).

System.out.printf is a standard method[6] which can be used for printing data on the 'standard output'. To be more precise, **printf** is a method which belongs to the *object* **System.out**; for now, the distinction is not important. For the most part, we will refer to the method simply as **printf**. In the example, the data to be printed consists of a *string* (a set of characters enclosed in double quotation marks).

Let us take a closer look at Program P1.1.

public class Welcome says that we are defining a public **class** whose name is **Welcome**. In this book, we begin class names with a capital letter but this is not *required* by Java. A public class is accessible to other classes. Our programs will have at least one public class.

Next comes a left brace (curly bracket), {; this indicates the start of the class. A matching right brace, }, (the last one) indicates the end of the class. In general, left and right braces are used to mark off blocks or sections of code.

The header of **main** comes next. After the header is a left brace indicating the start of the body of **main**. A matching right brace indicates the end of **main**. All methods have such matching braces; between them come the statements that comprise the method. This is illustrated as follows[7]:

```
<method header> {
   <statements of the method>
}
```

In this book, we use the *convention* of putting the left brace on the same line as the header. The above could have been written:

```
<method header>
{
   <statements of the method>
}
```

In Program P1.1, there is just one statement in **main**:

```
System.out.printf("Welcome to Trinidad & Tobago");
```

In Java, the semicolon is used to terminate a statement and is considered part of the statement. The string **"Welcome to Trinidad & Tobago"** is said to be an *argument* to the method **System.out.printf**. The argument is written within round brackets (parentheses).

---

[6] **printf** was introduced in JDK 5.0. It is much more versatile and flexible than the older **print** and **println** methods. In this book, we mainly use **printf**.

[7] In this book, we use the angle brackets, < and >, to specify a 'place-holder' for some item.

Elementary programming concepts

1.5.1 Running the program

Having written the program on paper, the next task is to get it running on a real computer. How this is done varies somewhat from one computer system to the next but, in general, the following steps must be performed:

(1) type the program to a file. The file should be named **Welcome.java** (make sure and use **W** instead of **w**). Java is *case-sensitive*; this means that it makes a difference if you use an uppercase as opposed to a lowercase letter. For example, **Welcome** is different from **welcome**. *Observe that the first part of the file name is the same as the name of the class.* This is required by Java.

(2) invoke your Java compiler to compile the program in the file **Welcome.java**. A typical command for doing this is:

    javac Welcome.java

where **javac** specifies that the Java compiler is required; it expects to find a file, **Welcome.java**, containing a Java program. If any (syntax) errors are detected during the compile phase, you must correct these errors and try again.

When there are no more syntax errors, the compiler will produce a 'class file' called **Welcome.class**, containing the Java bytecode equivalent to your Java program.

(3) run the program. A typical command is

    java Welcome

The Java interpreter looks for a file **Welcome.class** and executes the code in its **main** method. (Note that you must *not* type the **.class** part of the filename). When this program is run,

    Welcome to Trinidad & Tobago

is printed on the screen.

1.5.2 A word on program layout

Java does not require the program to be laid out as in the example. An equivalent program is

    public class Welcome {public static void main(String[] args) {
    System.out.printf("Welcome to Trinidad & Tobago"); } }

For this small program, it probably does not matter which version we use. However, as program size increases, it becomes imperative that the layout of the program highlight the logical structure of the program, thus improving its readability. Indentation and clearly indicating which right brace matches which

reccommend although not required

left brace can help in this regard. We will see the value of this principle as our programs become more substantial.

1.6 Writing output with printf

Suppose we want to write a program to print the lines[8]:

> Where the mind is without fear
> And the head is held high

Our initial attempt might be:

```
public class Gitanjali {
  public static void main(String[] args) {
    System.out.printf("Where the mind is without fear");
    System.out.printf("And the head is held high");
  }
}
```

However, when run, this program would print:

> Where the mind is without fearAnd the head is held high

Note that the two strings are joined together (we say the strings are *concatenated*). This happens because **printf** does not place output on a *new* line, unless this is specified explicitly. Put another way, **printf** does not automatically supply a *newline* character after printing its argument(s). A newline character would cause subsequent output to begin at the left margin of the next line.

In the example, a newline character is *not* supplied after **fear** is printed so that **And the head...** is printed on the same line as **fear** and immediately after it.

1.6.1 The newline character, \n (backslash n)

To get the desired effect, we must tell **printf** to supply a newline character after printing **...without fear**. We do this by using the character sequence **\n** (backslash n) as in Program P1.2, which *must* be saved in a file named **Gitanjali.java**.

```
                    Program P1.2
public class Gitanjali {
  public static void main(String[] args) {
    System.out.printf("Where the mind is without fear\n");
    System.out.printf("And the head is held high\n");
  }
}
```

---

[8] From *The Gitanjali* by Rabindranath Tagore

Elementary programming concepts

The first **\n** says to terminate the current output line; subsequent output will start at the left margin of the next line. Thus, **And the...** will be printed on a new line. The second **\n** has the effect of terminating the second line. If it were not present, the output will still come out right, but only because this is the last line of output.

A program prints all pending output just before it terminates. (This is also the reason why our first program, P1.1, worked without **\n**).

As an embellishment, suppose we want to put a blank line between our two lines of output, like this:

> Where the mind is without fear
>
> And the head is held high

Each of the following sets of statements will accomplish this:

(1) System.out.printf("Where the mind is without fear\n\n");
     System.out.printf("And the head is held high\n");

(2) System.out.printf("Where the mind is without fear\n");
     System.out.printf("\nAnd the head is held high\n");

(3) System.out.printf("Where the mind is without fear\n");
     System.out.printf("\n");
     System.out.printf("And the head is held high\n");

We just have to make sure we print two **\n**'s between **fear** and **And**. The first **\n** ends the first line; the second ends the second line, in effect, printing a blank line. Java gives us a lot of flexibility in how we write statements to produce a desired effect.

Note for those familiar with **System.out.print** *and* **System.out.println**: you get the same effect as **print** if you supply the same arguments to **printf**. You get the same effect as **println** if you supply the same arguments to **printf** and add "\n" as the last argument. For example, the following three statements produce the same effect:

    System.out.println("And the head is held high");
    System.out.printf("And the head is held high\n");
    System.out.printf("And the head is held high" + "\n");

Exercise: Write a program to print the lyrics of your favourite song.

1.6.2 Escape sequences

Within the string argument to **printf**, the backslash (\) signals that a special effect is needed at this point. The character following the backslash specifies what to do. This combination (\ followed by another character) is referred to as an *escape sequence*. The following are some escape sequences you can use in a string in a **printf** statement:

  \n   issue a newline character
  \f   issue a new page (formfeed) character
  \t   issue a tab character
  \"   print "
  \\   print \

For example, using an escape sequence is the only way to print a double quote as part of your output. Suppose we want to print the line

    Use " to begin and end a string

If we typed

    System.out.printf("Use " to begin and end a string\n");

then Java would assume that the double quote *after* **Use** ends the string (causing a subsequent error when it can't figure out what to do with **to**). Using the escape sequence \", we can correctly print the line with:

    System.out.printf("Use \" to begin and end a string\n");

Exercise: Write a statement to print the line:

    An escape sequence starts with \

1.6.3 Printing the value of a variable

So far, we have used **printf** to print the *value* of a string constant (that is, the characters of the string excluding the quotes). We now show how we can print the *value* of a variable ignoring, for the moment, *how* the variable gets its value. (We will see how in Chapter 2.) Suppose the integer variable **a** has the value 52. The statement:

    System.out.printf("The number of students = %d\n", a);

will print:

    The number of students = 52

This **printf** is a bit different from those we have seen so far. This one has *two* arguments—a string and a variable. The string, called the *format string*, contains a *format specification* %d. (In our previous examples, the format string contained no format specifications). The effect, in this case, is that the format string is printed as before, except that the %d is replaced by the *value* of the second argument, **a**. Thus, %d is replaced by 52, giving:

```
The number of students = 52
```

We will explain **printf** and format specifications in more detail in Chapter 2 but, for now, note that we use the specification %d if we want to print an integer value.

What if we want to print more than one value? This can be done provided that *each* value has a corresponding format specification. For example, suppose that **a** has the value 14 and **b** has the value 25. Consider,

```
System.out.printf("The sum of %d and %d is %d\n", a, b, a + b);
```

This **printf** has *four* arguments—the format string and three values to be printed: **a**, **b** and **a + b**. The format string *must* contain three format specifications: the first will correspond to **a**, the second to **b** and the third to **a + b**. When the format string is printed, each %d will be replaced by the *value* of its corresponding argument, giving:

```
The sum of 14 and 25 is 39
```

Exercise: What is printed by the following statement?

```
System.out.printf("%d + %d = %d\n", a, b, a + b);
```

1.7 Comments

All programming languages let you include *comments* in your programs. Comments can be used to remind yourself (and others) of what processing is taking place or what a particular variable is being used for. They can be used to explain or clarify any aspect of a program which may be difficult to understand by just reading the programming statements. This is very important since the easier it is to understand a program, the more confidence you will have that it is correct. It is worth adding anything which makes a program easier to understand.

Remember that a comment (or lack of it) has absolutely no effect on how the program runs. If you remove all the comments from a program, it will run exactly the same way as with the comments.

Each language has its own way of specifying how a comment must be written. In Java, we write a comment by enclosing it within /* and */, for example:

```
/* This program prints a greeting */
```

A comment extends from /* to the next */ and may span one or more lines. The following is a valid comment:

```
/* This program reads characters one at a time
   and counts the number of letters found */
```

Java also lets you use // to write one-line comments. The comment extends from // to the end of the line, for example:

> a = s * s;   //calculate area; store in a

In this book, we will use mainly one-line comments.

1.8 Programming with variables

To reinforce the ideas discussed so far, let us write a program which adds the numbers 14 and 25 and prints the sum.

We would need storage locations for the two numbers and the sum. The values to be stored in these locations are *integer* values. To refer to these locations, we make up the names **a**, **b** and **sum**, say. (Any other names would do. In Java, as in all programming languages, there are rules to follow for making up variable names, for instance, a name must start with a letter and cannot contain spaces. We will see the Java rules in the next chapter.)

One possible algorithm might look like this:

> set a to 14
> set b to 25
> set sum to a + b
> print sum

The algorithm consists of four statements. The following explains the meaning of each statement:

- **set a to 14**   store the number 14 in memory location **a**; this is an example of an *assignment statement*; we assign a value to a variable.
- **set b to 25**   store the number 25 in memory location **b**.
- **set sum to a + b**   add the numbers in memory locations **a** and **b** and store the sum in memory location **sum**. The result is that 39 is stored in **sum**.
- **print sum**   print (on the screen) the value in **sum**, i.e. 39.

Program P1.3 shows how we can write this algorithm as a Java program. Note that we have named the class **ProgramP1_3** and not, say, **ProgramP1.3**. As we will see in Chapter 2 when we discuss the rules for naming things, Java does not allow us to use a period in a class name (or a variable name, for that matter). However, the underscore (_) is allowed. When we name the class **ProgramP1_3**, it follows that the program *must* be stored in a file named **ProgramP1_3.java**. Of course, if we wished, we *could* have named the class **PrintSum**, say, and store the program in a file called **PrintSum.java**.

Elementary programming concepts

> **Program P1.3**
>
> ```
> // This program prints the sum of 14 and 25. It shows how
> // to declare variables in Java and assign values to them.
> public class ProgramP1_3 {
>    public static void main(String[] args) {
>       int a, b, sum; //declare the variables
>       a = 14;
>       b = 25;
>       sum = a + b;
>       System.out.printf("%d + %d = %d\n", a, b, sum);
>    }
> }
> ```

When run, this program will print

```
14 + 25 = 39
```

In Java, variables are declared as *integer* using the required word **int**. (In programming terminology, we say that **int** is a *reserved* word). Thus, the statement:

    int a, b, sum;

'declares' that **a**, **b** and **sum** are integer variables. In Java, all variables must be declared before they are used in a program. Note that the variables are separated by commas, with a semicolon after the last one. If we were declaring just one variable (**a**, say), we would write:

    int a;

The statement

    a = 14;

is Java's way of writing the *assignment statement*

    set a to 14

It is sometimes pronounced "a becomes 14". In Java, an assignment statement consists of a variable (**a** in the example), followed by an equals sign (**=**), followed by the value to be assigned to the variable (14 in the example), followed by a semicolon. In general, the value can be a constant (like 14), a variable (like **b**) or an expression (like **a + b**). Similarly,

set b to 25 is written as

    b = 25;

and **set sum to a + b** is written as

sum = a + b;

One final point: you may have gathered from page 19 that, for this problem, the variable **sum** is not really necessary. We *could*, for instance, have omitted **sum** from the program altogether and used:

```
int a, b;
a = 14;
b = 25;
System.out.printf("%d + %d = %d\n", a, b, a + b);
```

to give the same result since Java lets us use an expression (e.g. **a + b**) as an argument to **printf**. However, if the program were longer and we needed to use the sum in other places, it would be wise to calculate and store the sum once (in **sum**, say). Whenever the sum is needed, we use **sum** rather than recalculate **a + b** each time.

Now that we have a general idea of what is involved in writing a program, we are ready to get down to the nitty-gritty of Java programming.

Elementary programming concepts

Exercises 1

1. What makes it possible to do such a variety of things on a computer?
2. Computers can execute instructions written in what language?
3. Give two advantages of assembly language over machine language.
4. Give two advantages of a high-level language over assembly language.
5. Describe two main tasks performed by a compiler.
6. Describe the steps which must be performed for a problem to be solved by a computer.
7. Distinguish between an algorithm and a program.
8. Programming instructions fall into 3 main categories; what are they?
9. Distinguish between a syntax error and a logic error.
10. What is meant by "debugging a program"?
11. Name 5 data types commonly used in programming and give examples of constants of each type.
12. What are the different classes into which characters can be divided? Give examples in each class.
13. What is the purpose of comments in a program?
14. Write a program to print **Welcome to Java** on the screen.
15. Write a program to print the following:
    There is a tide in the affairs of men
    Which, taken at the flood, leads on to fortune
16. Write a program to print any 4 lines of your favourite song or poem.
17. Same as exercise 16, but print a blank line after each line.
18. If **a** is 29 and **b** is 5, what is printed by each of the following statements?
    System.out.printf("The product of %d and %d is %d\n", a, b, a * b);
    System.out.printf("%d + %d = %d\n", a, b, a + b);
    System.out.printf("%d - %d = %d\n", a, b, a - b);
    System.out.printf("%d x %d = %d\n", a, b, a * b);
19. If **a** is 29 and **b** is 14, what is printed by the following statements?
    System.out.printf("%d + \n", a);
    System.out.printf("%d\n", b);
    System.out.printf("--\n");
    System.out.printf("%d\n", a + b);
20. If **rate** = 15, what is printed by
    (a) System.out.printf("rate\n")?
    (b) System.out.printf("%d\n", rate)?

2 Java – the basics

In this chapter, we will explain:

- what is an alphabet, a character set and a token
- what is a syntax rule and a syntax error
- what is a reserved word
- how to create identifiers in Java
- what is a symbolic constant
- what are the Java basic data types
- how to write integer and floating-point expressions
- how to print an integer using a field width
- how to print a floating-point number to a required number of decimal places
- what happens when different types are mixed in the same expression
- what happens when we assign one type of value to a different type of variable
- how to declare a variable to hold a string
- how to assign a string value to a string variable
- some things to know about the assignment statement

In this chapter, we discuss some basic concepts you need to know in order to write programs in the Java programming language.

A programming language is similar to speaking languages in many respects. It has an *alphabet* (more commonly referred to as a *character set*) from which everything in the language is constructed. It has rules for forming *words* (also called *tokens*), rules for forming statements and rules for forming programs. These are called the *syntax rules* of the language and *must* be obeyed when writing programs. If you violate a rule, your program will contain a *syntax error*. When you attempt to compile the program, the compiler will inform you of the error. You must correct it and try again. *[handwritten: compile: translate programming → machine language]*

The first step in becoming a good programmer is learning the syntax rules of the programming language. This is the easy part and many people mistakenly believe that this makes them a programmer. It is like saying that learning some rules of English grammar and being able to write some correctly formed sentences make one a novelist. Novel-writing skills require much more than learning some rules of grammar. Among other things, it requires insight, creativity and a knack for using the right words in a given situation.

In the same vein, a good programmer must be able to creatively use the features of the language to solve a wide variety of problems in an elegant and efficient manner. This is the difficult part and can only be achieved by long, hard study of problem-solving algorithms and writing programs to solve a wide range of problems. But we must start with baby steps.

2.1 The Java alphabet

In Section 1.4 we introduced the idea of a character. We can think of the Java alphabet as consisting of all the characters one could type on a standard English keyboard, for example, the digits, uppercase and lowercase letters, and special characters such as **+**, **=**, **<**, **>**, **&** and **%**.

More formally, Java uses the ASCII (American Standard Code for Information Interchange, pronounced **ass-key**) character set[1]. This is a character standard which includes the letters, digits and special characters found on a standard keyboard. It also includes *control* characters such as backspace, tab, line feed, form feed and carriage return. Each character is assigned a numeric code. The ASCII codes run from 0 to 127.

The programs in this book will be written using the ASCII character set. The characters in the ASCII character set are shown in Appendix B.

Character handling will be discussed in detail in Chapter 6.

2.2 Java tokens

The *tokens* of a language are the basic building blocks which can be put together to construct programs. A token can be a reserved word (such as **int** or **while**), an identifier (such as **b** or **sum**), a constant (such as **25** or **"Alice in Wonderland"**), a delimiter (such as **{** or **;**) or an operator (such as **+** or **=**).

For example, consider the following portion of the program given at the end of the last chapter:

```
public class ProgramP1_3 {
   public static void main(String[] args) {
      int a, b, sum; //declare the variables
      a = 14;
      b = 25;
      sum = a + b;
```

---

[1] In reality, Java uses the Unicode character set. For starters, it includes the ASCII character set. But Unicode also includes all characters in all written languages in the world. In order to represent so many characters Unicode uses two bytes (16 bits) for storing each character. With 16 bits, one can store $2^{16} = 65,536$ different codes. Unicode is especially useful if one is writing a program for use by people speaking different languages. In this book, we use only the English alphabet.

Starting from the beginning, we can list the tokens in order:

`public`	reserved word
`class`	reserved word
`ProgramP1_3`	user identifier
`{`	left brace, delimiter
`public`	reserved word
`static`	reserved word
`void`	reserved word
`main`	user identifier
`(`	right parenthesis, delimiter
`String`	class name identifier
`[`	left square bracket, delimiter
`]`	right square bracket, delimiter
`args`	user identifier
`)`	right parenthesis, delimiter
`{`	left brace, delimiter
`int`	reserved word
`a`	user identifier
`,`	comma, delimiter
`b`	user identifier
`,`	comma, delimiter
`sum`	user identifier
`;`	semicolon, delimiter
`//`	delimiter, start of comment which extends to end-of-line
`a`	user identifier
`=`	equals sign, operator
`14`	constant
`;`	semicolon, delimiter

and so on. Thus we can think of a program as a 'stream of tokens', which is precisely how the compiler views it. So that, as far as the compiler is concerned, the above could have been written:

```
public class ProgramP1_3 { public static void main(String[] args) {
int a, b, sum; //declare the variables
a = 14; b = 25; sum = a + b;
```

The *order* of the tokens is exactly the same; to the compiler, it *is* the same program. To the computer, only the order of the tokens is important. However, layout and spacing are important to make the program more readable to human beings.

A word on spacing

Generally speaking, Java programs can be written using "free format". The language does not require us, for instance, to write one statement on a line. Even a simple statement like

```
a = 14;
```

can be written on four separate lines, like this:

```
        a
        =
        14
        ;
```

Only the order of the tokens is important. However, since 14 is one token, the 1 cannot be separated from the 4. You are not even allowed to put a space between 1 and 4.

Except within a string constant, spaces are not significant in Java. However, judicious use of spaces can dramatically improve the readability of your program. A general 'rule of thumb' is that wherever you can put one space, you can put any number of spaces without affecting the meaning of your program. The statement

> a = 14;

can be written as

> a=14;

or

> a = 14 ;

or

> a=   14;

The statement

> sum = a + b;

can be written as

> sum=a+b;

or

> sum= a + b ;

or

> sum = a+b;

Note, of course, that you cannot have spaces *within* the variable **sum**. It would be wrong to write **s um** or **su m**. In general, all the characters of a token must stay together.

2.2.1 Reserved words

The Java language uses a number of *keywords* such as **int**, **char** and **while**. A keyword has a special meaning in the context of a Java program and can be used for that purpose only. For example, **int** can be used only in those places where we need to specify that the type of some item is *integer*. All keywords are written in *lowercase letters* only. Thus **int** is a keyword but **Int** and **INT** are not. Keywords are reserved, that is, you cannot use them as *your* identifiers. As such, they are usually called *reserved words*. A list of Java keywords is given in Appendix A.

2.2.2 Identifiers

The Java programmer needs to make up names for things such as variables, method names (Chapter 7) and symbolic constants (see following page). A name that he makes up is called a *user identifier*. There are a few simple rules to follow in naming an identifier:

- it must start with a letter (a-z or A-Z) or underscore (_) or dollar sign ($);
- if other characters are required, they can be any combination of letters, digits (0-9), underscore or dollar sign;
- there is no limit to the length of an identifier.

Examples of valid identifiers:

```
r
R
sumOfRoots1and2
$1000
_XYZ
maxThrowsPerTurn
TURNS_PER_GAME
R2D2
root$1$2
```

Examples of invalid identifiers:

```
2hotToHandle    // does not start with a letter or _ or $
Net Pay    // contains a space
ALPHA;BETA    //contains an invalid character ;
$1,000    //contains an invalid character ,
```

Important points to note:

- Spaces are not allowed in an identifier. If you need one which consists of two or more words, use a combination of uppercase and lowercase letters (as in **numThrowsThisTurn**) or use the underscore to separate the words (as in **num_throws_this_turn**). We prefer the uppercase/lowercase combination.
- In general, Java is *case-sensitive* (an uppercase letter is considered different from the corresponding lowercase letter). Thus **r** is a different identifier from **R**. And **sum** is different from **Sum** is different from **SUM** is different from **SuM**.
- You cannot use a Java reserved word as one of your identifiers.

Some naming conventions

Other than the rules for creating identifiers, Java imposes no restriction on what names to use, or what format (uppercase or lowercase, for instance) to use.

However, good programming practice dictates that some common-sense rules should be followed.

An identifier should be meaningful. For example, if it's a variable, it should reflect the value being stored in the variable; **netPay** is a much better variable than **x** for storing someone's net pay, even though both are valid. If it's a method (Chapter 7), it should give some indication of what the method is supposed to do; **playGame** is a better identifier than **plg**.

It is a good idea to use upper and lower case combinations to indicate the kind of item named by the identifier. In this book, we use the following conventions:

- A *variable* is normally written in lowercase, for example, **sum**. If we need a variable consisting of two or more words, we start the second and subsequent words with an uppercase letter, for example, **voteCount** or **sumOfSeries**.
- A *symbolic* (or *named*) *constant* is an identifier which can be used in place of a constant such as 100. Suppose 100 represents the maximum number of items we wish to process in some program. We would probably need to use the number 100 in various places in the program. But suppose we change our mind and want to cater for 500 items. We would have to change all occurrences of 100 to 500. However, we would have to make sure that we do *not* change an occurrence of 100 used for some purpose other than the maximum number of items (in a calculation like **principal*rate/100**, say).

   To make it easy to change our mind, we can set the identifier **MaxItems** to 100 and use **MaxItems** whenever we need to refer to the maximum number of items. If we change our mind, we would just need to set **MaxItems** to the new value. We will begin a symbolic constant with an uppercase letter. If it consists of more than one word, we will begin each word with uppercase, as in **MaxThrowsPerTurn**.

We will see how to use symbolic constants in Section 4.5 (page 82).

2.3 Basic data types

In Section 1.3 we briefly touched on the concept of a data type. In Java, there are 8 basic data types. (We also call them *built-in* or *primitive* data types.) They are: **byte**, **short**, **int**, **long**, **float**, **double**, **char** and **boolean**. Each data type defines *constants* of that type. When we declare a variable to be of a particular type, we are really saying what kind of constants (values) can be stored in that variable. For example, if we declare the variable **num** to be **int**, we are saying that the value of **num** at any time can be an integer constant such as 25, -369 or 1024. If we declare the variable **found** to be **boolean**, we are saying that the value of **found** at any time can be either **true** or **false**.

2.4 The integer types – byte, short, int, long

An integer type is used to store an *integer* (whole number) value. An integer value is one of 0, ±1, ±2, ±3, ±4, etc. However, on a computer, the largest and smallest integers (and all those in between) which can be stored are determined by the *number of bits* used to store an integer. The more bits we use, the greater the range. The following shows the length and the range of integers which can be stored in each type.

byte	8 bits (1 byte)	-128 to +127
short	16 bits (2 bytes)	-32,768 to +32,767
int	32 bits (4 bytes)	-2,147,483,648 to +2,147,483,647
long	64 bits (8 bytes)	-9,223,372,036,854,775,808 to +9,223,372,036,854,775,807

In general, if n bits are used to store an integer, the range of numbers which can be stored is -2^{n-1} to $+2^{n-1} - 1$. Appendix C shows how integers can be represented on a computer.

Integer constants can be written in various ways. The most common form is the one we are all accustomed to, using *decimal* digits, for example, 354, -1, 32905 and 987654321. Note that you are allowed to use only a possible sign followed by digits 0 to 9. In particular, you cannot use commas as you might do to separate thousands; thus 1,713 is an *invalid* integer constant—you *must* write it as **1713**.

Octal constants are numbers written in base 8, using digits **0** to **7**. In Java, if a number begins with **0** (zero), it is considered an octal constant. For example, **047** is an octal number whose decimal equivalent is **39**.

Hexadecimal constants are numbers written in base 16, using digits **0** to **9** and letters **A** to **F** (or **a** to **f**) to represent the hexadecimal 'digits' 10 to 15. In Java, a hexadecimal number begins with **0x** or **0X** (zero ex). For example, **0x27** (or **0X27**) is a hexadecimal number whose decimal equivalent is **39**.

In this book, we will generally use decimal integers.

When you write an integer constant in a program, it is considered to be of type **int**. In the statement

    a = 14;

14 is considered an **int**.

If you want an integer constant to be **long**, you must end it with **L** or **l** (ell, not one —always use **L** to avoid confusion). Thus **39L** is a long constant. You may do this if you feel that your calculation might produce a result which is too large to fit in an **int** and you want to force it to be done using **long** precision. For example, if **j** is an **int**, the expression **j * 39** (meaning **j** multiplied by **39**; * denotes multiplication) is also an **int** but **j * 39L** is of type **long** (see **Integer expressions** below).

For most of this book, we will use **int** for working with integers.

2.4.1 Declaring variables

In Java, a variable is declared by specifying a type name followed by the variable. For example,

> int j;

declares **j** to be a variable of type **int**.

You can declare several variables *of the same type* in one statement as in:

> int a, b, c;   // declares 3 variables of type int

The variables are separated by commas, with a semicolon after the last one.

You can declare a variable and give it an initial value in one statement, as in:

> int j = 14;

This declares **j** to be **int** *and* gives it a value of 14.

2.4.2 Integer expressions

An integer constant is the simplest example of an integer *expression*. However, most of the time, we write integer expressions by combining constants and variables with the following *arithmetic operators*:

> +   add
> -   subtract
> *   multiply
> /   divide
> %   find remainder

For example, suppose we have the following declaration:

> int a, b, c;

then the following are all valid expressions:

> a + 39
> a + b - c * 2
> b % 10   //the remainder when b is divided by 10
> c + (a * 2 + b * 2) / 2

The operators **+**, **-** and ***** all give the expected results. However, **/** performs *integer division*; if there is any remainder, it is thrown away. We say integer division *truncates*. Thus **19 / 5** gives the value 3; the remainder 4 is discarded.

But what is the value of **-19 / 5**? The answer here is −3. The rule is that, in Java, integer division truncates *towards* zero. Since the exact value of −19 ÷ 5 is −3.8, truncating towards zero gives −3. (In Section 2.5.4, we show how to get the precise value for the division of one integer by another).

The % operator gives the *remainder* when one integer is divided by another; for example,

> 19 % 5 evaluates to 4;
>
> j % 7 gives the remainder when j is divided by 7;

You can use it to test, for instance, if a number **j** is even or odd. If **j % 2** is **0** then **j** is even; if **j % 2** is **1**, **j** is odd.

2.4.3 Precedence of operators

Java evaluates an expression based on the usual *precedence* of operators: multiplication and division are done *before* addition and subtraction. We say that multiplication and division have *higher precedence* than addition and subtraction. For example, the expression

> 5 + 3 * 4

is evaluated by *first* multiplying 3 by 4 (giving 12) and *then* adding 5 to 12, giving 17 as the value of the expression.

As usual, we can use brackets to force the evaluation of an expression in the order we want. For example,

> (5 + 3) * 4

first adds 5 and 3 (giving 8), and then multiplies 8 by 4, giving 32.

When two operators which have the *same* precedence appear in an expression, they are evaluated *from left to right*, unless specified otherwise by brackets. For example,

> 24 / 4 * 2

is evaluated as

> (24 / 4) * 2

(giving 12) and

> 12 - 7 + 3

is evaluated as

> (12 - 7) + 3

giving 8. However,

> 24 / (4 * 2)

is evaluated with the multiplication done first, giving 3, and

> 12 - (7 + 3)

is evaluated with the addition done first, giving 2.

In Java, the remainder operator % has the same precedence as multiplication (*) and division (/).

Exercise: What is printed by the following program? Check your answer by typing the program to a file **Exercise.java**. Compile the program and run it.

```
public class Exercise {
  public static void main(String[] args) {
    int a = 15;
    int b = 24;
    System.out.printf("%d %d\n", b - a + 7, b - (a + 7));
    System.out.printf("%d %d\n", b - a - 4, b - (a - 4));
    System.out.printf("%d %d\n", b % a / 2, b % (a / 2));
    System.out.printf("%d %d\n", b * a / 2, b * (a / 2));
    System.out.printf("%d %d\n", b / 2 * a, b / (2 * a));
  }
}
```

2.4.4 Printing an integer using a "field width"

We have seen that we can print an integer value by specifying the value (either by a variable or an expression) in a **printf** statement. When we do so, Java prints the value using as many "print columns" as needed. For instance, if the value is 782, it is printed using 3 print columns since 782 has 3 digits. If the value is -2345, it is printed using 5 print columns (one for the minus sign).

While this is usually sufficient for most purposes, there are times when it is useful to be able to tell Java how many print columns to use. For example, if we want to print the value of **n** in 5 print columns, we can do this by specifying a *field width* of 5, as in:

```
System.out.printf("%5d", n);
```

Instead of the specification **%d**, we now use **%5d**. The field width is placed between **%** and **d**. The value of **n** is printed "in a field width of 5".

Suppose **n** is 279; there are 3 digits to print so 3 print columns are needed. Since the field width is 5, the number 279 is printed with 2 spaces before it, thus: ◊◊279 (◊ denotes a space). We also say "printed with 2 leading blanks/spaces" and "printed padded on the left with 2 blanks/spaces".

A more technical way of saying this is "**n** is printed *right-justified* in a field width of 5". "Right-justify" means that the number is placed as far right as possible in the field and spaces added in *front* of it to make up the field width. If the number is placed as far *left* as possible and spaces are added *after* it to make up the field width, the number is *left-justified*. For example, 279◊◊ is left-justified in a field width of 5.

The minus sign can be used to specify *left-justification*; **%-wd** will print a value left-justified in a field width of **w**. For example, to print an integer value left-justified in field width of 5, we use **%-5d**.

For another example, suppose **n** is -7 and the field width is 5. Printing **n** requires two print columns (one for - and one for 7); since the field width is 5, it is printed with 3 leading spaces, thus: ◇◇◇-7.

You may ask, what will happen if the field width is too small? Suppose the value to be printed is 23456 and the field width is 3. Printing this value requires 5 columns which is greater than the field width 3. In this case, Java ignores the field width and simply prints the value using as many columns as needed (5, in this example).

In general, suppose the integer value **v** is printed with the format specification **%wd** where **w** is an integer, and suppose **n** columns are needed to print **v**. There are 2 cases to consider:

- If **n** is less than **w** (the field width is bigger), the value is padded on the left with (**w** - **n**) spaces. For example, if **w** is 7 and **v** is -345 so that **n** is 4, the number is padded on the left with (7-4) = 3 spaces and printed as ◇◇◇-345.
- If **n** is greater than or equal to **w** (field width is the same or smaller), the value is printed using **n** print columns. In this case, the field width is ignored.

A field width is useful when we want to line up numbers one below the other. Suppose we have three **int** variables **a**, **b** and **c** with values 9876, -3 and 501, respectively. The statements

```
System.out.printf("%d\n", a);
System.out.printf("%d\n", b);
System.out.printf("%d\n", c);
```

will print

9876
-3
501

Each number is printed using just the number of columns required. Since this varies from one number to the next, they do not line up. If we want to, we could get the numbers lined up using a field width of 5, say. The statements

```
System.out.printf("%5d\n", a);
System.out.printf("%5d\n", b);
System.out.printf("%5d\n", c);
```

will print (◇ denotes a space)

◇9876
◇◇◇-3
◇◇501

which will look like (without ◊)

```
9876
  -3
 501
```

all nicely lined up.

As a matter of interest, we don't really need 3 **printf** statements. We can replace the last 3 **printf** statements with

```
System.out.printf("%5d\n%5d\n%5d\n", a, b, c);
```

Each **\n** forces the following output onto a new line.

2.5 Floating-point numbers – the types float and double

A floating-point number is one which may have a fractional part. A *floating-point constant* can be written in one of two ways:

- the normal way, with an optional sign, and including a decimal point; for example, `-3.75, 0.537, 81.792, 47.0`;
- using *scientific* notation, with an optional sign, including a decimal point and including an 'exponent' part; for example, `-0.375E1` meaning "-0.375 multiplied by 10 to the power 1", that is, `-3.75`. Similarly, `0.537` can be written as `5.37e-1`, that is, "5.37×10^{-1}". The exponent can be specified using either **e** or **E**.

Note that there are several ways to write the same number. For example, the following all represent the same number `27.96`:

```
27.96E00  2.796E1  2.796E+1  2.796E+01  0.2796E+02  279.6E-1
```

In Java, we can declare a floating-point variable using either **float** or **double**. A **float** value is normally stored as a 32-bit floating-point number, giving about 6 or 7 significant digits. A **double** value is stored as a 64-bit floating-point number, giving about 15 significant digits.

A floating-point constant is of type **double** unless it is followed by **f** or **F**, in which case it is of type **float**. Thus `3.75` is of type **double** but `3.75f` (or `3.75F`) is of type **float**. Most calculations are done using **double** precision. The type **float** is useful if you need to store lots of floating-point numbers and you wish to use as little storage as possible (and do not mind living with 6 or 7 digits of precision).

In this book, we will use **double** mostly for working with floating-point numbers.

2.5.1 *Printing the values of* double *and* float *variables*

We have been using the *format specification* **%d** in a **printf** statement to print the value of an integer variable. If we wish to print the value of a **double** or **float** variable, we can use **%f**. For example, consider:

```
double d = 987.654321;
System.out.printf("%f \n", d);
```

The value of **d** will be printed to a pre-defined number of decimal places (usually 6, but could vary from one compiler to the next). In this case, the value printed will be 987.654321. However, if **d** were assigned 987.6543215, the value printed would be 987.654322 (rounded to 6 decimal places).

Similarly, if **x** was of type **float**, its value could be printed using:

```
System.out.printf("%f \n", x);
```

We just saw that the specification **%f** prints the number to a pre-defined number of decimal places. Most times, though, we want to say how many decimal places to print and, sometimes, how many columns to use. For example, if we want to print **d**, above, to 2 decimal places in a field width of 6, we can use:

```
System.out.printf("%6.2f \n", d);
```

Between **%** and **f**, we write **6.2**, that is, the field width, followed by a . (point), followed by the number of decimal places. The value is *rounded* to the stated number of decimal places and then printed. Here, the value printed will be 987.65, which occupies exactly 6 print columns. If the field width were bigger, the number will be padded on the left with spaces. If the field width were smaller, it is ignored, and the number printed using as many columns as necessary.

As another example, consider

```
b = 245.75;
System.out.printf("%6.1f \n", d);
```

In the specification **%6.1f**, 1 says to *round* the number to 1 decimal place; this gives 245.8, which requires 5 columns for printing.

6 says to print 245.8 in 6 columns; since only 5 columns are needed for printing the number, one space is added at the beginning to make up 6 columns, so the number is printed as ◊245.8 (◊ denotes a space).

Similarly,

```
System.out.printf("%6.0f \n", d);
```

will print **b** as ◊◊◊246 (rounded to 0 decimal places and printed in a field width of 6).

If the specification were **%3.1f** and the value to be printed is 245.8, it would be printed using 5 print columns, even though the field width is 3. Again, when the field width specified is *smaller* than the number of print columns required, Java ignores the field width and prints the value using as many columns as needed.

We can sometimes use this to our advantage. If we do not know how big a value might be, we can deliberately use a small field width to ensure it is printed using the exact number of print columns required for printing the value.

In general, suppose the **float** or **double** value **v** is to be printed with the specification **%w.df** where **w** and **d** are integers. Firstly, the value **v** is *rounded* to **d** decimal places; suppose the number of print columns required to print **v**, including a possible point[2] and a possible sign, is **n**. There are 2 cases to consider:

- If **n** is less than **w** (the field width is bigger), the value is padded on the left with (**w** - **n**) spaces. For example, if **w** is 7 and the value to be printed is -3.45 so that **n** is 5, the number is padded on the left with (7-5) = 2 spaces and printed as ◊◊-3.45.
- If **n** is greater than or equal to **w** (field width is the same or smaller), the value is printed using **n** print columns. In this case, the field width is ignored.

As with integers, a field width is useful when we want to line up numbers one below the other. Assume we have three **double** variables **a**, **b** and **c** with values 419.563, -8.7 and 3.25, respectively. Suppose we want to print the values to 2 decimal places, lined up on the decimal point, like this:

```
419.56
 -8.70
  3.25
```

Since the biggest number requires 6 print columns, we can line them up using a field width of at least 6. The following statements will line them up as above:

```
System.out.printf("%6.2f \n", a);
System.out.printf("%6.2f \n", b);
System.out.printf("%6.2f \n", c);
```

If we use a field width bigger than 6, the numbers will still line up but with leading spaces.

For example, if we use a field width of 8, we will get (◊ denotes a space)

◊◊419.56
◊◊◊-8.70
◊◊◊◊3.25

Again, we can use one **printf** instead of three to achieve the same effect:

```
System.out.printf("%6.2f \n%6.2f \n%6.2f \n", a, b, c);
```

---

[2] There will be no point if d = 0 (the value is to be rounded to a whole number)

Each **\n** forces the following output onto a new line.

2.5.2 Assignment between double and float

As expected, you can store a **float** value in a **float** variable and a **double** value in a **double** variable. Since **float** is smaller than **double**, Java allows you to store a **float** value in a **double** variable without any problems. However, if you try to assign a **double** value to a **float** variable, Java will complain. Consider:

```
double d = 987.654321;
float x = d;  //this is wrong; can't assign double to float
```

The second statement will give an error message since Java will recognize that precision could be lost when assigning a "bigger" value (**double**) to a "smaller" variable (**float**). However, if we are sure that that is what we want to do, we can use a *cast* to tell Java that we know what we are doing and are aware of the risk. We must write the statement as:

```
float x = (float) d;
```

The construct **(float)** is called a *cast* and it forces the **double** value **d** to be converted to **float**. A cast consists of a type name enclosed in brackets.

However, since a **float** variable allows only about 6 or 7 digits of precision, we should expect that the value of **d** may not be assigned precisely to **x**. Indeed, when run using one compiler, the value 987.654297 was assigned to **x**. When **d** was changed to 987654321.12345, the value assigned was 987654336.000000. In both cases, about 6 or 7 digits of precision were retained.

As an exercise, see what values would be printed using your compiler.

We must also be careful with statements such as:

```
float x = 3.64; //wrong
```

Since 3.64 is a **double** constant, Java will not allow us to assign it directly to a **float** variable. We can make the assignment valid by using either of the following:

```
x = (float) 3.64; //use a cast to convert to float
x = 3.64f; //write 3.64 as a float constant
```

2.5.3 Floating-point expressions

Floating-point expressions can be written using the following operators:

- \+   addition
- \-   subtraction
- *   multiplication
- /   division

These operate as expected; in particular, division is performed in the usual way so that, for example, 19.0/5.0 gives the value 3.8.

If **op1** and **op2** are the two operands of an operator, the following shows the type of calculation performed:

op1	op2	type of calculation
float	float	float
float	double	double
double	float	double
double	double	double

Thus **float** is performed only if both operands are **float**; otherwise **double** is performed.

2.5.4 Expressions with integer and floating-point values

It is quite common to use expressions involving both integer and floating-point values, for example,

    a / 3   where a is float
    n * 0.25   where n is int

In Java, the rule for such expressions is:

If either operand of an arithmetic operator is floating-point, the calculation is done in floating-point arithmetic. The calculation is done in **double** unless *both* operands are **float**, in which case the calculation is done in **float**.

In the first example above, the integer 3 is converted to **float** and the calculation is done in **float**. In the second example, **n** is converted to **double** (since 0.25 is **double**) and the calculation is done in **double**.

How do we get the exact value of an integer division, 19/5, say? We can force a double precision calculation by writing one or both constants as **double**, thus: 19/5.0, 19.0/5 or 19.0/5.0. We can also use a cast, as in

    (double) 19 / 5

A cast allows us to force the conversion of one type to another. Here, the **int** 19 is cast to **double**, forcing 5 to be converted to **double** and a double precision division is performed.

However, we must be careful with a construct like

    (double) (19 / 5)

since it may not do what we think. This does NOT do a floating-point division. Since both constants are integer, the expression inside the brackets is evaluated as an integer division, giving 3; *this* value is converted to **double**, giving 3.0.

2.5.5 *Assigning integer types to* double/float

Java is a *strongly typed* language. This means that the compiler keeps a close check on operations requested by a program and forbids anything questionable. In particular, it checks that the type of value being assigned to a variable is compatible with the type of the variable.

In general, Java does not complain if try to assign a value, v, to a variable whose type supports a range that includes v. In other words, there is usually no problem going from a smaller type to a bigger type. So, for instance, we can assign an **int** value to a **long** variable or a **float** value to a **double** variable without having to do anything special. But what happens if we try to assign an integer type to a **float** or **double** or vice versa?

Assigning a **byte** to a **float** or **double** is allowed and causes no problems since the range of a **byte** could be easily accommodated in a **float** or **double**; similarly for **short**.

Assigning an **int** to a **double** is allowed and causes no problems since the range of an **int** could be easily accommodated in a **double**. However, even though assigning an **int** to a **float** is allowed, you must be aware that you could lose precision.

The reason is that the largest **int** contains 10 digits whereas a **float** has only 6 or 7 significant digits. For example, consider the following:

```
float f = 123456789;
int k = (int) f;  // k becomes 123456792
```

When the value 123456789 is assigned to a **float** and then reassigned to an **int**, the value changes to 123456792; precision is lost. Be careful when assigning an **int** to a **float**.

Assigning a **long** to a **float**/**double** is allowed but, since the number of significant digits of a **long** (about 19) is greater than that for both **float** and **double**, you could run into the same problem as above. For example, when the following is executed,

```
float f = 8589934288L; //L needed since number is too big for int
long g = (long) f;
System.out.printf("%d \n", g);
```

8589934080 is printed.

In summary, any integer type could be assigned to a floating-point type. However, in some cases, precision could be lost.

2.5.6 Assigning double/float to integer types

Java does *not* let us assign a floating-point value (**float** or **double**) directly to an integer variable (**byte**, **short**, **int** or **long**).

For example, consider:

```
int n = 987.654321;    //cannot assign double to int
long m = 3.24f; //cannot assign float to long
```

None of these statements is valid in Java. We can use a cast to make them valid, as in:

```
int n = (int) 987.654321;
long m = (long) 3.24f;
```

Now, 987 is assigned to **n** and 3 is assigned to **m**.

When we assign a floating-point value to an integer type, the fractional part, if any, is dropped (not rounded) and the resulting integer value is assigned. It is up to us to ensure that the integer obtained is small enough to fit in the integer type. If not, the resulting value is unpredictable.

For example, the largest **byte** value is 127. The statement

```
byte b = (byte) 300.75;
```

is valid and will attempt to store the value 300 in the **byte** variable **b**. Since this is too big to fit in **b**, the value assigned is unpredictable[3]. In this case, the value assigned is 44.

As another example, the statement

```
short s = (short) 65585.36;
```

will store 49 in **s**; 65585 is too big to fit in a **short** variable. Here, the low-order 16 bits of 65585 (which happens to be 49) is stored in **s**.

Suppose the **double** variable **d** has the value 987.654321. If we want the *rounded* value of **d** (988) stored in the **int** variable **n**, we could do this with

```
n = (int) (d + 0.5);
```

If the first digit after the point in **d** is 5 or more, adding 0.5 would add 1 to the whole number part. If the first digit after the point is less than 5, adding 0.5 would not change the whole number part.

For example, if **d** is 245.75, adding 0.5 would give 246.25 and 246 would be assigned to **n**. But if **d** were 245.49, adding 0.5 would give 245.99 and 245 would be assigned to **n**.

---

[3] Not quite unpredictable; the binary equivalent of 300 is 100101100. Since a **byte** can hold 8 bits, the low-order 8 bits are stored in **b**; thus 00101110, which is 44 in decimal, is stored in **b**.

2.6 The type char

Most of us are familiar with a computer or typewriter keyboard (called the *standard English keyboard*). On it, we can type the letters of the alphabet (both uppercase and lowercase), the digits and other 'special' characters like **+**, **=**, **<**, **>**, **&** and **%** – these are the so-called *printable* characters.

On a computer, each character is assigned a unique integer value, called its *code*. This code may be different from one computer to another depending on the *character set* being used. For example, the code for A might be 33 on one computer but 65 on another.

Inside the computer, this integer code is stored as a sequence of bits; for example, the 6-bit code for 33 is **100001** and the 7-bit code for 65 is **1000001**.

Nowadays, most computers use the ASCII (American Standard Code for Information Interchange) character set[4] for representing characters. This is a 7-bit character standard which includes the letters, digits and special characters found on a standard keyboard. It also includes *control* characters such as backspace, tab, line feed, form feed and carriage return.

The ASCII codes run from 0 to 127 (the range of numbers which can be stored using 7 bits). The ASCII character set is shown in Appendix B. Interesting features to note are:

- the digits **0** to **9** occupy codes **48** to **57**
- the uppercase letters **A** to **Z** occupy codes **65** to **90**
- the lowercase letters **a** to **z** occupy codes **97** to **122**

Note, however, that even though the ASCII set is *defined* using a 7-bit code, it is *stored* on most computers in 8-bit bytes—a 0 is added at the front of the 7-bit code. For example, the 7-bit ASCII code for A is **1000001**; on a computer, it is stored as **01000001**, occupying one byte.

A character constant is a single character enclosed in single quotes such as **'A'**, **'+'** and **'5'**. The *value* of a character constant is the character without the quotes. Thus, the value of **'A'** is **A**.

Java allows us to declare variables of type **char**. A variable of type **char** can take a character constant as its value. For example, the statement

    char ch;

declares **ch** as a **char** variable. We can assign a character constant to it with

    ch = 'R';

---

[4] As mentioned before, Java uses the (very large) Unicode character set but the ASCII set, a subset of Unicode, will suffice for our purposes.

The *value* of **ch** is the value of '**R**' which is **R**.

Java uses an *escape sequence* to represent certain special characters. These, with their codes, are:

\b	backspace	code 8
\f	formfeed	code 12
\n	newline	code 10
\r	carriage return	code 13
\t	tab	code 9
\'	single quote	code 39
\"	double quote	code 34
\\	backslash	code 92
\ddd	character whose code is the octal value **ddd** (d is one of 0-7) **ddd** cannot exceed 377.	

If we need to use one of these special characters as a character constant, it must be enclosed in single quotes. For example, if **ch** is a variable of type **char**, we can write statements such as:

```
ch = '\"';  // assign " to ch
ch = '\n';  // assign the newline character to ch
```

In Chapter 6, we will explain how to work with characters.

2.7 The type boolean

A *Boolean expression*[5] is one that is either true or false. The simplest kinds of Boolean expressions are those that compare one value with another. Examples are

j is equal to 999
a is greater than 100
$a^2 + b^2$ is equal to c^2
b^2 is greater than or equal to 4ac
s is not equal to 0

Each of these can be either true or false.

Boolean expressions are normally used to control the flow of program execution. For example, we may have a variable (**j**, say) which starts off with a value of 0. We keep increasing it by 1 and we want to know when its value exceeds 100. We say we wish to know when the *condition* **j > 100** is true. A condition is the common name for a Boolean expression.

Java uses the keyword **boolean** to declare variables whose values can be either **true** or **false**. In other words, there are exactly two **boolean** constants—**true** and **false**. We can, for instance, declare a variable **found** and set it to **false** with:

---
[5] Named after the famous English mathematician, George Boole

```
         boolean found = false;
```

We will see how to use Boolean expressions in our programs starting in Chapter 4.

2.8 Strings

So far, we have seen several examples of string constants in **printf** statements.

A *string constant* is any sequence of characters enclosed in double quotes. Examples are:

```
"Once upon a time"
"645-2001"
"Are you OK?"
"c:\\data\\castle.in"
```

The opening and closing quotes *must* appear *on the same line*. In other words, Java does not allow a string constant to continue on to another line. However, a long string can be broken up into pieces, with each piece on one line. The pieces can be joined together using **+**. For example,

```
System.out.printf("Part of a long string can be placed on one line and " +
        "the other part placed on the next line. The pieces are " +
        "joined together using the + operator.\n");
```

The *value* of a string constant is the sequence of characters without the beginning and ending quotes. Thus, the value of **"Are you OK?"** is **Are you OK?**.

If you want the double quote to be part of a string, you must write it using the escape sequence \", as in

```
"\"Don't move!\", he commanded"
```

The value of this string is **"Don't move!", he commanded**. Each \" is replaced by " and the beginning and ending quotes are dropped.

For working with strings, Java provides the type **String**[6] (note the uppercase **S**).

When we write a statement such as:

```
System.out.printf("Welcome");
```

we create the string **"Welcome"** *implicitly*. Java stores the string somewhere in memory and uses a *reference* to the string (the string's address) in **printf**. Since we do not know what this address is, we have no direct control over the string. Strings we create implicitly are sometimes called *transient* strings.

---

[6] Strictly speaking, in Java, a string is an *object* belonging to the class **String**. But, for the time being, we will think of **String** as simply a type (similar to the basic types) we can use to declare variables to hold strings.

We can create a string *explicitly* by declaring a **String** variable and assigning a string to it, as in:

```
String str;              // declare the variable
str = "Welcome";         // assign a string to it
```

As usual, the two statements can be combined into one:

```
String str = "Welcome";
```

When this statement is executed, the following occurs:

- the characters **Welcome** are stored somewhere in memory (at location 3029, say); the quotes are not stored;
- the address 3029 is stored in **str**.

This can be depicted as follows:

So, strictly speaking, **str** contains the *address* of the string, not the string itself. However, for the most part, we will talk as if **str** contains the string, as follows:

```
str | Welcome
```

When we need to make the distinction as to what **str** actually holds, we will do so.

We can print **str** as in:

```
System.out.printf(str + " to Java\n");
```

which will print:

Welcome to Java

As another example, consider:

```
str += " tiger";    // str = str + " tiger"
```

The **+** operator, when applied to strings, concatenates them (joins them together). The statement creates a new string "**Welcome tiger**" and this becomes the new value of **str**[7]; the old value (the address of the first string) is lost.

Suppose we wish to store the name **Alice Wonder** in some variable **name**. We can do this with:

```
String name = "Alice Wonder";
```

---

[7] Again, for the record, Java stores the new string somewhere in memory, and stores the address on this new string in **str**, replacing the address of the old string.

This stores the characters from **A** to **r**, including the space, in **name**. The quotes are *not* stored. Once this is done, we could print the value of **name** using the specification **%s** in **printf**, thus:

> System.out.printf("Hello, %s\n", name);

This will print

> Hello, Alice Wonder

The *value* of **name** replaces **%s**.

In Section 3.3 (page 57), we will see how to read a string value into a variable.

2.9 The assignment statement

In Section 1.8, we introduced the *assignment statement*. Recall that an assignment statement consists of a *variable* followed by an equals sign (=) followed by the *value* to be assigned to the variable, followed by a semicolon. We could write this as:

> <variable> = <value>;

<value> must be *compatible* with <variable> otherwise we will get an error. For example, if <variable> is **int**, we must be able to derive an integer from <value>. And if <variable> is **double**, we must be able to derive a floating-point value from <value>. If **n** is **int** and **x** is **double**, we cannot, for instance, write

> n = "Hi there";   //cannot assign string to int
> x = "Be nice";   //cannot assign string to double

It is useful to think of the assignment statement being executed as follows: the value on the right-hand side of = is evaluated. The value obtained is stored in the variable on the left-hand side. The old value of the variable, if any, is lost. For example, if **score** had the value 25, then after the statement

> score = 84;

the value of **score** would be 84; the old value 25 is lost. We can picture this as:

> score | ~~25~~ 84 |

A variable can take on any of several values, but *only one at a time*. As another example, consider

> score = score + 5;

and suppose **score** has the value 84 before this statement is executed. What is the value after execution?

Java – the basics

First, the right-hand side **score + 5** is evaluated using the current value of **score**, 84. The calculation gives 89—this value is then stored in the variable on the left-hand side; it happens to be **score**. The end result is that the value of **score** is increased by 5 to 89. The old value 84 is lost.

It is possible that even though an assignment statement is *valid*, it could produce an error when the program is run. Consider the following:

```
int a, b, c, d, e;
a = 12;
b = 5;
c = (a - b) * 2;
d = c + e;
```

Each of these is a correctly formed assignment statement. However, when these statements are executed, an error will result. Can you see how?

The first statement assigns 12 to **a**; the second assigns 5 to **b**; the third assigns 14 to **c**; no problem so far. However, when the computer attempts to execute the fourth statement, it runs into a problem: there is no value for **e**, so the expression **c + e** cannot be evaluated. We say that **e** is *undefined*—it has no value.

Before we can use any variable in an expression, it must have been assigned a value by some previous statement. If not, we will get an "undefined variable" error and our program will halt.

The moral of the story is: a *valid* program is not necessarily a *correct* program.

Exercise: What is printed by the following?

```
a = 13;
b = a + 12;
System.out.printf("%d %d\n", a, b);
c = a + b;
a = a + 11;
System.out.printf("a = %d b = %d c = %d\n", a, b, c);
```

2.10 printf

We have seen several examples of the **printf** statement. We have used it to print string constants, integer values and floating-point values. And we have printed values with and without field widths. We have also seen how to use the escape sequence **\n** to force output onto a new line.

printf is a relatively new addition to Java[8]. Technically, it is a method (Java's name for a function) belonging to the **System.out** and **PrintWriter** classes. At this

---
[8] Older versions of Java used **print/println**. With **printf**, there is hardly any need for **print/println**.

time, it is not important that you know precisely what this means in order to use it. For now, just use **System.out.printf(...)**. In Section 5.8 (page 110), we will see how to use **PrintWriter**.

It is worth emphasizing that the characters in the format string are printed exactly as they appear except that a format specification is replaced by its corresponding value. For example, if **a** is 25 and **b** is 847, the statement

    System.out.printf("%d%d\n", a, b);

will print

    25847

The numbers are stuck together and we cannot tell what is **a** and what is **b**! This is so because the specification **%d%d** says to print the numbers next to each other. If we want them separated by one space, say, we must put a space between **%d** and **%d**, like this:

    System.out.printf("%d %d\n", a, b);

This will print

    25 847

If we want more spaces between the numbers, we simply put how many we want between **%d** and **%d**.

Exercise: What is printed by the following?

    System.out.printf("%d\n %d\n", a, b);

The following are some useful things to know about format specifications.

Suppose **num** is **int** and its value is 75:

- the specification **%d** will print 75 using 2 print columns: **75**
- the specification **%5d** will print 75 with 3 leading spaces: ◊◊◊**75**
- the specification **%-5d** will print 75 with 3 trailing spaces: **75**◊◊◊
- the specification **%05d** will print 75 with 3 leading zeroes: **00075**

For an example in which leading 0's might be useful, the statement

    System.out.printf("Pay this amount: $%04d\n", num);

will print

    Pay this amount: $0075

This is better than printing

    Pay this amount: $ 75

since someone can insert numbers between **$** and **7**.

Java – the basics

In general, the minus sign specifies left-justification and a 0 in front of the field width specifies 0 (zero, rather than a space) as the padding character.

Exercises 2

1. In the ASCII character set, what is the range of codes for (a) the digits (b) the uppercase letters and (c) the lowercase letters?
2. What is a token? Give examples.
3. Spaces are normally not significant in a program. Give an example showing where spaces *are* significant.
4. What is a reserved word? Give examples.
5. Give the rules for making up an identifier.
6. What is a symbolic constant and why is it useful?
7. Give examples of integer constants, floating-point constants and string constants.
8. Name 5 operators which can be used for writing integer expressions and give their precedence in relation to each other.
9. Give the value of (a) **39 % 7** (b) **88 % 4** (c) **100 % 11** (d) **-25 % 9**
10. Give the value of (a) **39 / 7** (b) **88 / 4** (c) **100 / 11** (d) **-25 / 9**
11. Write a statement which prints the value of the **int** variable **sum**, right justified in a field width of 6.
12. You are required to print the values of the **int** variables **b, j** and **n**. Write a statement which prints **b** with its rightmost digit in column 10, **j** with its rightmost digit in column 20 and **n** with its rightmost digit in column 30.
13. Write statements which print the values of **b, j** and **n** lined up one below the other with their rightmost digits in column 8.
14. Using scientific notation, write the number **345.72** in 4 different ways.
15. Write a statement which prints the value of the **double** variable **total** to 3 decimal places, right justified in a field width of 9.
16. You need to print the values of the **float** variables **a, b** and **c** to 1 decimal place. Write a statement which prints **a** with its rightmost digit in column 12, **b** with its rightmost digit in column 20 and **c** with its rightmost digit in column 32.
17. What kind of variable would you use to store a telephone number? Explain.
18. Write statements to print the values of 3 **double** variables **a, b** and **c**, to 2 decimal places, The values must be printed one below the other, with their rightmost digits in column 12.
19. How can you print the value of a **double** variable, rounded to the nearest whole number?
20. What happens if you try to print a number (**int, float** or **double**) with a field width and the field width is too small? What if the field width is too big?
21. Name some operators which can be used for writing floating-point expressions.
22. Describe what happens when we attempt to assign an **int** value to a **float** variable.

49

23. Describe what happens when we attempt to assign a **float** value to an **int** variable.
24. Write a statement to print **Use \n to end a line of output**.
25. Write a statement to increase the value of the **int** variable **quantity** by 10.
26. Write a statement to decrease the value of the **int** variable **quantity** by 5.
27. Write a statement to double the value of the **int** variable **quantity**.
28. Write a statement to set **a** to 2 times **b** plus 3 times **c**.
29. The **double** variable **price** holds the price of an item. Write a statement to increase the price by (a) $12.50 (b) 25%.
30. What will happen when the computer attempts to execute the following:

    ```
    p = 7;
    q = 3 + p;
    p = p + r;
    System.out.printf("%d\n", p);
    ```

31. Suppose **rate = 15**. What is printed by each of the following?

    (a) System.out.printf("Maria earns rate dollars an hour\n");

    (b) System.out.printf("Maria earns %d dollars an hour\n", rate);

32. If **m** is 3770 and **n** is 123, what is printed by each of the following?

    (a) System.out.printf("%d%d\n", n, m);

    (b) System.out.printf("%d\n%d\n", n, m);

3 Writing programs using sequence logic

In this chapter, we will explain:

- how to read data supplied by a user
- how to read integers using **nextInt**
- how to read floating-point data using **nextDouble** and **nextFloat**
- how to read string data using **nextLine** and **next**
- important principles of program writing using several examples

In the last chapter, we introduced some of Java's data types and used simple statements to illustrate their use. We now go a step further and introduce several programming concepts by writing programs using these types.

The programs in this chapter will be based on *sequence* logic—that simply means that the statements in the programs are executed one after the other, from the first to the last. This is the simplest kind of logic, also called *straight-line* logic. In the next chapter we will write programs which use *selection* logic—the ability of a program to test some *condition* and take different courses of action based on whether the condition is true or false.

3.1 How to read data supplied by a user

Consider, again, Program P1.3 from page 21.

```
Program P1.3
// This program prints the sum of 14 and 25. It shows how
// to declare variables in Java and assign values to them.
public class ProgramP1_3 {
   public static void main(String[] args) {
      int a, b, sum; //declare the variables
      a = 14;
      b = 25;
      sum = a + b;
      System.out.printf("%d + %d = %d\n", a, b, sum);
   }
}
```

Since Java allows us to declare a variable and give it an initial value in one statement, we could write the program more concisely (without the comment) as Program P3.1:

> **Program P3.1**
>
> ```
> public class ProgramP3_1 {
>   public static void main(String[] args) {
>     int a = 14;
>     int b = 25;
>     int sum = a + b;
>     System.out.printf("%d + %d = %d\n", a, b, sum);
>   }
> }
> ```

And since, as discussed on page 22, we do not really need the variable **sum**, this program can be written as Program P3.2:

> **Program P3.2**
>
> ```
> public class ProgramP3_2 {
>   public static void main(String[] args) {
>     int a = 14;
>     int b = 25;
>     System.out.printf("%d + %d = %d\n", a, b, a + b);
>   }
> }
> ```

This program is very restrictive. If we wish to add two other numbers, we will have to change the numbers 14 and 25 in the program to the ones required. We would then have to re-compile the program. And each time we want to add two different numbers, we would have to change the program. This can become very tedious.

It would be nice if we could write the program in such a way that when we *run* the program, we will have the opportunity to tell the program which numbers we wish to add. In this way, the numbers would not be tied to the program, and the program would be more *flexible*. When we 'tell' the program the numbers, we say we are supplying *data* to the program. But how do we get the program to 'ask' us for the numbers and how do we 'tell' the program what the numbers are?

We can get the program to *prompt* us for a number by printing a message such as:

    Enter first number:

using a **printf** statement. The program must then wait for us to type the number and, when it is typed, *read* it. This can be done with **nextInt** (explained shortly). Before first, let us rewrite the algorithm using these new ideas:

    prompt for the first number
    read the number

prompt for the second number
read the number
find the sum
print the sum

We can *implement* this algorithm in Java as Program P3.3.

Program P3.3

```
//prompt for two numbers and find their sum
import java.util.*;
public class ProgramP3_3 {
   public static void main(String[] args) {
      Scanner in = new Scanner(System.in);
      System.out.printf("Enter first number: ");
      int a = in.nextInt();
      System.out.printf("Enter second number: ");
      int b = in.nextInt();
      System.out.printf("%d + %d = %d\n", a, b, a + b);
   }
}
```

The **Scanner** class was introduced in Java 5.0 (officially, Java 2 Standard Editon 5.0). Before that, a simple thing like reading a number from the input was a very complicated affair. It is now simpler but still not as easy as it could be. In order to use the **Scanner** class, your program must be preceded by the line

   import java.util.*;

This says that your program has access to the classes (one of which is **Scanner**) in the *package* **java.util**.

In Java, **System.in** is used to refer to the *standard input*, usually the keyboard. The statement

   Scanner in = new Scanner(System.in);

creates a new **Scanner** *object* called **in** which will let us read data typed at the keyboard using the *methods* (functions) from the **Scanner** class. One such method is called **nextInt** and the statement

   int a = in.nextInt();

reads the next integer from the "input stream", **in** (in this case, the keyboard), and stores it in the variable **a**. We say that **nextInt** *returns* the next integer.

Note that we write **nextInt()**—the empty brackets, which must be present, indicate that **nextInt** is a method which takes no arguments.

The above explanation may not make much sense to you at this stage but don't worry. You do not need to understand it all in order to read numbers from the input. For now, just think of the **import** and **Scanner in...** statements as a necessary evil for being able to get data from a user.

When the program is run, the first **printf** statement will print:
    Enter first number:

The **nextInt** function will then cause the computer to wait for the user to type a number.

Suppose she types 23; the screen will look like this:

```
Enter first number: 23
```

When she presses the "Enter" or "Return" key on the keyboard, **nextInt** *reads* the number and stores it in the variable **a**.

The next **printf** statement then prompts:
    Enter second number:

In the statement
    int b = in.nextInt();

nextInt causes the computer to wait for the user to enter a number. Suppose she enters 18; **nextInt** reads the number and stores it in the variable **b**. At this stage, the number 23 is stored in **a** and 18 is stored in **b**. We can picture this as:

    a | 23 | b | 18 |

The program then executes the last **printf** statement and prints:
    23 + 18 = 41

At the end, the screen will look as follows. Underlined items are typed by the user, everything else is printed by the computer:

```
Enter first number: 23
Enter second number: 18
23 + 18 = 41
```

Since the user is free to enter *any* numbers, the program will work for whatever numbers are entered provided the numbers entered and their sum are within the range of numbers which can be stored in an **int** variable. If they are not, strange results will be printed.

When using **nextInt**, it is important that the next item in the data be an integer. If it is not, your program will crash. For example, in this program, if the user enters

Writing programs using sequence logic

23.0, say, the program will crash since 23.0 is not an integer (because of the decimal point).

Spaces, tabs and blank lines (so-called *whitespace*) do not matter; **nextInt** will simply keep reading data, ignoring spaces, tabs and blank lines, until it finds the next integer. However, if any invalid character is encountered, the program will crash. For instance, if the user types

    18.0

or

    =42

the program will crash. In the first case, the decimal point is invalid since an integer is expected and, in the second case, = is not a valid character for an integer.

3.2 How to read data into a double/float variable

If we wish to read a floating-point number from the input stream, **in**, into a **double** variable **x**, we can use

    x = in.nextDouble();

When executed, **nextDouble** expects to find a valid floating-point constant in the data. For example, any of the following will be acceptable:

    4.265
    -707.96
    2.345E+1

In the last case, there must be no spaces, for instance, between the 5 and the E or between the E and the + or between the + and the 1. The following will all be invalid for reading the number 23.45:

    2.345 E+1
    2.345E +1
    2.345E+ 1

If we wish to read a floating-point number into a **float** variable **y**, we can use

    y = in.nextFloat();

When executed, **nextFloat** expects to find a valid floating-point constant in the data. For example, any of the following will be acceptable:

    3.125
    -7201.69
    23.45E-2

Surprisingly, a **float** constant written with an **f** or **F** is invalid *as data*; you cannot supply 23.4, say, as 23.4f or 23.4F.

When entering data for a **float/double** variable, an integer is acceptable. If you enter 42, say, it will be interpreted as `42.0`. But, as discussed above, you cannot enter a floating-point constant for an **int** variable; if you do, your program will crash.

Consider the statements

```
int item = in.nextInt();
double price = in.nextDouble();
int quantity = in.nextInt();
```

When executed, they expect to find 3 numbers next in the data.

- The first must be an **int** constant which will be stored in **item**.
- The second must be a **double** (or **int**) constant which will be stored in **price**.
- The third must be an **int** constant which will be stored in **quantity**.

The following are all valid data for these statements:

```
4000   7.99   8
3575   10     44        price will be interpreted as 10.00
5600   25.0   1
```

As usual, any amount of whitespace may be used to separate the numbers.

The following are all invalid data for these statements:

```
4000   7.99   8.5       8.5 is not an integer constant
35.75  10     44        35.75 is not an integer constant
560    25     amt = 7   a is not a valid numeric character
```

After a number is read, we can imagine a 'pointer' poised just after the number; a subsequent **nextInt** or **nextDouble** will continue to read data from that point. To illustrate, suppose some data is typed as

```
4000 7.99 8
```

and consider the above statements.

Initially, think of the pointer as positioned before 4000. The first statement will store 4000 in **item**. On completion, the pointer is positioned at the space after 4000.

The next statement will continue reading from that point and will store `7.99` in **price**. On completion, the pointer is positioned at the space after `7.99`.

The third statement will continue reading from that point and store 8 in **quantity**. The pointer will be positioned at the character after 8; this may be a space or the *end-of-line* character. Any subsequent reading of data will start from that charater. We will refer to this imaginary pointer as the *data pointer*, or, simply, pointer.

3.3 How to read strings

On page 45, we saw how to declare a variable to hold a string value. For example, the declaration

        String tool = "Yellow Wheelbarrow";

stores a string value in **tool**.

Now we show you how to read a value from the input into **tool**. There are several ways to do this in Java. We will use the **nextLine** method (function), also found in the **Scanner** class. The statement

        String tool = in.nextLine();

reads characters and stores them in **tool** starting from the current position of the data pointer until the end-of-line is reached. The end-of-line character is *not* stored. The data pointer is positioned at the beginning of the next line.

For example, if the data line is

    Red Hammer

then the string **Red Hammer** is stored in **tool**. The *effect* is the same as if we had written

        String tool = "Red Hammer";

Of course, *this* statement *always* assigns **Red Hammer** to **tool**, whereas the one above will assign *whatever* is typed by the user.

Consider the following:

        System.out.printf("Hi, what's your name? ");
        String name = in.nextLine();
        System.out.printf("Delighted to meet you, %s\n", name);

When executed,

- the first **printf** statement will ask for your name
- the next statement will wait for you to type your name. You must press the "Enter" or "Return" key to indicate you are finished typing. The name you type will be stored in the variable **name**
- **printf** will then print a greeting using your name

Your computer screen will look as follows (assuming **Kelvin Singh** is typed as the name):

    Hi, what's your name? <u>Kelvin Singh</u>
    Delighted to meet you, Kelvin Singh

As mentioned, **nextLine** will store whatever is typed (except "Enter" or "Return") in **name**. But suppose we want the program to run as follows:

> Hi, what's your name? <u>Kelvin Singh</u>
> Delighted to meet you, Kelvin

We want to print only the person's first name in our response. To do this, we will need to get the first name and last name separately. We can do this with the method **next**, also from the **Scanner** class. Consider the following:

```
                          Program P3.4
import java.util.*;
public class Greeting {
   public static void main(String[] args) {
      Scanner in = new Scanner(System.in);
      System.out.printf("Hi, what's your name? ");
      String firstName = in.next();  //read the first name
      String lastName = in.next();   //read the last name
      System.out.printf("Delighted to meet you, %s\n", firstName);
   }
}
```

When run, this program will work as above. In general, **next** returns "the next token" in the input. On page 25, we described what tokens are. Assuming that at least one space was typed between the first and last names, then the first name would be one token and the last name would be another. The space after the first name indicates the end of that token and the end-of-line character indicates the end of the second token. We can think that a token starts with the next non-whitespace character and ends with the first whitespace character after that; the whitespace character that ends the token is not part of the token.

As a matter of interest, the statement

   System.out.printf("Delighted to meet you, Mr. %s\n", lastName);

would print

   Delighted to meet you, Mr. Singh

3.4 Examples

We now write programs to solve a few problems. You should try solving the problems before looking at the solutions. In the sample runs, the underlined items are typed by the user; everything else is printed by the computer.

Writing programs using sequence logic

Problem 1

Write a program to request 3 integers and print their average to 1 decimal place. The program should work as follows:

```
Enter 3 integers: 23 7 10
Their average is 13.3
```

A solution is shown as Program P3.5.

Program P3.5
```java
import java.util.*;
public class Average3 {
   public static void main(String[] args) {
   //request 3 integers; print their average
      Scanner in = new Scanner(System.in);
      System.out.printf("Enter 3 integers: ");
      int a = in.nextInt();
      int b = in.nextInt();
      int c = in.nextInt();
      double average = (a + b + c) / 3.0;
      System.out.printf("\nTheir average is %3.1f\n", average);
   }
}
```

Points to note about Program P3.5:

- The variable **average** is declared as **double** instead of **int** since the average may not be a whole number.
- If whole numbers are not entered in the data, the program will crash or, at best, give incorrect results.
- We use 3.0 instead of 3 in calculating the average. This forces a floating-point division to be performed. If we had used 3, an integer division would be performed, giving 13.0 as the answer for the sample data, above.
- In the last **printf**, the first \n is used to print the blank line in the output.
- The variable **average** is not really necessary in this program. We could calculate and print the average in the **printf** statement with

    System.out.printf("\nTheir average is %3.1f\n", (a + b + c) / 3.0);

Problem 2

Write a program to request a whole number and print the number and its square. The program should work as follows:

```
Enter a whole number: 6
Square of 6 is 36
```

A solution is shown as Program P3.6.

Program P3.6
```java
import java.util.*;
public class Square {
    public static void main(String[] args) {
    //request a whole number; print its square
        Scanner in = new Scanner(System.in);
        System.out.printf("Enter a whole number: ");
        int num = in.nextInt();
        int numSq = num * num;
        System.out.printf("\nSquare of %d is %d\n", num, numSq);
    }
}
```

Points to note about Program P3.6:

- To make the output readable, in the last statement, note the space after **f** and the spaces around **is**. If these spaces are omitted, the sample output will be

    ```
    Square of6is36
    ```

- The variable **numSq** is not really necessary. It can be omitted altogether and the same output printed with

    ```
    System.out.printf("\nSquare of %d is %d\n", num, num * num);
    ```

- The program assumes an integer will be entered; if anything other than an integer is entered, the program will crash or give incorrect results. To cater for numbers with a point, declare **num** (and **numSq**, if used) as **double**.

Problem 3

The following data are given for a customer in a bank: name, account number, average balance and number of transactions made during the month. It is required to calculate the interest earned and service charge.

The interest is calculated by

Writing programs using sequence logic

> interest = 6% of average balance

and the service charge is calculated by

> service charge = 50 cents per transaction

Write a program to read the data for the customer, calculate the interest and service charge, and print the customer's name, average balance, interest and service charge.

The following is a sample run of the program:

```
Name? Alice Wonder
Account number? 4901119250056048
Average balance? 2500
Number of transactions? 13

Name: Alice Wonder
Average balance: $2500.00
Interest: $150.00
Service charge: $6.50
```

A solution is shown as Program P3.7.

Program P3.7

```java
import java.util.*;
public class Banking {
   public static void main(String[] args) {
   //calculate interest and service charge for bank customer
      Scanner in = new Scanner(System.in);

      System.out.printf("Name? ");
      String name = in.nextLine();
      System.out.printf("Account number? ");
      String acctNum = in.nextLine();
      System.out.printf("Average balance? ");
      double avgBalance = in.nextDouble();
      System.out.printf("Number of transactions? ");
      int numTrans = in.nextInt();

      double interest = avgBalance * 0.06;
      double service = numTrans * 0.50;

      System.out.printf("\nName: %s\n", name);
      System.out.printf("Average balance: $%3.2f\n", avgBalance);
      System.out.printf("Interest: $%3.2f\n", interest);
      System.out.printf("Service charge: $%3.2f\n", service);
   }
}
```

This problem is more complicated than those we have seen so far. It involves more data and more processing. But we can simplify its solution if we tackle it in small steps.

First, let us outline an algorithm for solving the problem. This can be:

> prompt for and read each item of data
> calculate interest earned
> calculate service charge
> print required output

The logic here is fairly straightforward and a little thought should convince us that these are the steps required to solve the problem.

Next, we must choose variables for the data items we need to store.

- For the customer's name, we need a string variable—we call it **name**.
- We may be tempted to use an integer variable for the account number but this is not a good idea for two reasons: an account number may contain letters (as in CD55887700) or it may be a very long integer, too big to fit in an **int** variable. For these reasons, we use a string variable which we call **acctNum**.
- The average balance may contain a decimal point and should be stored in a **double** variable; we call it **avgBalance**.
- The number of transactions is a whole number so we use an **int** variable, **numTrans**.

Next, we need variables to store the interest and service charge. Since these may contain a decimal point, we must use **double** variables—we call them **interest** and **service**.

Prompting for and reading the data are fairly straightforward, given what we have covered so far. We need only emphasize that when numeric data is being entered, it must be a numeric constant. We cannot, for instance, enter the average balance as $2500 or as 2,500. We must enter it as 2500 or 2500.0 or 2500.00.

The calculation of the interest and service charge presents the biggest challenge. We must specify the calculation in a form which the computer can understand and execute.

We cannot, for instance, write

> interest = 6% of avgBalance;

or even

> interest = 6% * avgBalance;

or

> service = 50 cents per transaction;

We must express each right-hand side as a proper arithmetic expression, using appropriate constants, variables and operators. Hence,

"6% of average balance" must be expressed as **avgBalance * 0.06** or **0.06 * avgBalance** and

"50 cents per transaction" must be expressed as **numTrans * 0.50** or **0.5 * numTrans** or something similar, even **numTrans / 2.0**.

Printing the output is fairly straightforward. Even though, for example, we cannot use $ when entering data for average balance, we can print a dollar sign in front of it when we print its value. All we need to do is print $ as part of a string. How this is done is shown in the program. Similarly, we print the interest and service charge labelled with a dollar sign.

We use the specification %3.2f for printing **avgBalance**. We intentionally use a small field width of 3 so that **avgBalance** is printed using only the exact number of print columns needed for printing its value. This ensures that its value is printed right next to the dollar sign. Similar remarks apply to **interest** and **service**.

Problem 4

At a football match, tickets are sold in 3 categories: reserved, stands and grounds. For each of these categories, you are given the ticket price and the number of tickets sold. Write a program to prompt for these values and print the amount of money collected from each category of tickets. Also print the total number of tickets sold and the total amount of money collected.

We will write the program to operate as follows when run:

```
Reserved price and tickets sold? 100 500
Stands price and tickets sold? 75 4000
Grounds price and tickets sold? 40 8000

Reserved sales: $50000.00
Stands sales: $300000.00
Grounds sales: $320000.00

12500 tickets were sold
Total money collected: $670000.00
```

As shown, we prompt for and read two values at a time, the price and the number of tickets sold.

For each category, the sales is calculated by multiplying the ticket price by the number of tickets sold.

The total number of tickets sold is calculated by adding the number of tickets sold for each category.

The total money collected is calculated by adding the sales for each category.

An outline of the algorithm for solving the problem is:

prompt for and read reserved price and tickets sold
calculate reserved sales
prompt for and read stands price and tickets sold
calculate stands sales
prompt for and read grounds price and tickets sold
calculate grounds sales
calculate total tickets
calculate total sales
print required output

A solution is shown as Program P3.8. The price can be entered as an integer or **double** constant; the number of tickets *must* be entered as an integer constant.

Program P3.8

```
import java.util.*;
public class TicketSales {
  public static void main(String[] args) {
  //calculate ticket sales for football match
    Scanner in = new Scanner(System.in);
    double rPrice, sPrice, gPrice;
    double rSales, sSales, gSales, tSales;
    int rTickets, sTickets, gTickets, tTickets;

    System.out.printf("Reserved price and tickets sold? ");
    rPrice = in.nextDouble();
    rTickets = in.nextInt();
    rSales = rPrice * rTickets;
    System.out.printf("Stands price and tickets sold? ");
    sPrice = in.nextDouble();
    sTickets = in.nextInt();
    sSales = sPrice * sTickets;
    System.out.printf("Grounds price and tickets sold? ");
    gPrice = in.nextDouble();
    gTickets = in.nextInt();
    gSales = gPrice * gTickets;

    tTickets = rTickets + sTickets + gTickets;
    tSales = rSales + sSales + gSales;

    System.out.printf("\nReserved sales: $%3.2f\n", rSales);
    System.out.printf("Stands sales: $%3.2f\n", sSales);
    System.out.printf("Grounds sales: $%3.2f\n", gSales);
    System.out.printf("\n%d tickets were sold\n", tTickets);
    System.out.printf("Total money collected: $%3.2f\n", tSales);
  }
}
```

In our previous examples, we declared variables as they were needed. This program illustrates a slightly different programming style. Here, we declare all our variables first and, then, just use them when they are needed. Which is better? Neither, really—it's just a matter of personal style. Both are acceptable as good programming practice. In fact, some languages *require* that you declare all your variables at the head of your program. Java is a bit more flexible.

Exercises 3

1. For each of the following, give examples of data which will be read correctly and examples of data which will cause the program to crash: (assume the declarations **int i, j ; double x, y;**)

    (a) i = in.nextInt(); j = in.nextInt();
    (b) x = in.nextDouble(); y = in.nextDouble();
    (c) i = in.nextInt(); x = in.nextDouble(); j = in.nextInt();

2. For 1(c), state what will be stored in **i, x** and **j** for each of the following sets of data:

    (a) 14 11 52
    (b) -7 2.3 52
    (c) 0 6.1 7.0
    (d) 1.0 8 -1

3. Write a program which requests a user to enter a weight in kilograms, and converts it to pounds. (1 kilogram = 2.2 pounds).

4. Write a program which requests a length in centimetres and converts it to inches. (1 inch = 2.54 cm).

5. Assuming that **12** and **5** are entered as data, identify the logic error in the following statements (**a, b, c, d** and **e** are **int**):

    ```
    a = in.nextInt();
    b = in.nextInt();
    c = (a - b) * 2;
    d = e + a;
    e = a / (b + 1);
    System.out.printf("%d %d %d\n", c, d, e);
    ```

    When the error is corrected, what is printed?

6. What is printed by the following (**a, b,** and **c** are **int**)?

    ```
    a = 13;
    b = a + 12;
    System.out.printf("%d %d\n", a, b);
    c = a + b;
    a = a + 11;
    System.out.printf("%d %d %d\n", a, b, c);
    ```

7. Write a program which requests a price and a discount percent. The program prints the original price, the discount amount and the amount the customer must pay.

8. Same as 7, but assume that 15% tax must be added on to the amount the customer must pay.

9. Write a program to calculate electricity charges for a customer. The program requests a name, previous meter reading and current meter reading. The difference in the two readings gives the number of units of electricity used. The customer pays a fixed charge of $25 plus 20 cents for each unit used.

   Print all the data, the number of units used and the amount the customer must pay, appropriately labelled.

10. Modify 9 so that the program requests the fixed charge and the rate per unit.

11. Write a program to request a student's name and marks in 4 subjects. The program must print the name, total marks and average mark, appropriately labelled.

12. Write a program which requests a person's gross salary, deductions allowed and rate of tax (e.g. 25, meaning 25%) and calculates his net pay as follows:

    tax is calculated by applying the rate of tax to the gross salary minus the deductions;

    net pay is calculated by gross salary minus tax.

    Print the gross salary, tax deducted and net pay, appropriately labelled.

    Also print the percentage of the gross salary that was paid in tax.

    Make up appropriate sets of data for testing the program.

13. Write a program which, when run, works as follows:

    > Hi, what's your name? **Alice**
    > Welcome to our show, Alice
    > How old are you? **27**
    > Hmm, you don't look a day over 22
    > Tell me, Alice, where do you live? **Princes Town**
    > Oh, I've heard Princes Town is a lovely place

14. A ball is thrown vertically upwards with an initial speed of **U** metres per second. Its height **H** after time **T** seconds is given by

    $$H = UT - 4.9T^2$$

    Write a program which requests **U** and **T** and prints the height of the ball after **T** seconds.

15. Write a program to calculate the cost of carpeting a rectangular room in a house. The program must
    - request the length and breadth of the room (assume they are in metres)
    - request the cost per square metre of the carpet
    - calculate the area of the room
    - calculate the cost of the carpet for the room
    - print the area and the cost, appropriately labelled

16. Write a program which, given a length in inches, converts it to yards, feet and inches. (1 yard = 3 feet, 1 foot = 12 inches). For example, given **100** inches, the program should print **2 yd 2 ft 4 in**.

4 Writing programs using selection logic

In this chapter, we will explain:

- what are Boolean expressions
- how to write programs using **if**
- how to write programs using **if...else**
- where semicolons are required, where they are optional and where they must *not* be put
- how a program should be tested
- why symbolic constants are useful and how to use them in a Java program

In the last chapter, we showed how to write programs using sequence logic—programs whose statements are executed "in sequence" from the first to the last.

In this chapter, the programs will use *selection* logic—they will *test* some *condition* and take different courses of action based on whether the condition is true or false. In Java, selection logic is implemented using the **if** and the **if...else** statements.

4.1 Boolean expressions

In Section 2.7, we briefly touched on Boolean expressions. We now look at them in more detail.

The following are examples of Boolean expressions:

> j is equal to 999
> a is greater than 100
> $a^2 + b^2$ is equal to c^2
> b^2 is greater than or equal to 4ac
> s is not equal to 0

Each of these can be either true or false. These are examples of a special kind of Boolean expression called *relational expressions*. Such expressions simply check if one value is equal to, not equal to, greater than, greater than or equal to, less than and less than or equal to another value. We write them using *relational operators*.

The Java relational operators (with examples) are:

==	equal to	j == 999, a*a + b*b == c*c
!=	not equal to	s != 0, a != b + c
>	greater than	a > 100
>=	greater than or equal to	b*b >= 4.0*a *c
<	less than	n < 0
<=	less than or equal to	score <= 65

Boolean expressions are normally used to control the flow of program execution. For example, we may have a variable (j, say) which starts off with a value of 0. We keep increasing it by 1 and we want to know when its value reaches 100. We say we wish to know when the *condition* j == 100 is true. A condition is the common name for a Boolean expression.

The real power of programming lies in the ability of a program to *test* a *condition* and decide whether it is true or false. If it is true, the program can perform one set of actions and if it is false, it can perform another set, or simply do nothing at all.

For example, suppose the variable **score** holds the score obtained by a student in a test, and the student passes if her score is 50 or more and fails if it is less than 50. A program can be written to *test* the *condition*

    score >= 50

If it is true, the student passes; if it is false, the student fails. In Java, this can be written as:

    if (score >= 50) System.out.printf("Pass\n");
    else System.out.printf("Fail\n");

When the computer gets to this statement, it compares the current value of **score** with 50. If the value is greater than or equal to 50, we say that the condition **score >= 50** is true. In this case the program prints **Pass**. If the value of **score** is less than 50, we say that the condition **score >= 50** is false. In this case, the program prints **Fail**.

In this chapter, we will see how Boolean expressions are used in **if** and **if...else** statements and, in the next chapter, we will see how they are used in **while** and **for** statements.

With the relational operators, we can create *simple* conditions. But sometimes, we need to ask if one thing is true AND another thing is true. We may also need to know if one of two things is true. For these situations, we need *compound* conditions. To create compound conditions, we use the *logical operators* AND, OR and NOT.

For example, suppose we want to know if the value of **h** lies between 1 and 99, inclusive. We want to know if **h** is greater than or equal to 1 AND if **h** is less than or equal to 99. In Java, we express this as:

(h >= 1) && (h <= 99)

The symbol for AND is **&&**.

Note the following:

- the variable **h** *must be repeated* in both conditions. It is tempting, but wrong, to write

    h >= 1 && <= 99   //this is wrong

- The brackets around **h >= 1** and **h <= 99** are not *required*, but it is not wrong to put them. This is so since **&&** (and **||**, see next) have lower precedence than the relational operators. Without the brackets,

    h >= 1 && h <= 99

    would be interpreted by Java as

    (h >= 1) && (h <= 99)

    the same as with the brackets.

If **n** is an integer representing a month of the year, we can check if **n** is invalid by testing if **n** is less than 1 OR **n** is greater than 12. In Java, we express this as:

(n < 1) || (n > 12)

In Java, the symbol for OR is **||**. As discussed above, the brackets are not required and we could write the expression as

n < 1 || n > 12

This tests if **n** is invalid. Of course, we can test if **n** is valid by testing if

n >= 1 && n <= 12

Which test we use depends on how *we* wish to express our logic. Sometimes it's convenient to use the valid test, sometimes the invalid one.

If **p** is some Boolean expression, then **NOT p** reverses the truth value of p. In others words, if **p** is true then **NOT p** is false; if **p** is false, **NOT p** is true. In Java, the symbol for NOT is the exclamation mark, **!**. Using the above example, since

n >= 1 && n <= 12

tests for valid **n**, the condition **NOT (n >=1 && n <= 12)** tests for invalid **n**. This is written in Java as

! (n >= 1 && n <= 12)

This is equivalent to **n < 1 || n > 12**.

In general, if **p** and **q** are Boolean expressions, then:

- **p && q** is **true** when both **p** and **q** are **true** and **false**, otherwise;

- p || q is **true** when either **p** is **true** or **q** is **true** and **false** only when both **p** and **q** are **false**;
- !p is true when **p** is **false** and **false** when **p** is **true**.

Most of the programs in this book will use simple conditions. A few will use compound conditions.

4.2 The if construct

Let us write a program for the following problem:

A computer repair shop charges $100 per hour for labour plus the cost of any parts used in the repair. However, the minimum charge for any job is $150. Prompt for the number of hours worked and the cost of parts (which could be $0) and print the charge for the job.

We will write the program so that it works as follows:

```
Hours worked? 2.5
Cost of parts? 20

Charge for the job: $270.00
```

or

```
Hours worked? 1
Cost of parts? 25

Charge for the job: $150.00
```

The following algorithm describes the steps required to solve the problem:

```
prompt for and read the hours worked
prompt for and read the cost of parts
calculate charge = hours worked * 100 + cost of parts
if charge is less than 150 then set charge to 150
print charge
```

This is another example of an algorithm written in *pseudocode*—an informal way of specifying programming logic.

The algorithm introduces a new statement—the **if** statement. The expression **charge is less than 150** is an example of a *condition*. If the condition is **true**, the statement after **then** (called the *then part*) is executed; if it is **false**, the statement after **then** is *not* executed.

Program P4.1 shows how to express this algorithm as a Java program.

Writing programs using selection logic

Program P4.1

```java
import java.util.*;
public class JobCharge {
   public static void main(String[] args) {
   //print job charge based on hours worked and cost of parts
      Scanner in = new Scanner(System.in);
      double hours, parts, jobCharge;

      System.out.printf("Hours worked? ");
      hours = in.nextDouble();
      System.out.printf("Cost of parts? ");
      parts = in.nextDouble();
      jobCharge = hours * 100 + parts;
      if (jobCharge < 150) jobCharge = 150;
      System.out.printf("\nCharge for the job: $%3.2f\n", jobCharge);
   }
}
```

For this program, we choose to use 3 variables—**hours, parts** and **jobCharge**, all of type **double** since we may need to enter floating-point values for hours worked and cost of parts.

It is very important that you make an extra effort to understand the **if** statement since it is one of the most important statements in programming. It is the **if** statement that can make a program appear to think.

The condition **charge is less than 150** of the pseudocode algorithm is expressed in our program as **jobCharge < 150**. When the program is executed, the job charge is calculated in the normal way (**hours * 100 + parts**). The **if** statement then tests if this value, **jobCharge**, is less than 150; if it is, then **jobCharge** is set to 150. If it is not less than 150, **jobCharge** remains as it is. The statement

   if (jobCharge < 150) jobCharge = 150;

is a simple example of the **if** *construct*. Observe that the word **then** is *not* used in Java. In general, the construct takes the following form in Java:

> if (<condition>) <statement>
>
> The word **if** and the brackets around **<condition>** are *required* by Java. You must supply **<condition>** and **<statement>** where **<condition>** is a Boolean expression and **<statement>** can be either a one-line statement or a block[1]. If **<condition>** is **true**, **<statement>** is executed; if **<condition>** is **false**, **<statement>** is **not** executed. In either case, the program continues with the statement, if any, after **<statement>**.

---

[1] One or more statements enclosed by { and }

In the program, <condition> is **jobCharge < 150** and <statement> is **jobCharge = 150;**.

To give an example where <statement> is a block, suppose we want to exchange the values of two variables **a** and **b** but only if **a** is bigger than **b**. This can be done with (using as an example **a** = 15, **b** = 8):

```
if (a > b)
{
   c = a;   //store a in a temporary variable c; c becomes 15
   a = b;   //store b in a; a becomes 8
   b = c;   //store c, the old value of a, in b; b becomes 15
}
```

Here, <statement> is the part from **{** to **}**, a block containing 3 assignment statements. If **a** is greater than **b**, the block is executed (and the values are exchanged); if **a** is **not** greater than **b**, the block is **not** executed (and the values remain as they are). In passing, be aware that exchanging the values of two variables requires *three* assignment statements; it cannot be done with *two*. If you are not convinced, try it.

In general, if there are several things that we want to do if a condition is true, we must enclose them within **{** and **}** to create a block. This will ensure that we satisfy Java's rule that <statement> is a single statement or a block.

It is good programming practice to *indent* the statements in the block. This makes it easy to see at a glance which statements are in the block. If we had written the above as

```
if (a > b)
{
c = a;   //store a in a temporary variable c; c becomes 15
a = b;   //store b in a; a becomes 8
b = c;   //store c, the old value of a, in b; b becomes 15
}
```

the structure of the block is not so easy to see.

When we are writing *pseudocode*, we normally use the following format:

```
if <condition> then
   <statement1>
   <statement2>
   etc.
endif
```

The construct is terminated with **endif**, a convention used by many programmers. Note, again, that we indent the statements to be executed if <condition> is true. We emphasize that **endif** is not a Java word but merely a convenient word used by programmers in writing pseudocode.

Writing programs using selection logic

The example illustrates one style of writing a block in an **if** statement. This style matches **{** and **}** as follows:

```
if (<condition>)
{
   <statement1>;
   <statement2>;
      etc.
}
```

Here, **{** and **}** line up with **if** and the statements are indented. This makes it easy to recognize what's in the body. For a small program, it probably doesn't matter, but as program size increases, it will become more important for the layout of the code to reflect its structure. In this book, we will use the following style[2]:

```
if (<condition>) {
   <statement1>;
   <statement2>;
      etc.
}
```

We will put **{** on the first line after the right bracket and let **}** match up with **if**; the statements in the block are indented. We believe this is as clear as the first style and it's one less line in the program! Which style you use is a matter of personal preference; choose one and use it consistently.

Example – finding the sum of two lengths

Suppose that a length is given in metres and centimetres, for example, 3m 75cm. You are given two pairs of integers representing two lengths. Write a program to prompt for two lengths and print their sum such that the centimetre value is less than 100.

For example, the sum of 3m 25cm and 2m 15cm is 5m 40cm, but the sum of 3m 75cm and 5m 50cm is 9m 25cm.

Assume the program works as follows:

```
Enter values for m and cm: 3 75
Enter values for m and cm: 5 50
Sum is 9m 25cm
```

Observe that the data must be entered with digits only. If, for instance, we type 3m 75cm we will get an error since 3m is not a valid integer constant. Our program will assume that the first number entered is the metre value and the second number is the centimetre value.

---

[2] As you would know by now, the *compiler* doesn't care which style is used.

We find the sum by adding the two metre values and adding the two centimetre values. If the centimetre value is less than 100, there is nothing more to do. But if it is not, we must subtract 100 from it and add 1 to the metre value. This logic is expressed by

```
m = sum of metre values
cm = sum of centimetre values
if cm >= 100 then
    subtract 100 from cm
    add 1 to m
endif
```

As a 'boundary' case, we must check that our program works if **cm** is exactly 100. As an exercise, verify that it does.

Program P4.2 solves the problem as described.

Program P4.2

```java
import java.util.*;
public class SumOfLengths {
   public static void main(String[] args) {
   //find the sum of two lengths given in metres and cm
      Scanner in = new Scanner(System.in);
      int m1, cm1, m2, cm2, mSum, cmSum;

      System.out.printf("Enter values for m and cm: ");
      m1 = in.nextInt();
      cm1 = in.nextInt();
      System.out.printf("Enter values for m and cm: ");
      m2 = in.nextInt();
      cm2 = in.nextInt();

      mSum = m1 + m2;  //add the metres
      cmSum = cm1 + cm2;  //add the centimetres
      if (cmSum >= 100) {
         cmSum = cmSum - 100;
         mSum = mSum + 1;
      }
      System.out.printf("\nSum is %dm %dcm\n", mSum, cmSum);
   }
}
```

We use the variables **m1** and **cm1** for the first length, **m2** and **cm2** for the second length, and **mSum** and **cmSum** for the sum of the two lengths.

The code assumes that the **cm** part of the given lengths is less than 100 and works correctly if this is so. But what if the lengths were 3m 150cm and 2m 200cm?

The program will print 6m 250cm. (As an exercise, follow the logic of the program to see why.) While this is correct, it is not in the correct format since we require the centimetre value to be less than 100. We can modify our program to work in these cases as well by using integer division and % (remainder operator).

The following pseudocode shows how:

```
m = sum of metre values
cm = sum of centimetre values
if cm >= 100 then
    add cm / 100 to m
    set cm to cm % 100
endif
```

In this example, **m** is set to 5 and **cm** is set to 350. Since **cm** is greater than 100, we work out **350 / 100** (the number of 100s in 350) which is 3, using integer division; this is added to **m**, giving 8. The next line sets **cm** to **350 % 100** which is 50. So the answer we get is **8m 50cm**, which is correct *and* in the correct format.

The above pseudocode is expressed in Program 4.2 as:

```
mSum = m1 + m2;  //add the metres
cmSum = cm1 + cm2;  //add the centimetres
if (cmSum >= 100) {
    mSum = mSum + cmSum / 100;
    cmSum = cmSum % 100;
}
```

Note that the statements in the 'then part' *must* be written in the order shown. We must use the (original) value of **cm** to work out **cm / 100** before changing it in the next statement to **cm % 100**. As an exercise, work out what value will be computed for the sum if these statements are reversed. (The answer will be 5m 50cm, which is wrong. Can you see why?)

With these changes, the program will run as follows:

```
Enter values for m and cm: 3 150
Enter values for m and cm: 2 200

Sum is 8m 50cm
```

The astute reader may recognize that we do not even need the **if** statement.

Consider:

```
mSum = m1 + m2;   //add the metres
cmSum = cm1 + cm2;  //add the centimetres
mSum = mSum + cmSum / 100;
cmSum = cmSum % 100;
```

where the last two statements come from the **if** statement.

We know therefore that this will work if **cmSum** is greater than or equal to 100 since, when that is the case, these four statements are executed.

What if **cmSum** is less than 100? Originally, the last two statements would not have been executed since the **if** condition would have been false. *Now* they are executed. Let us see what happens. Using the example of 3m 25cm and 2m 15cm, we get **mSum** as 5 and **cmSum** as 40.

In the next statement **40 / 100** is 0 so **mSum** does not change and in the last statement **40 % 100** is 40 so **cmSum** does not change. So the answer will be printed correctly as

```
Sum is 5m 40cm
```

You should begin to realize by now that there is usually more than one way to express the logic of a program. With experience and study, you will learn which ways are better and why.

4.3 The if...else construct

Let us write a program for the following problem:

A student is given 3 tests, each marked out of 100. The student passes if his average mark is greater than or equal to 50 and fails if his average mark is less than 50. Prompt for the 3 marks and print **Pass** if the student passes and **Fail** if he fails.

We will write the program assuming it works as follows:

```
Enter 3 marks: 60 40 56
Average is 52.0 Pass
```

or

```
Enter 3 marks: 40 60 36
Average is 45.3 Fail
```

The following algorithm describes the steps required to solve the problem:

```
prompt for the 3 marks
calculate the average
if average is greater than or equal to 50 then
   print "Pass"
else
   print "Fail"
endif
```

The part from **if** to **endif** is an example of the **if...else** *construct*.

Writing programs using selection logic

The condition **average is greater than or equal to 50** is another example of a relational expression. If the condition is **true**, the statement after **then** (the *then part*) is executed; if it is **false**, the statement after **else** (the *else part*) is executed.

The whole *construct* is terminated with **endif**.

When you write pseudocode, what is important is that the logic intended is unmistakably clear. Note again how indentation can help by making it easy to identify the **then** part and the **else** part.

In the end, though, you must express the code in some programming language for it to be run on a computer. Program P4.3 shows how to do this for the above algorithm.

Program P4.3

```
import java.util.*;
public class StudentTest {
  public static void main(String[] args) {
  //request 3 marks; print their average and Pass/Fail
    Scanner in = new Scanner(System.in);
    System.out.printf("Enter 3 marks: ");
    int mark1 = in.nextInt();
    int mark2 = in.nextInt();
    int mark3 = in.nextInt();
    double average = (mark1 + mark2 + mark3) / 3.0;
    System.out.printf("\nAverage is %3.1f", average);
    if (average >= 50) System.out.printf(" Pass\n");
    else System.out.printf(" Fail\n");
  }
}
```

Study carefully the **if...else** construct in the program. It reflects the logic expressed in the pseudocode above. Note, again, that the word **then** is omitted in Java.

In general, the **if...else** construct in Java takes the form shown below.

---

if (<condition>) <statement1> else <statement2>

The words **if** and **else**, and the brackets, are *required* by Java. You must supply <condition>, <statement1> and <statement2>. Each of <statement1> and <statement2> can be a one-line statement or a block. If <condition> is **true**, <statement1> is executed and <statement2> is skipped; if <condition> is **false**, <statement1> is skipped and <statement2> is executed. Note that when the **if** construct is executed, *either* <statement1> *or* <statement2> is executed, but not both.

If ‹statement1› and ‹statement2› are one-line statements, you can use the layout

```
if (‹condition›) ‹statement1›
else ‹statement2›
```

If ‹statement1› and ‹statement2› are blocks, you can use the layout

```
if (‹condition›) {
   ...
}
else {
   ...
}
```

In describing the various constructs in Java, we normally use the phrase "where ‹statement› can be a one-line statement or a block".

It is useful to remember that, in Java, for one-line statements, the semicolon is considered *part of* the statement. Examples are:

```
a = 5;
System.out.printf("Pass\n");
c = in.nextInt();
```

So, in those cases where one-line statements are used, the semicolon, being part of the statement, must be present. In Program P4.3, in the **if...else** statement, ‹statement1› is **System.out.printf("Pass\n");** (semicolon included) and ‹statement2› is **System.out.printf("Fail\n");** (semicolon included).

However, for a block or compound statement, the right brace, **}**, ends the block. So, in those cases where a block is used, there is no need for an additional semicolon to end the block.

It is sometimes useful to remember that the entire **if...else** construct (from **if** to ‹statement2›) is considered by Java to be *one* statement and can be used in any place where one statement is required.

Example – calculating pay

For an example requiring blocks, suppose we have values for hours worked and rate of pay (the amount paid per hour) and wish to calculate a person's regular pay, overtime pay and net pay based on the following:

> if hours worked is less than or equal to 40, regular pay is calculated by multiplying hours worked by rate of pay and overtime pay is 0. If hours worked is greater than 40, regular pay is calculated by multiplying 40 by the rate of pay and overtime pay is calculated by multiplying the hours *in excess of* 40 by the rate of pay by 1.5. Net pay is calculated by adding regular pay and overtime pay.

Writing programs using selection logic

For example, if hours is 36 and rate is 20 dollars per hour, regular pay is $720 (36 times 20) and overtime pay is $0. Net pay is $720.

And if hours is 50 and rate is 12 dollars per hour, regular pay is $480 (40 times 12) and overtime pay is $180 (excess hours 10 times 12 times 1.5). Net pay is $660 (480 + 180).

The above description could be expressed in pseudocode as:

```
if hours is less than or equal to 40 then
   set regular pay to hours x rate
   set overtime pay to 0
else
   set regular pay to 40 x rate
   set overtime pay to (hours - 40) x rate x 1.5
endif
set net pay to regular pay + overtime pay
```

We use indentation to highlight the statements to be executed if the condition "hours is less than or equal to 40" is true and those to be executed if the condition is false. The whole *construct* is terminated with **endif**.

The next step is to convert the pseudocode to Java. When we do, we have to make sure that we stick to Java's rules for writing an **if...else** statement. In this example, we have to ensure that both the **then** and **else** parts are written as blocks since they both consist of more than one statement.

Using the variables **hours** (hours worked), **rate** (rate of pay), **regPay** (regular pay), **ovtPay** (overtime pay) and **netPay** (net pay), we write

```
if (hours <= 40) {
   regPay = hours * rate;
   ovtPay = 0;
}    //no semicolon here; } ends the block
else {
   regPay = 40 * rate;
   ovtPay = (hours - 40) * rate * 1.5;
}    //no semicolon here; } ends the block
netPay = regPay + ovtPay;
```

Note the two comments. It would be wrong to put a semicolon after the first } since the **if** statement continues with an **else** part. If we were to put one, it effectively ends the **if** statement and Java assumes there is no **else** part. When it finds the word **else**, there will be no **if** with which to match it and the program will give a "misplaced else" error.

There is no need for a semicolon after the second } but putting one would do no harm.

Problem: write a program to prompt for hours worked and rate of pay. The program then calculates and prints regular pay, overtime pay and net pay, based on the above description.

The following algorithm outlines the overall logic of the solution:

```
prompt for hours worked and rate of pay
if hours is less than or equal to 40 then
   set regular pay to hours x rate
   set overtime pay to 0
else
   set regular pay to 40 x rate
   set overtime pay to (hours - 40) x rate x 1.5
endif
set net pay to regular pay + overtime pay
print regular pay, overtime pay and net pay
```

This algorithm is implemented as Program P4.4. All the variables are declared as **double** so that fractional values can be entered for hours worked and rate of pay.

Program P4.4

```java
import java.util.*;
public class CalcPay {
  public static void main(String[] args) {
    Scanner in = new Scanner(System.in);
    double hours, rate, regPay, ovtPay, netPay;

    System.out.printf("Hours worked? ");
    hours = in.nextDouble();
    System.out.printf("Rate of pay? ");
    rate = in.nextDouble();

    if (hours <= 40) {
      regPay = hours * rate;
      ovtPay = 0;
    }
    else {
      regPay = 40 * rate;
      ovtPay = (hours - 40) * rate * 1.5;
    }
    netPay = regPay + ovtPay;

    System.out.printf("\nRegular pay: $%3.2f\n", regPay);
    System.out.printf("Overtime pay: $%3.2f\n", ovtPay);
    System.out.printf("Net pay: $%3.2f\n", netPay);
  }
}
```

A sample run of this program is shown below. You should verify that the results are indeed correct.

```
Hours worked? 50
Rate of pay? 12

Regular pay: $480.00
Overtime pay: $180.00
Net pay: $660.00
```

Note that even though **hours** and **rate** are **double**, *data* for them can be supplied in any valid numeric format—here we use the integers 50 and 12. These values would be converted to **double** format before being stored in the variables. We could, if we wished, have typed 50.0 and 12.00, for example.

4.4 On program testing

When we write a program we should test it thoroughly to ensure that it is working correctly. As a minimum, we should test *all paths* through the program. This means that our *test data* must be chosen so that each statement in the program is executed at least once.

For Program P4.4, the sample run tests only when the hours worked is greater than 40. Based on this test alone, we cannot be sure that our program will work correctly if the hours worked is less than or equal to 40. To be sure, we must run another test in which the hours worked is less than or equal to 40. The following is such a sample run:

```
Hours worked? 36
Rate of pay? 20

Regular pay: $720.00
Overtime pay: $0.00
Net pay: $720.00
```

These results are correct which gives us greater assurance that our program is correct. We should also run a test when the hours is exactly 40; we must always test a program at its 'boundaries'. For this program, 40 is a boundary—it is the value at which overtime begins to be paid.

What if the results are incorrect? For example, suppose overtime pay is wrong. We say the program contains a *bug* (an error), and we must *debug* (remove the error from) the program. In this case, we can look at the statement(s) which calculate the overtime pay to see if we have specified the calculation correctly. If this fails to uncover the error, we must painstakingly 'execute' the program by hand using the test data which produced the error. If done properly, this will usually reveal the cause of the error.

4.5 Using symbolic constants in Java

In Program P4.1, we used two constants—100 and 150—denoting the labour charge per hour and the minimum job cost, respectively. What if these values change after the program has been written? We would have to find all occurrences of them in the program and change them to the new values.

This program is fairly short so this would not be too difficult to do. But imagine what the task would be like if the program contained hundreds or even thousands of lines of code. It would be difficult, time-consuming and error-prone to make all the required changes.

We can make life a little easier by using *symbolic constants*[3]—identifiers which we set to the required constants in one place. If we need to change the value of a constant, the change would have to be made in one place only. For example, in Program P4.1, we could use the symbolic constants **ChargePerHour** and **MinJobCost**. We would set **ChargePerHour** to 100 and **MinJobCost** to 150.

We rewrite P4.1 as P4.5 to illustrate how to use symbolic constants in Java.

```
Program P4.5
//This program illustrates the use of symbolic constants
import java.util.*;
public class JobCharge1 {
   final static double ChargePerHour = 100;
   final static double MinJobCost = 150;

   public static void main(String[] args) {
   //print job charge based on hours worked and cost of parts
      Scanner in = new Scanner(System.in);
      double hours, parts, jobCharge;

      System.out.printf("Hours worked? ");
      hours = in.nextDouble();
      System.out.printf("Cost of parts? ");
      parts = in.nextDouble();
      jobCharge = hours * ChargePerHour + parts;
      if (jobCharge < MinJobCost) jobCharge = MinJobCost;
      System.out.printf("\nCharge for the job: $%3.2f\n", jobCharge);
   }
}
```

The statement

final static double ChargePerHour = 100;

---

[3] Some people use the term *manifest constant* or *named constant*

defines **ChargePerHour** as a symbolic constant with a value of 100. The word **final** makes it a constant; the value assigned is final and cannot be changed. For now, take it that the word **static** is required to ensure that storage is allocated for **ChargePerHour** when the class is first loaded into memory.

In **main**, we use **ChargePerHour** instead of 100. Similar remarks apply to **MinJobCost**. Notice that, nowhere in **main**, do we see any numeric constants. This is a good sign that the program is flexible. If the charge per hour or the minimum job cost changes, it would be easy to modify the program to cater for the changes.

In this book, we will use the *convention* of starting a symbolic constant identifier with an uppercase letter. Note, however, that Java allows you to use any valid identifier.

So far, our programs have consisted of a **main** method only. But, in general, a Java program, defined by a **class**, can consist of one or more methods. If we wanted to use a symbolic constant in several methods, we would need to declare it *outside* of all the methods[4]; we have to make it what is called a *class variable* (also called a *static* variable, hence the required word **static**).

In this example, we place the **static** declarations just after the **class** heading and before **main**. This ensures that those symbolic constants are available to any method in the class; in this case, they are available to **main**.

For a slightly bigger example, consider Program P4.4 (page 80). Here, we used two constants—40 and 1.5—denoting the maximum regular hours and the overtime rate factor, respectively. We rewrite Program P4.4 as Program P4.6 (next page) using the symbolic constants **MaxRegularHours** (set to 40) and **OvertimeFactor** (set to 1.5).

Suppose, for instance, the maximum regular hours changes from 40 to 35. Program P4.6 would be easier to change than Program P4.4, since we would need to change the value in the declaration only, thus:

```
final static double MaxRegularHours = 35;
```

No other changes would be needed.

The numbers 40 and 1.5 used in Program P4.4 are referred to as *magic numbers*—they appear in the program for no apparent reason, as if by magic. Magic numbers are a good sign that a program may be restrictive, tied to those numbers. As far as possible, we must write our programs without magic numbers. Using symbolic constants can help to make our programs more flexible and easier to maintain.

---

[4] If we declared it *inside* any method, it would belong to *that* method only.

Program P4.6

```java
import java.util.*;
public class CalcPay1 {
   final static double MaxRegularHours = 40;
   final static double OvertimeFactor = 1.5;

   public static void main(String[] args) {
      Scanner in = new Scanner(System.in);
      double hours, rate, regPay, ovtPay, netPay;

      System.out.printf("Hours worked? ");
      hours = in.nextDouble();
      System.out.printf("Rate of pay? ");
      rate = in.nextDouble();

      if (hours <= MaxRegularHours) {
         regPay = hours * rate;
         ovtPay = 0;
      }
      else {
         regPay = 40 * rate;
         ovtPay = (hours - MaxRegularHours) * rate * OvertimeFactor;
      }
      netPay = regPay + ovtPay;

      System.out.printf("\nRegular pay: $%3.2f\n", regPay);
      System.out.printf("Overtime pay: $%3.2f\n", ovtPay);
      System.out.printf("Net pay: $%3.2f\n", netPay);
   }
}
```

4.6 More examples

We now write programs to solve two more problems. Their solutions will illustrate how to use **if...else** statements to determine which of several alternatives to take. In the sample runs, the underlined items are typed by the user; everything else is printed by the computer.

Example – printing a letter grade

Write a program to request a score in a test and print a letter grade based on the following:

```
score < 50           F
50 ≤ score < 75      B
score ≥ 75           A
```

The program should work as follows:

```
Enter a score: 70
Grade B
```

A solution is shown as Program P4.7.

Program P4.7

```java
//request a score; print letter grade
import java.util.*;
public class PrintGrade {
  public static void main(String[] args) {
    Scanner in = new Scanner(System.in);

    System.out.printf("Enter a score: ");
    int score = in.nextInt();
    System.out.printf("\nGrade ");
    if (score < 50) System.out.printf("F\n");
    else if (score < 75) System.out.printf("B\n");
    else System.out.printf("A\n");
  }
}
```

The second **printf** prints a blank line followed by the word **Grade** followed by one space but does not end the line. When the letter grade *is* determined, it will be printed on this same line.

We saw that the **if...else** statement takes the form

> if (<condition>) <statement1> else <statement2>

where <statement1> and <statement2> can be any statements. In particular, either one (or both) can be an **if...else** statement. This allows us to write so-called *nested if* statements. This is especially useful when we have several related conditions to test, as in this example. In the program, we can think of the part:

> if (score < 50) System.out.printf("F\n");
> else if (score < 75) System.out.printf("B\n");
> else System.out.printf("A\n");

as

> if (score < 50) System.out.printf("F\n");
> else <statement>

where <statement> is the **if...else** statement

> if (score < 75) System.out.printf("B\n");
> else System.out.printf("A\n");

If **score** is less than 50, the program prints **F** and ends. If not, it follows that **score** must be greater than or equal to 50.

Knowing this, the first **else** part checks if **score** is less than 75. If it is, the program prints **B** and ends. If not, it follows that **score** must be greater than or equal to 75.

Knowing this, the second **else** part (which matches the second **if**) prints **A** and ends.

To make sure the program is correct, you should run it with at least 3 different scores (e.g. 70, 45, 83) to verify that each of the 3 grades is printed correctly.

Note the preferred style for writing **else if**'s. If we had followed our normal indenting style, we would have written

```
if (score < 50) printf("F\n");
else
    if (score < 75) printf("B\n");
    else printf("A\n");
```

which would, of course, still be correct. However, if we had more cases, the indentation would go too deep and would look awkward. Also, since the different ranges for **score** are really *alternatives* (rather than one being within the other), it is better to keep them at the same indentation level.

The statements here were all one-line **printf** statements so we chose to write them on the same line as **if** and **else**. However, if they were blocks, it would be better to write it like this:

```
if (score < 50) {
    ...
}
else if (score < 75) {
    ...
}
else {
    ...
}
```

As an exercise, extend the program to print the correct grade based on:

```
score  <  50           F
50  ≤  score  <  65    C
65  ≤  score  <  80    B
score  ≥   80          A
```

Writing programs using selection logic

Example – classifying a triangle

Given three integer values representing the sides of a triangle, print:

- **Not a triangle** if the values cannot be the sides of any triangle. This is so if any value is negative or zero, or if the length of any side is greater than or equal to the sum of the other two;
- **Scalene** if the triangle is scalene (all sides different);
- **Isosceles** if the triangle is isosceles (two sides equal);
- **Equilateral** if the triangle is equilateral (three sides equal).

The program should work as follows:

```
Enter 3 sides of a triangle: 7 4 7
Isosceles
```

A solution is shown as Program P4.8.

Program P4.8

```java
import java.util.*;
public class Triangle {
   public static void main(String[] args) {
   //request 3 sides; determine type of triangle
      Scanner in = new Scanner(System.in);
      System.out.printf("Enter 3 sides of a triangle: ");
      int a = in.nextInt();
      int b = in.nextInt();
      int c = in.nextInt();
      if (a <= 0 || b <= 0 || c <= 0) System.out.printf("\nNot a triangle\n");
      else if (a >= b + c || b >= c + a || c >= a + b)
         System.out.printf("\nNot a triangle\n");
      else if (a == b && b == c) System.out.printf("\nEquilateral\n");
      else if (a == b || b == c || c == a) System.out.printf("\nIsosceles\n");
      else System.out.printf("\nScalene\n");
   }
}
```

The first task is to establish that we, in fact, have a valid triangle. The first **if** checks if any of the sides is negative or zero. If so, **Not a triangle** is printed. If they are all positive, we go to the **else** part which itself consists of an **if...else** statement.

Here, the **if** checks if any one side is greater than or equal to the sum of the other two. If so, **Not a triangle** is printed. If not, then we have a valid triangle and must determine its type by executing the **else** part beginning **if (a == b ...**

It is easiest to do this by first checking if it is equilateral. If two different *pairs of sides* are equal—**if (a == b && b == c)**—then all three are equal and we have an equilateral triangle.

If it is not equilateral, then we check if it is isosceles. If any two sides are equal—**if (a == b || b == c || c == a)**—we have an isosceles triangle.

If it is not isosceles, then it must be scalene.

As an exercise, extend the program to determine if the triangle is right-angled. It is right-angled if the sum of the squares of two sides is equal to the square of the third side.

Exercises 4

1. An auto repair shop charges as follows. Inspecting the vehicle costs $75. If no work needs to be done, there is no further charge. Otherwise, the charge is $75 per hour for labour plus the cost of parts, with a minimum charge of $120. If any work is done, there is no charge for inspecting the vehicle.

    Write a program to read values for hours worked and cost of parts (either of which could be 0) and print the charge for the job.

2. Write a program which requests two weights in kilograms and grams and prints the sum of the weights. For example, if the weights are 3kg 500g and 4kg 700g, your program should print 8kg 200g.

3. Write a program which requests two lengths in feet and inches and prints the sum of the lengths. For example, if the lengths are 5 ft. 4 in. and 8 ft. 11 in., your program should print 14ft. 3 in. (1 ft. = 12 in.)

4. A variety store give a 15% discount on sales totalling $300 or more. Write a program to request the cost of 3 items and print the amount the customer must pay.

5. Write a program to read two pairs of integers. Each pair represents a fraction. For example, the pair 3 5 represents the fraction 3/5. Your program should print the sum of the given fractions. For example, give the pairs 3 5 and 2 3, your program should print 19/15, since

    $$\frac{3}{5} + \frac{2}{3} = \frac{19}{15}$$

    Modify the program so that it prints the sum with the fraction reduced to a proper fraction; for this example, your program should print 1 4/15.

6. Write a program to read integer values for **month** and **year** and print the number of days in the month. For example, 4 2005 (April 2005) should print 30; 2 2004 (February 2004) should print 29 and 2 1900 (February 1900) should print 28.

    A leap year, *n*, is divisible by 4; however, if *n* is divisible by 100 then it is a leap year only if it is also divisible by 400. So 1900 is not a leap year but 2000 is.

Writing programs using selection logic

7. Write a program to read a person's name, hours worked, hourly rate of pay and tax rate (a number representing a percentage, e.g. 25 meaning 25%). The program must print the name, gross pay, tax deducted and net pay.

   Gross pay is calculated as described for net pay on page 78. The tax deducted is calculated by applying the tax rate to 80% of gross pay. And the net pay is calculated by subtracting the tax deducted from the gross pay.

   For example, if the person works 50 hours at $20/hour and the tax rate is 25%, his gross pay would be $(40 \times 20) + (10 \times 20 \times 1.5) = \$1100$. He pays 25% tax on 80% of $1100, that is, 25% of $880 = $220. His net pay is 1100 - 220 = $880.

8. In an English class, a student is given 3 term tests (marked out of 25) and an end-of-term test (marked out of 100). The end-of-term test counts the same as the 3 term tests in determining the final mark (out of 100). Write a program to read marks for the 3 term tests followed by the mark for the end-of-term test. The program then prints the final mark and an indication of whether the student passes or fails. To pass, the final mark must be 50 or more.

   For example, given the data 20 10 15 56, the final mark is calculated by

   $$\frac{(20 + 10 + 15)}{75} \times 50 + \frac{56}{100} \times 50 = 58$$

9. Write a program to request two times given in 24-hour clock format and find the time (in hours and minutes) that has elapsed between the first time and the second time. You may assume that the second time is later than the first time. Each time is represented by two numbers: e.g. **16 45** means the time **16:45**, that is 4:45 p.m.

   For example, if the two given times are **16 45** and **23 25** your answer should be **6** hours **40** minutes.

   Modify the program so that it works as follows: if the second time is sooner than the first time, take it to mean a time for the *next* day. For example, given the times **20:30** and **6:15**, take this to mean 8.30 p.m. to 6.15 a.m. of the next day. Your answer should be **9** hours **45** minutes.

10. A bank pays interest based on the amount of money deposited. If the amount is less than $5,000, the interest is 4% per annum. If the amount is $5,000 or more but less than $10,000, the interest is 5% per annum. If the amount is $10,000 or more but less than $20,000, the interest is 6% per annum. If the amount is $20,000 or more, the interest is 7% per annum.

    Write a program to request the amount deposited and print the interest earned for one year.

11. Write a program to prompt for the name of an item, its previous price and its current price. Print the percentage increase or decrease in the price. For example, if the previous price is $80 and the current price is $100, you should print **increase of 25%**; if the previous price is $100 and the current price is $80, you should print **decrease of 20%**.

12. For any **year** between 1900 and 2099, inclusive, the **month** and **day** on which Easter Sunday falls can be determined by the following algorithm:

    ```
    set a to year minus 1900
    set b to the remainder when a is divided by 19
    set c to the integer quotient when 7b + 1 is divided by 19
    set d to the remainder when 11b + 4 - c is divided by 29
    set e to the integer quotient when a is divided by 4
    set f to the remainder when a + e + 31 - d is divided by 7
    set g to 25 minus the sum of d and f
    if g is less than or equal to 0 then
      set month to 'March'
      set day to 31 + g
    else
      set month to 'April'
      set day to g
    endif
    ```

    Write a program which requests a year between 1900 and 2099, inclusive, and checks if the year is valid. If it is, print the day on which Easter Sunday falls in that year. For example, if the year is **1999**, your program should print **April 4**.

13. A country charges income tax as follows based on one's gross salary. No tax is charged on the first 20% of salary. The remaining 80% is called *taxable income*. Tax is paid as follows:

    - 10% on the first $15,000 of taxable income;
    - 20% on the *next* $20,000 of taxable income;
    - 25% on all taxable income in excess of $35,000;

    Write a program to read a value for a person's salary and print the amount of tax to be paid. Also print the *average tax rate*, that is, the percentage of salary that is paid in tax. For example, on a salary of $20,000, a person pays $1700 in tax. The average tax rate is `1700/20000*100 = 8.5%`.

5 Writing programs using repetition logic

In this chapter, we will explain:

- how to use the **while** construct to perform 'looping' in a program
- how to find the sum and average of an arbitrary set of numbers
- how to get a program to 'count'
- how to find the largest and smallest of an arbitrary set of numbers
- how to read data from a file
- how to write output to a file
- how to use the **for** construct to perform 'looping' in a program
- how to produce tables using **for**

In Chapter 3, we showed you how to write programs using *sequence* logic—programs whose statements are executed "in sequence" from the first to the last. In Chapter 4, we showed you how to write programs for problems which require *selection* logic. These programs used the **if** and the **if...else** statements.

In this chapter, we discuss problems which require *repetition* logic. The idea is to write statements once and get the computer to execute them repeatedly as long as some condition is true. We will see how to express repetition logic using the **while** and **for** statements.

5.1 The while construct

Consider the problem of writing a program to find the sum of some numbers which the user enters one at a time. The program will prompt the user to enter numbers as follows:

```
Enter a number: 13
Enter a number: 8
Enter a number: 16
```

and so on. We want to let the user enter as many number as he wishes. Since we can have no idea how many that will be, and the amount could vary from one run of the program to the next, we must let the user 'tell' us when he wishes to stop entering numbers.

How does he 'tell' us? Well, the only time the user 'talks' to the program is when he types a number in response to the prompt. If he wishes to stop entering numbers, he can enter some 'agreed upon' value; when the program reads this value, it will know that the user wishes to stop.

In this example, we can use 0 as the value which tells the program that the user wishes to stop. When a value is used this way, it is referred to as a *sentinel* or *end-of-data* value. It is sometimes called a *rogue* value—the value is not to be taken as one of the actual data values.

What can we use as a sentinel value? Any value that cannot be confused with an actual data value would be okay. For example, if the data values are all positive numbers, we can use 0 or -1 as the sentinel value. When we prompt the user, it is a good idea to remind him what value to use as the sentinel value.

Assume we want the program to run as follows:

```
Enter a number (0 to end): 24
Enter a number (0 to end): 13
Enter a number (0 to end): 55
Enter a number (0 to end): 32
Enter a number (0 to end): 19
Enter a number (0 to end): 0
The sum is 143
```

How do we get the program to run like that? We want to be able to express the following logic

As long as the user does not enter 0, keep prompting him for another number and add it to the sum

It seems obvious that we must, at least, prompt him for the first number. If this number is 0, we must print the sum (which, of course, would be 0 at this time). If the number is not 0, we must add it to the sum and prompt for another number. If *this* number is 0, we must print the sum. If this number is not 0, we must add it to the sum and prompt for another number. If *this* number is 0..., and so on.

The process will come to an end when the user enters 0.

This logic is expressed quite neatly using a **while** construct (informally, we say a **while** loop):

```
//Algorithm for finding sum
set sum to 0
get a number, num
while num is not 0 do
   add num to sum
   get another number, num
endwhile
print sum
```

Note, particularly, that we get a number *before* we enter the **while** loop. This is to ensure that the **while** condition makes sense the first time. (It would not make sense if **num** had no value).

To find the sum, we need to:

- Choose a variable to hold the sum; we will use **sum**.
- Initialize **sum** to 0 (before the **while** loop).
- Add a number to **sum** (inside the **while** loop). One number is added each time through the loop.

On exit from the loop, **sum** contains the sum of all the numbers entered.

The **while** construct lets us execute one or more statements repeatedly as long as some condition is true. Here, the two statements

> add num to sum
> get another number, num

are executed repeatedly as long as the condition **num is not 0** is true.

In *pseudocode*, the **while** construct is usually written as follows:

> while <condition> do
>   statements to be executed repeatedly
> endwhile

The statements to be executed repeatedly are called the *body* of the **while** construct. The construct is executed as follows:

(1)   <condition> is tested;
(2)   if **true**, the body is executed and we go back to step (1);
      if **false**, we continue with the statement, if any, after **endwhile**.

Below, we show how the algorithm is executed using the sample data entered above. For easy reference, the data was entered in the order:

> 24   13   55   32   19   0

When a **while** construct is being executed, we say the program is *looping* or the **while** *loop* is being executed.

Execution of algorithm for finding sum with data: 24 13 55 32 19 0

Initially, **num** is undefined and **sum** is 0. We show this as:

> num [   ]   sum [0]

24 is entered and stored in **num**;
num is not 0 so we enter the **while** loop;
num (24) is added to **sum** (0), giving:

13 is entered and stored in **num**;
num is not 0 so we enter the **while** loop;
num (13) is added to **sum** (24), giving:

num | 13 | **sum** | 37 |

55 is entered and stored in **num**;
num is not 0 so we enter the **while** loop;
num (55) is added to **sum** (37), giving:

num | 55 | **sum** | 92 |

32 is entered and stored in **num**;
num is not 0 so we enter the **while** loop;
num (32) is added to **sum** (92), giving:

num | 32 | **sum** | 124 |

19 is entered and stored in **num**;
num is not 0 so we enter the **while** loop;
num (19) is added to **sum** (124), giving:

num | 19 | **sum** | 143 |

0 is entered and stored in **num**;
num *is* 0 so we exit the **while** loop and go to **print sum** with

num | 0 | **sum** | 143 |

sum is now 143 so the algorithm prints 143.

It remains to show how to express this algorithm in Java. Program P5.1 (next page) shows how.

Of particular interest is the **while** statement. The pseudocode

```
while num is not 0 do
   add num to sum
   get another number, num
endwhile
```

> **Program P5.1**
> ```
> import java.util.*;
> public class SumNumbers {
>    public static void main(String[] args) {
>       //print the sum of several numbers entered by a user
>       Scanner in = new Scanner(System.in);
>
>       int num, sum = 0;
>       System.out.printf("Enter a number (0 to end): ");
>       num = in.nextInt();
>       while (num != 0) {
>          sum = sum + num;
>          System.out.printf("Enter a number (0 to end): ");
>          num = in.nextInt();
>       }
>       System.out.printf("\nThe sum is %d\n", sum);
>    }
> }
> ```

is expressed in Java as

```
while (num != 0) {
   sum = sum + num;
   System.out.printf("Enter a number (0 to end): ");
   num = in.nextInt();
}
```

When the program is run, what would happen if the very first number entered was 0? Since **num** *is* 0, the **while** condition is immediately **false** so we drop out of the **while** loop and continue with the **printf** statement. The program will print the correct answer:

```
The sum is 0
```

In general, if the **while** condition is **false** the first time it is tested, the body is not executed at all.

Formally, the **while** construct in Java is defined as follows:

> while (<condition>) <statement>
>
> The word **while** and the brackets are required; you must supply <condition> and <statement>; <statement> must be a single statement or a block[1]. First, <condition> is tested; if **true**, <statement> is executed and <condition> is tested again. This is repeated until <condition> becomes **false**. When <condition> becomes **false**, execution continues with the statement, if any, after <statement>. If <condition> is **false** the first time, <statement> is *not* executed and execution continues with the following statement, if any.

In Program P5.1, <condition> is **num != 0** and <statement> is the block

```
{
    sum = sum + num;
    System.out.printf("Enter a number (0 to end): ");
    num = in.nextInt();
}
```

Whenever we want to execute several statements if <condition> is true, we must enclose the statements by **{** and **}**; effectively, this makes them into one statement, a *compound* statement, satisfying Java's syntax rule which requires one statement as the body.

Example – finding the highest common factor

Let us write a program to find the highest common factor[2] (HCF) of two numbers. The program will run as follows:

```
Enter two numbers: 42 24
Their HCF is 6
```

We will use Euclid's algorithm for finding the **HCF** of two integers, **m** and **n**. The algorithm is as follows:

1. if n is 0, the HCF is m—stop
2. set r to the remainder when m is divided by n
3. set m to n
4. set n to r
5. go to step 1

---

[1] Recall that a block, also called a compound statement, is one or more statements enclosed by **{** and **}**.
[2] Also known as the greatest common divisor (GCD)

Writing programs using repetition logic

Using **m** as 42 and **n** as 24, step through the algorithm and verify that it gives the correct answer, 6.

Steps 2, 3 and 4 are executed as long as **n** is not 0. Hence, this algorithm can be expressed using a **while** loop as follows:

```
while n is not 0 do
    set r to m % n
    set m to n
    set n to r
endwhile
HCF is m
```

We can now write Program P5.2 which finds the highest common factor of two numbers entered.

Program P5.2
```java
import java.util.*;
public class HCF {
    public static void main(String[] args) {
        //find the HCF of two numbers entered by a user
        Scanner in = new Scanner(System.in);
        System.out.printf("Enter two numbers: ");
        int m = in.nextInt();
        int n = in.nextInt();
        while (n != 0) {
            int r = m % n;
            m = n;
            n = r;
        }
        System.out.printf("\nTheir HCF is %d\n", m);
    }
}
```

Note that the **while** condition is **n != 0** and the **while** body is the block

```
{
    int r = m % n;
    m = n;
    n = r;
}
```

The algorithm and, hence, the program, works whether **m** is bigger than **n** or not. Using the example above, if **m** is 24 and **n** is 42, when the loop is executed the first time, it will set **m** to 42 and **n** to 24. In general, if **m** is smaller than **n**, the first thing the algorithm does is swap their values.

5.2 Keeping a count

Program P5.1 finds the sum of a set of numbers entered. Suppose we want to *count* how many numbers were entered, not counting the end-of-data 0. We could use an integer variable **n** to hold the count. To get the program to keep a count, we need to do the following:

- Choose a variable to hold the count; we choose **n**.
- Initialize **n** to 0.
- Add 1 to **n** in the appropriate place. Here, we need to add 1 to **n** each time the user enters a non-zero number.
- Print the count.

Program P5.3 is the modified program for counting the numbers.

Program P5.3

```java
import java.util.*;
public class SumNumbers1 {
    public static void main(String[] args) {
        //print the sum of several numbers entered by a user
        Scanner in = new Scanner(System.in);

        int num, sum = 0, n = 0;
        System.out.printf("Enter a number (0 to end): ");
        num = in.nextInt();
        while (num != 0) {
            sum = sum + num;
            n = n + 1;
            System.out.printf("Enter a number (0 to end): ");
            num = in.nextInt();
        }
        System.out.printf("\n%d numbers were entered\n", n);
        System.out.printf("\nThe sum is %d\n", sum);
    }
}
```

The following is a sample run of the program:

```
Enter a number (0 to end): 24
Enter a number (0 to end): 13
Enter a number (0 to end): 55
Enter a number (0 to end): 32
Enter a number (0 to end): 19
Enter a number (0 to end): 0

5 numbers were entered
The sum is 143
```

Writing programs using repetition logic

Comments on Program P5.3

- We declare and initialize **n** and **sum** to 0 *before* the **while** loop.
- The statement

    n = n + 1;

    adds 1 to **n**. We say that **n** is *incremented* by 1. Suppose **n** has the value 3. When the right hand side is evaluated, the value obtained is 3 + 1 = 4. This value is stored in the variable on the left hand side, i.e. **n**. The net result is that 4 is stored in **n**.

    This statement is placed *inside* the loop so that **n** is incremented each time the loop body is executed. Since the loop body is executed when **num** is not 0, the value of **n** is always the amount of numbers entered so far.

- When we exit the **while** loop, the value in **n** will be the amount of numbers entered, not counting 0. This value is then printed.
- Observe that if the first number entered were 0, the **while** condition would be immediately false and control will go directly to the first **printf** statement with **n** and **sum** both having the value 0. The program will print, correctly:

    ```
    0 numbers were entered
    The sum is 0
    ```

- If one number (15, say) is entered and then 0, the program will print:

    ```
    1 numbers were entered
    The sum is 15
    ```

    The mathematics is correct but the English leaves a lot to be desired. We can fix this by using an **if...else** statement, thus:

    ```
    if (n == 1) System.out.printf("\n%d number was entered\n", n);
    else System.out.printf("\n%d numbers were entered\n", n);
    ```

Finding the average

Program P5.3 can be easily modified to find the average of the numbers entered. As we saw above, on exit from the **while** loop, we know the sum (**sum**) and how many numbers were entered (**n**). We can add a **printf** statement to print the average to 2 decimal places, thus:

```
System.out.printf("The average is %3.2f\n", (double) sum/n);
```

For the data in the sample run, the output will be

```
5 numbers were entered
The sum is 143
The average is 28.60
```

Note the use of the cast **(double)** to force a floating-point calculation. Without it, since **sum** and **n** are **int**, an integer division would be performed, giving 28. Alternatively, we could declare **sum** as **double**, and print the sum and average with:

```
System.out.printf("The sum is %3.0f\n", sum);
System.out.printf("The average is %3.2f\n", sum/n);
```

However, there is still a problem. If the user enters 0 as the first number, execution will reach the last **printf** statement with **sum** having the value 0 and **n** having the value 0. The program will attempt to divide 0 by 0, giving the error "Attempt to divide by 0". This is an example of a *run-time* (or *execution*) error.

To cater for this situation, we could use the following after the **while** loop:

```
if (n == 0) System.out.printf("\nNo numbers entered\n");
else {
   System.out.printf("\n%d numbers were entered\n", n);
   System.out.printf("The sum is %d\n", sum);
   System.out.printf("The average is %3.2f\n", (double) sum/n);
}
```

The moral of the story is that, whenever possible, you should try to anticipate the ways in which your program might fail and cater for them. This is an example of what is called *defensive programming*.

5.3 Increment and decrement operators

There are a number of operators that originated with C and incorporated in Java. The best known of these is the increment operator, **++**. In the last program, we used

```
n = n + 1;
```

to add 1 to **n**. The statement

```
n++;
```

does the same thing. The operator **++** adds 1 to its argument, which *must* be a variable. It can be written as a prefix (**++n**) or as a suffix (**n++**).

Even though **++n** and **n++** both add 1 to **n**, in certain situations, the *side-effect* of **++n** is different from **n++**. This is so because **++n** increments **n** *before* using its value, whereas **n++** increments **n** *after* using its value. As an example, suppose **n** has the value 7. The statement

```
a = ++n;
```

first increments **n** and *then assigns* the value (8) to **a**. But the statement

```
a = n++;
```

first assigns the value 7 to **a** and *then increments* **n** to 8. In both cases, though, the end result is that **n** is assigned the value 8.

As an exercise, what is printed by the following?

```
n = 5;
System.out.printf("Suffix: %d\n", n++);
System.out.printf("Prefix: %d\n", ++n);
```

The decrement operator **--** is similar to **++** except that it *subtracts* 1 from its variable argument. For example, **--n** and **n--** are both equivalent to

```
n = n - 1;
```

As explained above, **--n** *subtracts* 1 and *then uses* the value of **n**; **n--** *uses* the value of **n** and *then subtracts* 1 from it. It would be useful to do the above exercise with **--** replaced by **++**.

5.4 Assignment operators

So far, we have used the assignment operator, **=**, to assign the value of an expression to a variable, as in:

```
c = a + b
```

The entire construct consisting of the variable, **=** and the expression is referred to as an *assignment expression*. When the expression is followed by a semicolon, it becomes an *assignment statement*. The *value* of an assignment expression is simply the value assigned to the variable. For example, if **a** is 15 and **b** is 20, then the assignment expression

```
c = a + b
```

assigns the value 35 to **c**. The value of the assignment expression is also 35.

Multiple assignments are possible, as in

```
a = b = c = 13
```

The operator **=** evaluates from right to left, so the above is equivalent to

```
a = (b = (c = 13))
```

The rightmost assignment is done first, followed by the one to the left, and so on.

Java provides other assignment operators, of which **+=** is the most widely used. In Program P5.3, above, we used the statement

```
sum = sum + num;
```

to add the value of **num** to **sum**. This can be written more neatly using **+=** as:

```
sum += num;   //add num to sum
```

To add 3 to **n**, we could write **n += 3**, which is the same as **n = n + 3**.

Other assignment operators include **-=**, ***=**, **/=** and **%=**. If **op** represents any of **+**, **-**, *****, **/** or **%**, then

```
variable op= expression
```

is equivalent to

variable = variable op expression

We point out that we could write all our programs without using increment, decrement or the special assignment operators. However, sometimes, they permit us to express certain operations more concisely or more conveniently.

5.5 Finding the largest

Suppose we want to write a program which works as follows: the user will type some numbers and the program will find the largest number typed. The following is a sample run of the program (underlined items are typed by the user):

```
Enter a number (0 to end): 36
Enter a number (0 to end): 17
Enter a number (0 to end): 43
Enter a number (0 to end): 52
Enter a number (0 to end): 50
Enter a number (0 to end): 0

The largest is 52
```

The user will be prompted to enter numbers, one at a time. We will assume that the numbers entered are all positive integers. We will let the user enter as many numbers as she likes. However, in this case, she will need to tell the program when she wishes to stop entering numbers. To do so, she will type 0.

Finding the largest number involves the following steps:

- Choose a variable to hold the largest number; we choose **bigNum**.
- Initialize **bigNum** to a very small value. The value chosen should be such that no matter what number is entered, *its* value would be greater than this initial value. Since we are assuming that the numbers entered would be positive, we can initialize **bigNum** to 0.
- As each number (**num**, say) is entered, it is compared with **bigNum**; if **num** is greater than **bigNum**, then we have a bigger number and **bigNum** is set to this new number.
- When all the numbers have been entered and checked, **bigNum** will contain the largest one.

These ideas are expressed in the following algorithm:

```
set bigNum to 0
get a number, num
while num is not 0 do
   if num is bigger than bigNum, set bigNum to num
   get a number, num
endwhile
print bigNum
```

Like before, we get the first number *before* we enter the **while** loop. This is to ensure that the **while** condition makes sense (*is defined*) the first time. It would not make sense if **num** had no value. If it is not 0, we enter the loop. Inside the loop, we process the number (compare it with **bigNum**, etc.) after which we get another number. *This* number is then used in the next test of the **while** condition. When the **while** condition is **false** (**num** *is* 0), the program continues with the **print** statement *after* the loop.

This algorithm is implemented as shown in Program P5.4.

```
                        Program P5.4
    import java.util.*;
    public class Largest {
      public static void main(String[] args) {
      //find the largest of a set of numbers entered
        Scanner in = new Scanner(System.in);
        int num, bigNum = 0;
        System.out.printf("Enter a number (0 to end): ");
        num = in.nextInt();
        while (num != 0) {
          if (num > bigNum) bigNum = num;  //is this number bigger?
          System.out.printf("Enter a number (0 to end): ");
          num = in.nextInt();
        }
        System.out.printf("\nThe largest is %d\n", bigNum);
      }
    }
```

Let us 'step through' this program using the sample data entered at the beginning of this section. For easy reference, the data was entered in the order:

    36 17 43 52 50 0

Initially, **num** is undefined and **bigNum** is 0. We show this as:

    num ▢   bigNum ▢ 0

36 is entered and stored in **num**;
num is not 0 so we enter the **while** loop;
num (36) is compared with **bigNum** (0);
36 is bigger so **bigNum** is set to 36, giving:

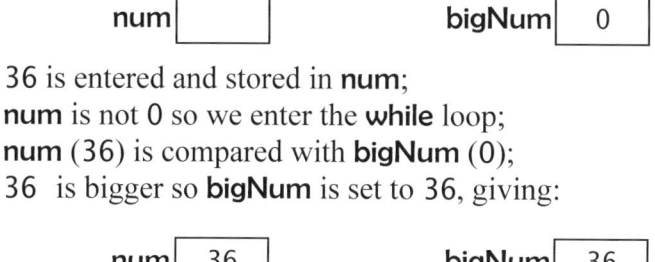

17 is entered and stored in **num**;
num is not 0 so we enter the **while** loop;

num (17) is compared with **bigNum** (36);
17 is not bigger so **bigNum** remains at 36, giving:

$$\text{num} \boxed{17} \qquad \text{bigNum} \boxed{36}$$

43 is entered and stored in **num**;
num is not 0 so we enter the **while** loop;
num (43) is compared with **bigNum** (36);
43 is bigger so **bigNum** is set to 43, giving:

$$\text{num} \boxed{43} \qquad \text{bigNum} \boxed{43}$$

52 is entered and stored in **num**;
num is not 0 so we enter the **while** loop;
num (52) is compared with **bigNum** (43);
52 is bigger so **bigNum** is set to 52, giving:

$$\text{num} \boxed{52} \qquad \text{bigNum} \boxed{52}$$

50 is entered and stored in **num**;
num is not 0 so we enter the **while** loop;
num (50) is compared with **bigNum** (52);
50 is not bigger so **bigNum** remains at 52, giving:

$$\text{num} \boxed{50} \qquad \text{bigNum} \boxed{52}$$

0 is entered and stored in **num**;
num *is* 0 so we exit the **while** loop and go to **printf** with

$$\text{num} \boxed{0} \qquad \text{bigNum} \boxed{52}$$

bigNum is now 52 and the **printf** statement prints

```
The largest is 52
```

5.6 Finding the smallest

In addition to finding the largest of a set of items, we are sometimes interested in finding the smallest. We will find the smallest of a set of integers. To do so involves the following steps:

- Choose a variable to hold the smallest number; we choose **smallNum**.
- Initialize **smallNum** to a very big value. The value chosen should be such that no matter what number is entered, *its* value would be *smaller* than this initial value. To do so, we should have an idea of the numbers we will get.

For instance, if we know that the numbers will contain at most 4 digits, we can use an initial value such as 10000. If we do not know this, we can set **smallNum** to the largest integer value defined by the compiler (2147483647 for **int**). Similarly, when we are finding the largest, we can initialize **bigNum** (say) to a very small number like -2147483647.

Another possibility is to read the first number and set **smallNum** (or **bigNum**) to it. For our program, we will set **smallNum** to 2147483647.

- As each number (**num**, say) is entered, it is compared with **smallNum**; if **num** is smaller than **smallNum**, then we have a smaller number and **smallNum** is set to this new number.
- When all the numbers have been entered and checked, **smallNum** will contain the smallest one.

These ideas are expressed in the following algorithm:

```
set smallNum to 2147483647
get a number, num
while num is not 0 do
    if num is smaller than smallNum, set smallNum to num
    get a number, num
endwhile
print smallNum
```

This algorithm is implemented as shown in Program P5.5.

Program P5.5

```java
import java.util.*;
public class Smallest {
  public static void main(String[] args) {
  //find the smallest of a set of numbers entered
    Scanner in = new Scanner(System.in);
    int num, smallNum = 2147483647;
    System.out.printf("Enter a number (0 to end): ");
    num = in.nextInt();
    while (num != 0) {
      if (num < smallNum) smallNum = num;
      System.out.printf("Enter a number (0 to end): ");
      num = in.nextInt();
    }
    System.out.printf("\nThe smallest is %d\n", smallNum);
  }
}
```

When run, if numbers are entered in the following order:

    36   17   43   52   50   0

the program will print

```
The smallest is 17
```

and if the numbers entered are

```
36  -17  43  -52  50  0
```

the program will print

```
The smallest is -52
```

5.7 How to read data from a file

So far, we have written our programs assuming that data to be supplied is typed at the keyboard. We have fetched the data using statements like **in.nextInt()** where **in** was set to refer to the keyboard using the statement

```
Scanner in = new Scanner(System.in);
```

Typically, a program prompts the user for data and waits for the user to type the data. When the data is typed, the program reads it, stores it in a variable and continues with its execution. This mode of supplying data is called *interactive* since the user is interacting with the program.

We say we have been reading data from the "standard input". Java uses **System.in** to refer to the standard input, the keyboard and **System.out** to refer to the standard output, the screen. So far, our programs have written output to the screen.

We can also supply data to a program by storing the data in a file. When the program needs data, it fetches it directly from the file, without user intervention. Of course, we have to ensure that the appropriate data has been stored in the file in the correct order and format. This mode of supplying data is normally referred to as *batch*[3] mode.

For example, suppose we need to supply an item number (**int**) and a price (**double**) for several items. If the program is written assuming that the data file contains several pairs of numbers (an **int** constant followed by a **double** constant) then we must ensure that the data in the file conforms to this.

Suppose we create a file called **input.txt** and **type** data in it. This file is a *file of characters* or a *text* file. To be able to read data from **input.txt**, we must first inform Java with a statement such as:

```
Scanner in = new Scanner(new FileReader("input.txt"));
```

FileReader is one of Java's standard I/O (input/output) classes which lets us read data from a file. We use **in** here but any other identifier will do, such as **infile**,

---

[3] The term is historical and comes from the old days when data had to be 'batched' before being submitted for processing.

inputFile, payData. The argument to **FileReader** is the name of the file enclosed in double quotes.

Once this is done, the "data pointer" (see page 56) associated with **in** will be positioned at the beginning of the file. Now, if we write, say

        int first = in.nextInt();

the next integer from the file **input.txt** will be read and assigned to **first**. All we have said so far about reading data still apply except that reading is done from the file rather than the keyboard. Put another way, the only difference is the *source* of the data.

It is up to us to ensure that the file exists and contains the appropriate data. If not, we will get an error message such as "File not found". If we need to, we can specify the *path* to the file.

Suppose the file is located at: **C:\testdata\input.txt**.

We can tell Java we will be reading data from the file with:

        Scanner in = new Scanner(new FileReader("C:\\testdata\\input.txt"));

Recall that the escape sequence \\ is used to represent \ within a string. If the file is on a diskette, we can use:

        Scanner in = new Scanner(new FileReader("A:\\input.txt"));

When we have finished reading data from the file, we should *close* it. This is done with

        in.close();

After this, **in** is no longer connected with **input.txt**. If we wish, we can connect it with another file (**paydata.txt**, say) using:

        Scanner in = new Scanner(new FileReader("paydata.txt"));

Now, a statement such as

        double rate = in.nextDouble();

will fetch the next number from **paydata.txt**.

Finding the average of some numbers in a file

To illustrate how to read data from a file, let us modify Program P5.3 to read several numbers from a file and find their average. On page 99, we discussed how to find the average. We just need to make the changes to read the numbers from a file. Suppose the file is called **input.txt** and contains several positive integers with 0 indicating the end, for example,

        24 13 55 32 19 0

Program P5.6 (next page) shows how to define the file as the place from which the data will be read and how to find the average.

Program P5.6

```java
import java.util.*;
import java.io.*;
public class ReadFromFile {
   public static void main(String[] args) throws IOException {
   //read numbers from a file and find their average; 0 ends the data
      Scanner in = new Scanner(new FileReader("input.txt"));

      int num, sum = 0, n = 0;
      num = in.nextInt();
      while (num != 0) {
         n = n + 1;
         sum = sum + num;
         num = in.nextInt();
      }
      if (n == 0) System.out.printf("\nNo numbers supplied\n");
      else {
         System.out.printf("\n%d numbers were supplied\n", n);
         System.out.printf("The sum is %d\n", sum);
         System.out.printf("The average is %3.2f\n", (double) sum/n);
      }
      in.close();
   } //end main
} //end class
```

In the same way that we wrote **import java.util.*;** so that our programs can have access to the **Scanner** class, we must now also write **import java.io.*;** so that we can use **FileReader**.

Note also that the header for **main** has changed slightly with the addition of the phrase **throws IOException**. Why is this necessary? The easy answer is that if you want to write a method (such as **main**) which uses the classes (such as **FileReader**) in **java.io**, you must use this phrase.

Why this is really necessary is a bit complicated and beyond the scope of this book, but we offer a simplified explanation. When programs are run, it is possible to get a *run-time* error. For example, if a program expects an integer and the user enters 3.5, say, the program will halt abruptly giving a "type mismatch" error. In Java, we say the program "throws an InputMisMatch exception" and halts.

In other words, Java "throws" an "exception" when it encounters a run-time problem. As another example, suppose at the time a program attempts to do the calculation **sum/n**, the value of **n** is 0. The program will throw an "arithmetic exception", caused by the attempt to divide by 0.

In the present example, suppose the user forgot to create the file, **input.txt**. When the program tries to execute the statement

Scanner in = new Scanner(new FileReader("input.txt"));

it will not find the file and, hence, cannot proceed. The program will throw an "input file not found" exception. Java *requires* us to declare this possibility by including the phrase **throws IOException**[4].

Other comments on Program P5.6

- Since data is being read directly from the file, the need to prompt for data does not arise. We have removed the **printf** statements which prompted for data.
- The program makes sure that **n** is not 0 before attempting to find the average.
- When run, the program reads the data from the file and prints the results *without any user intervention.*
- If the data file contains
    24 13 55 32 19 0

  the output will be
    5 numbers were supplied
    The sum is 143
    The average is 28.60

- The numbers in the file could be supplied in "free format"—any amount could be put on a line. For example, the sample data could have been typed on one line as above or as follows:
    24   13
    55 32
              19 0
  or
    24   13
    55
         32 19
      0
  or
    24
    13
    55
    32
    19
    0

As an exercise, add statements to the program so that it also prints the largest and smallest numbers in the file.

File cannot be found: when you try to run this program, it may not run properly because it cannot find the file **input.txt**. This may be because the compiler is looking for the file in the wrong place. Some compilers expect to find the file in the same folder/directory as the program file. Others expect to find it in the same

---

[4] Java also allows us to "catch" the exception but that is beyond the scope of this book.

folder/directory as the compiler. Try placing **input.txt** in each of these folders, in turn, and run the program. If this does not work then you will need to specify the complete path to the file as the argument to **FileReader**. For example, if the file is in the folder **data** which is in the folder **CS10E** which is on the **C:** drive, you will need to use the statement:

```
Scanner in = new Scanner(new FileReader("C:\\CS10E\\data\\input.txt"));
```

5.8 How to send output to a file

So far, our programs have read data from the standard input (the keyboard) and sent output to the standard output (the screen). We have just seen how to read data from a file. We now show you how you can send output to a file.

This is important because when we send output to the screen, it is lost when we exit the program or when we switch off the computer. If we need to save our output, we must write it to a file. Then the output is available as long as we wish to keep the file.

Suppose we wish to send output to a file, **output.txt**. We can use **PrintWriter** and **FileWriter**, both found in **java.io**, as follows:

```
PrintWriter out = new PrintWriter(new FileWriter("output.txt"));
```

This tells Java to "prepare the file **output.txt** to receive output" and it connects the identifier **out** with **output.txt**. We could use any other identifier in place of **out**. We say the statement "opens the file for writing".

When this statement is executed, the file **output.txt** is created if it does not already exist. If it exists, its contents are destroyed. In other words, whatever you write to the file will *replace* its original contents. Be careful that you do not "open for writing" a file whose contents you wish to keep.

We can now use **out.printf** to send output to the file. It is used in exactly the same way as **System.out.printf**. For example, if **sum** is **int** with value 143, the statement

```
out.printf("The sum is %d\n", sum);
```

will write

```
The sum is 143
```

to the file **output.txt**.

When we are done writing output to the file, we must *close* it. This is especially important for output files since, the way some compilers operate[5], this is the only way to ensure that all output is sent to the file. We close the file as follows:

---

[5] For instance, they send output to a temporary buffer in memory and only when the buffer is full is it sent to the file. If you do not close the file, some output may be left in the buffer and never sent to the file.

Writing programs using repetition logic

```
out.close();
```

This statement breaks the connection of **out** with the file **output.txt**. If we need to, we could now link the identifier **out** with another file (**payroll.txt**, say) using:

```
out = new PrintWriter(new FileWriter("payroll.txt"));
```

Note that since **out** has been declared before, we do not need **PrintWriter out**. Subsequent **out.printf(...)** statements will send output to the file **payroll.txt**.

For an example, we re-write Program P5.6 as Program P5.7 to send the output to the file **output.txt**.

Program P5.7

```java
import java.util.*;
import java.io.*;
public class WriteToFile {
   public static void main(String[] args) throws IOException {
   //read numbers from a file and find their average; 0 ends the data
      Scanner in = new Scanner(new FileReader("input.txt"));
      PrintWriter out = new PrintWriter(new FileWriter("output.txt"));
      int num, sum = 0, n = 0;
      num = in.nextInt();
      while (num != 0) {
         n = n + 1;
         sum = sum + num;
         num = in.nextInt();
      }
      if (n == 0) out.printf("No numbers supplied\n");
      else {
         out.printf("%d numbers were supplied\n", n);
         out.printf("The sum is %d\n", sum);
         out.printf("The average is %3.2f\n", (double) sum/n);
      }
      in.close();
      out.close();
   } //end main
} //end class
```

As explained on page 107, you can, if you wish, specify the complete path to your file. For instance, if you want to send the output to a diskette, you can use

```
PrintWriter out = new PrintWriter(new FileWriter("a:\\output.txt"));
```

When you run Program P5.7, it will appear as if nothing has happened. However, if you check your file system you will find the file **output.txt**. Open it to view your results.

How to avoid System.out

So far, we have used **System.out.printf** whenever we needed to print output to the screen. But it gets tiresome having to write **System.out** all the time. We can get around this with the statement

> PrintWriter out = new PrintWriter(System.out);

Again, we can use any other identifier instead of **out**. And, in order to use the class **PrintWriter**, we must precede our program with **import java.io.*;**.

This statement connects the standard output, **System.out**, with the identifier **out**. Now, a statement like

> out.printf("The sum is %d\n", sum);

will send the output to the screen.

Generally, everything will work as before. However, there is a slight difference when prompting for input. Consider the following:

> out.printf("Enter a number: ");
> int n = in.nextInt();

We would expect that this would prompt the user with

> Enter a number:

and wait for the user to type the number. But whereas the computer will wait for the user to type, the prompt will not be displayed, yet. The reason is that **printf** will put the output in a buffer and print the buffer only when the buffer is full, the program ends or we close the output stream with **out.close()**.

We can also tell Java to *flush* the buffer (force it to print its contents) with **out.flush();**. We can force the prompt to be displayed with

> out.printf("The sum is %d\n", sum); out.flush();

If you find that some of your output is not being displayed, maybe you need to flush the buffer.

5.9 Example – payroll

We expand our 'calculating pay' example from page 78 to illustrate many of the ideas discussed so far in this chapter. Specifically, we will write a program to process pay data for several employees.

The data for each employee consists of a first name, a last name, the number of hours worked and the rate of pay. The data will be stored in a file **paydata.txt** and output will be sent to the file **payroll.txt**.

We will assume that the data is stored in the file as follows:

```
Maggie May 50 12.00
Akira Kanda 40 15.00
Richard Singh 48 20.00
Jamie Khan 30 18.00
END
```

We use the "first name" **END** as the end-of-data marker.

Regular pay, overtime pay and net pay will be calculated as described on page 78. The employee name, hours worked, rate of pay, regular pay, overtime pay and net pay are printed under a suitable heading. In addition, we will write the program to do the following:

- count how many employees are processed
- calculate the total wage bill (total net pay for all employees)
- determine which employee earned the highest pay and how much. We will ignore the possibility of a tie.

For the sample data, the output should look like this:

```
Name              Hours   Rate   Regular  Overtime    Net

Maggie May        50.0    12.00   480.00    180.00   660.00
Akira Kanda       40.0    15.00   600.00      0.00   600.00
Richard Singh     48.0    20.00   800.00    240.00  1040.00
Jamie Khan        30.0    18.00   540.00      0.00   540.00

Number of employees: 4
Total wage bill: $2840.00
Richard Singh earned the most pay of $1040.00
```

An outline of the algorithm for reading the data is:

```
read firstName
while firstName is not "END" do
    read lastName, hours, rate
    do the calculations
    print results for this employee
    read firstName
endwhile
```

We will read the name using **next()** as described on page 58. However, in order to get the output to line up neatly as shown above, it would be more convenient to have the entire name stored in one variable (**name**, say). Suppose **Robin** is stored in **firstName** and **Hood** is stored in **lastName**. We will use

String name = firstName + " " + lastName;

to store the full name, **Robin Hood**, in **name**. The operator **+** is used to join strings; we say *concatenate* them.

When faced with a program which requires so many things to be done, it is best to start by working on part of the problem, getting it right and then tackling the other parts. For this problem, we can start by getting the program to read and process the data without counting, finding the total or finding the highest-paid employee.

Program P5.8 does this and is based on P4.6 (page 84).

Program P5.8

```java
import java.util.*;
import java.io.*;
public class Payroll {
   final static double MaxRegularHours = 40;
   final static double OvertimeFactor = 1.5;

   public static void main(String[] args) throws IOException {
      Scanner in = new Scanner(new FileReader("paydata.txt"));
      PrintWriter out = new PrintWriter(new FileWriter("payroll.txt"));
      String firstName, lastName, name;
      double hours, rate, regPay, ovtPay, netPay;

      out.printf("Name         Hours  Rate Regular Overtime   Net\n\n");
      firstName = in.next();
      while (!firstName.equals("END")) {
         lastName = in.next();
         hours = in.nextDouble();
         rate = in.nextDouble();
         if (hours <= MaxRegularHours) {
            regPay = hours * rate;
            ovtPay = 0;
         }
         else {
            regPay = MaxRegularHours * rate;
            ovtPay = (hours - MaxRegularHours) * rate * OvertimeFactor;
         }
         netPay = regPay + ovtPay;

         //make one name out of firstName and lastName
         name = firstName + " " + lastName;

         out.printf("%-15s %5.1f %6.2f", name, hours, rate);
         out.printf("%9.2f %9.2f %7.2f\n", regPay, ovtPay, netPay);
         firstName = in.next();
      } //end while
      in.close();
      out.close();
   } //end main
} //end class
```

In P5.8, we use the specification **%-15s** to print **name**. This will print **name** left-justified in a field width of 15. In other words, all names will be printed using 15 print columns. This is necessary for the output to line up neatly. To cater for longer names, you can increase the field width.

Our program needs to check if the value in **firstName** is the string **"END"**. Ideally, we would like to say something like

> while (firstName != "END") { //this will not work in Java

but we cannot do so since Java does not allow us to compare *strings* using the relational operators. What we *can* do is use the "**equals** method in the **String** class". If **s1** and **s2** are two strings (constants or variables), then the expression

> s1.equals(s2)

is **true** if **s1** is identical to **s2** and **false**, otherwise. For example, "hello".equals("hi") is **false** but "allo".equals("allo") is **true**.

The expression **firstName.equals("END")** is **true** only when **firstName** contains **END**. In the **while** condition, we need to check if **firstName** does *not* contain **END** so we write **!firstName.equals("END")** (literally, not first name equals "END").

Other comments on Program P5.8:

- Since data is being read from a file, prompts are not required.
- We print a heading with the statement

  out.printf("Name   Hours   Rate Regular Overtime   Net\n\n");

  To get the output to line up nicely, you will need to fiddle with the spaces between the words and the field widths in the statements which print the results. For example, there are 12 spaces between **e** and **H**, 3 spaces between **s** and **R**, 2 between **e** and **R**, 2 between **r** and **O** and 5 between **e** and **N**.

  You should experiment with the field widths in the last two **printf** statements (which write one line of output) to see what effect it has on your output.
- We use a **while** loop to process several employees. When the "first name" **END** is read, the program knows it has reached the end of the data. It closes the files and stops.

Now that we've got the basic processing right, we can add the statements to perform the other tasks. Program P5.9 (next page) is the complete program which counts the employees, calculates the total wage bill and determines the employee who earned the highest salary. In order for the program to fit on one page, we have removed blank lines and, in some cases, put two statements on one line.

Counting the employees and finding the total wage bill are fairly straightforward. We use the variables **numEmp** and **wageBill** which are initialized to 0 *before* the loop. They are incremented *inside* the loop and their final values are printed *after*

Program P5.9

```java
import java.util.*; import java.io.*;
public class Payroll1 {
  final static double MaxRegularHours = 40;
  final static double OvertimeFactor = 1.5;
  public static void main(String[] args) throws IOException {
    Scanner in = new Scanner(new FileReader("paydata.txt"));
    PrintWriter out = new PrintWriter(new FileWriter("payroll.txt"));
    String firstName, lastName, name, bestPaid = "";
    double hours, rate, regPay, ovtPay, netPay;
    double wageBill = 0, mostPay = 0;
    int numEmp = 0;
    out.printf("Name         Hours  Rate Regular Overtime    Net\n\n");
    firstName = in.next();
    while (!firstName.equals("END")) {
      numEmp++;
      lastName = in.next();
      hours = in.nextDouble();
      rate = in.nextDouble();
      if (hours <= MaxRegularHours) {
        regPay = hours * rate;
        ovtPay = 0;
      }
      else {
        regPay = MaxRegularHours * rate;
        ovtPay = (hours - MaxRegularHours) * rate * OvertimeFactor;
      }
      netPay = regPay + ovtPay;
      //make one name out of firstName and lastName
      name = firstName + " " + lastName;
      out.printf("%-15s %5.1f %6.2f", name, hours, rate);
      out.printf("%9.2f %9.2f %7.2f\n", regPay, ovtPay, netPay);
      if (netPay > mostPay) {mostPay = netPay; bestPaid = name; }
      wageBill += netPay;
      firstName = in.next();
    } //end while
    out.printf("\nNumber of employees: %d\n", numEmp);
    out.printf("Total wage bill: $%3.2f\n", wageBill);
    out.printf("%s earned the most pay of $%3.2f\n",bestPaid, mostPay);
    in.close(); out.close();
  } //end main
} //end class
```

the loop. If you have difficulty following the code, you need to re-read Sections 5.1 and 5.2. We use **numEmp++** to add 1 to **numEmp** and **wageBill += netPay** to add **netPay** to **wageBill**.

The variable **mostPay** holds the most pay earned by any employee. It is initialized to 0. Each time we calculate **netPay** for the current employee, we compare it with **mostPay**. If it is bigger, we set **mostPay** to the new amount *and* save the name of the employee (**name**) in **bestPaid**.

Note the declaration **String bestPaid = ""**. If we do not initialize **bestPaid** (we use the empty string here), Java will complain that **bestPaid** "might not have been initialized" when it tries to execute the last **printf**. This is possible but only if no data was supplied. In this case, the statement **bestPaid = name;** will never be executed so **bestPaid** never gets set to anything so it would be wrong to try and print its value.

5.10 The for construct

In Chapters 3, 4 and 5 we showed you three kinds of logic which can be used for writing programs—sequence, selection and repetition. Believe it or not, with these three, you have all the logic control structures you need to express the logic of any program. It has been proven that these three structures are all you need to formulate the logic to solve any problem that can be solved on a computer.

It follows that all you need are **if** and **while** statements to write the logic of any program. However, many programming languages provide additional statements because they allow you to express some kinds of logic *more conveniently* than using **if** and **while**. The **for** statement is a good example.

Whereas **while** lets you repeat statements as long as some condition is true, **for** lets you repeat statements *a specified number of times* (25 times, say). Consider the following *pseudocode* example of the **for** construct (more commonly called the *for loop*):

```
for j = 1 to 5 do
    print "I must not sleep in class"
endfor
```

This says to execute the **print** statement 5 times, with **j** assuming the values 1, 2, 3, 4 and 5, one value for each of the 5 times. The effect is to print:

```
I must not sleep in class
I must not sleep in class
I must not sleep in class
I must not sleep in class
I must not sleep in class
```

The construct consists of:

- the word **for**
- the *loop variable* (j, in the example)
- =
- the *initial value* (1, in the example)
- the word **to**
- the *final value* (5, in the example)
- the word **do**
- one or more statements to be executed each time through the loop; these statements make up the *body* of the loop
- the word **endfor**, indicating the end of the construct

We emphasize that **endfor** is not a Java word and does not appear in any Java program. It is just a convenient word used by programmers when writing pseudocode to indicate the end of a **for** loop.

In order to highlight the structure of the loop and make it more readable, we line up **for** and **endfor**, and indent the statements in the body.

The part of the construct between **for** and **do** is called the *control part* of the loop. This is what determines how many times the body is executed. In the example, the control part is **j = 1 to 5**. This works as follows:

- j is set to 1 and the body (**print**) is executed
- j is set to 2 and the body (**print**) is executed
- j is set to 3 and the body (**print**) is executed
- j is set to 4 and the body (**print**) is executed
- j is set to 5 and the body (**print**) is executed

The net effect is that, in this case, the body is executed 5 times.

In general, if the control part is **j = first to last**, it is executed as follows:

- if **first > last**, the body is not executed at all; execution continues with the statement, if any, after **endfor**; otherwise
- j is set to **first** and the body is executed
- 1 is added to j; if the value of j is less than or equal to **last**, the body is executed again
- 1 is added to j; if the value of j is less than or equal to **last**, the body is executed again
- and so on

When the value of j reaches **last**, the body is executed for the last time and control goes to the statement, if any, after **endfor**.

The net effect is that the body is executed for each value of **j** between **first** and **last**, inclusive.

The *for* statement in Java

The pseudocode construct

```
for j = 1 to 5 do
   print 'I must not sleep in class'
endfor
```

is implemented in Java as

```
for (int j = 1; j <= 5; j++)
   System.out.printf("I must not sleep in class\n");
```

In Java, the body must be a single statement or a block. In the example, it is the single **printf** statement. If it were a block, we would write it in the form

```
for (int j = 1; j <= 5; j++) {
   <statement1>
   <statement2>
   etc.
}
```

Program P5.10 illustrates how the **for** statement is used to print

```
I must not sleep in class
```

5 times. As you could probably figure out, if you want to print 100 lines, say, all you have to do is change 5 to 100 in the **for** statement.

Program P5.10

```java
public class Sleep {
   public static void main(String[] args) {
      for (int j = 1; j <= 5; j++)
         System.out.printf("I must not sleep in class\n");
   }
}
```

The general form of the **for** statement in Java is

```
for (<expr1>; <expr2>; <expr3>)
   <statement>
```

The word **for**, the brackets and the semicolons are required by Java. You must supply <expr1>, <expr2>, <expr3> and <statement>.

In detail, the **for** statement consists of

- the word **for**
- a left bracket, (

- **<expr1>**, called the initialization step; this is the first step performed when the **for** is executed.
- a semicolon, ;
- **<expr2>**, the *condition* which controls whether or not **<statement>** is executed.
- a semicolon, ;
- **<expr3>**, called the re-initialization step
- a right bracket,)
- **<statement>**, called the *body* of the loop. This can be a simple statement or a block.

When a **for** statement is encountered, it is executed as follows:

(1) **<expr1>** is evaluated.
(2) **<expr2>** is evaluated. If it is **false**, execution continues with the statement, if any, after **<statement>**. If it is **true**, **<statement>** is executed, followed by **<expr3>**, and this step (2) is repeated.

This can be expressed more concisely as follows:

```
<expr1>;
while (<expr2>) {
   <statement>;
   <expr3>;
}
```

In the following

```
for (int j = 1; j <= 5; j++)
   System.out.printf("I must not sleep in class\n");
```

- **int j = 1** is **<expr1>**
- **j <= 5** is **<expr2>**
- **j++** is **<expr3>**
- **<statement>** is **System.out.printf(...);**

This code is executed as follows:

- **j** is set to 1
- the test **j <= 5** is performed. It is **true**, so the body of the loop is executed (one line is printed). The re-initialization step **j++** is then performed, so **j** is now 2.
- the test **j <= 5** is again performed. It is **true**, so the body of the loop is executed (a second line is printed); **j++** is performed, so **j** is now 3.
- the test **j <= 5** is again performed. It is **true**, so the body of the loop is executed (a third line is printed); **j++** is performed, so **j** is now 4.
- the test **j <= 5** is again performed. It is **true**, so the body of the loop is executed (a fourth line is printed); **j++** is performed, so **j** is now 5.

- the test **j <= 5** is again performed. It is **true**, so the body of the loop is executed (a fifth line is printed); **j++** is performed, so **j** is now 6.
- the test **j <= 5** is again performed. It is now **false**, so execution of the **for** loop ends and the program continues with the statement, if any, after **printf(...)**.

On exit from the **for** loop, the value of **j** (6, in this case) is *not* available. In fact, since **j** was declared within the **for** statement, it is unknown outside of this statement. If we need the value of **j** after the **for**, we must declare it before the **for**, as in:

```
int j;
for (j = 1; j <= 5; j++)
   System.out.printf("I must not sleep in class\n");
```

Now, when we exit the **for**, the value of **j** (6, in this case) *is* available.

If we need a loop to count backwards (from 5 down to 1, say), we can write

```
for (int j = 5; j >= 1; j--)
```

The loop body is executed with **j** taking on the values 5, 4, 3, 2 and 1. After the loop, **j** is unknown.

We can also count upwards in steps other than 1. For example, the statement

```
for (int j = 10; j <= 20; j += 3)
```

will execute the body with **j** taking on the values 10, 13, 16 and 19. After the loop, **j** is unknown.

In general, we can use whatever expressions we need to get a desired effect.

In Program P5.10, **j** takes on the values 1, 2, 3, 4 and 5 inside the loop. We have not used **j** in the body but it *is* available, if needed. We show a simple use in Program P5.11 in which we number the lines by printing the value of **j**.

```
                    Program P5.11
public class Sleep1 {
   public static void main(String[] args) {
      for (int j = 1; j <= 5; j++)
         System.out.printf("%d. I must not sleep in class\n", j);
   }
}
```

When run, this program will print

```
1. I must not sleep in class
2. I must not sleep in class
3. I must not sleep in class
4. I must not sleep in class
5. I must not sleep in class
```

The initial and final values in the **for** statement do not have to be constants; they can be variables or expressions. For example, consider

    for (j = 1; j <= n; j++) ...

How many times would the body of this loop be executed? We cannot answer unless we know the value of **n** when this statement is encountered. If **n** has the value 7, then the body would be executed 7 times.

This means that *before* the computer gets to the **for** statement, **n** must have been assigned some value and it is *this* value which determines how many times the loop is executed. If a value has not been assigned to **n**, the **for** statement would not make sense and the program will crash (or, at best, give some nonsensical output).

To illustrate, we can modify Program P5.11 to ask the user how many lines she wants to print. The number entered is then used to control how many times the loop is executed and, hence, how many lines are printed.

The changes are shown in Program P5.12.

Program P5.12

```java
import java.util.*;
public class Sleep2 {
   public static void main(String[] args) {
      Scanner in = new Scanner(System.in);
      System.out.printf("How many lines to print? ");
      int n = in.nextInt();
      System.out.printf("\n"); //print a blank line
      for (int j = 1; j <= n; j++)
         System.out.printf("%d. I must not sleep in class\n", j);
   }
}
```

A sample run is shown below. We will show shortly how to neaten the output.

```
How many lines to print? 12

1. I must not sleep in class
2. I must not sleep in class
3. I must not sleep in class
4. I must not sleep in class
5. I must not sleep in class
6. I must not sleep in class
7. I must not sleep in class
8. I must not sleep in class
9. I must not sleep in class
10. I must not sleep in class
11. I must not sleep in class
12. I must not sleep in class
```

Note that we do not (and cannot) know beforehand what number the user will type. However, that is not a problem. We simply store the number in a variable (**n** is used) and use **n** as the "final value" in the **for** statement. Thus, the number the user types will determine how many times the body is executed.

Now the user can change the number of lines printed simply by entering the desired value in response to the prompt. No change is needed in the program. Program P5.12 is much more *flexible* than P5.11.

A bit of aesthetics[6]

In the above run, while the output is correct, the *numbers* do not line up very nicely with the result that the **I**'s do not line up properly. We can get things to line up by using a field width when printing **j**. For this example, 2 will do. However, if the number could run into the hundreds, we must use at least 3 and for thousands at least 4, and so on.

In Program P5.12, if we change the **printf** statement to

```
System.out.printf("%2d. I must not sleep in class\n", j);
```

the following output would be much nicer to look at:

```
How many lines to print? 12
 1. I must not sleep in class
 2. I must not sleep in class
 3. I must not sleep in class
 4. I must not sleep in class
 5. I must not sleep in class
 6. I must not sleep in class
 7. I must not sleep in class
 8. I must not sleep in class
 9. I must not sleep in class
10. I must not sleep in class
11. I must not sleep in class
12. I must not sleep in class
```

5.11 Producing multiplication tables

The **for** statement is quite handy for producing multiplication tables. To illustrate, let us write a program to produce a "2 times" table from 1 to 12. The following should be printed by the program:

---

[6] aesthetic - showing good taste or appreciation of beauty

```
 1 x 2 =  2
 2 x 2 =  4
 3 x 2 =  6
 4 x 2 =  8
 5 x 2 = 10
 6 x 2 = 12
 7 x 2 = 14
 8 x 2 = 16
 9 x 2 = 18
10 x 2 = 20
11 x 2 = 22
12 x 2 = 24
```

A look at the output reveals that each line consists of 3 parts:

1. a number on the left which increases by 1 for each new line;
2. a fixed part " x 2 = " (note the spaces) which is the same for each line;
3. a number on the right, which is derived by multiplying the number on the left by 2.

We can produce the numbers on the left by using

```
for (m = 1; m <= 12; m++)
```

and printing **m** each time through the loop. And we can produce the number on the right by multiplying **m** by 2.

Program P5.13 shows how to write it. When run, it will produce the table above.

Program P5.13

```java
public class Times2 {
   public static void main(String[] args) {
      for (int m = 1; m <= 12; m++)
         System.out.printf("%2d x 2 = %2d\n", m, m * 2);
   }
}
```

Note the use of the field width 2 for printing **m** and **m * 2**. This is to ensure that the numbers line up as shown in the output. Without the field width, the table would not look neat—try it and see.

What if we want to print a "7 times" table? What changes would be needed? We would just need to change the **printf** statement to

```
System.out.printf("%2d x 7 = %2d\n", m, m * 7);
```

Similarly, if we want a "9 times" table, we would have to change the 7's to 9's. And we would have to keep changing the program for each table that we want.

A better approach is to let the user tell the computer which table he wants. The program will then use this information to produce the table requested. Now when the program is run, it will prompt:

```
Enter type of table:
```

If the user wants a "7 times" table, he will enter 7. The program will then go ahead and produce a "7 times" table. Program P5.14 shows how.

Program P5.14
```java
import java.util.*;
public class TimesTable {
    public static void main(String[] args) {
        Scanner in = new Scanner(System.in);
        System.out.printf("Type of table? ");
        int factor = in.nextInt();
        System.out.printf("\n"); //print a blank line
        for (int m = 1; m <= 12; m++)
            System.out.printf("%2d x %d = %2d\n", m, factor, m * factor);
    }
}
```

Since we do not know beforehand what type of table would be requested, we cannot use **7**, say, in the *format string*, since the user may want a "9 times" table. We must print the variable **factor** which holds the type of table.

The following is a sample run:

```
Type of table? 7
 1 x 7 =  7
 2 x 7 = 14
 3 x 7 = 21
 4 x 7 = 28
 5 x 7 = 35
 6 x 7 = 42
 7 x 7 = 49
 8 x 7 = 56
 9 x 7 = 63
10 x 7 = 70
11 x 7 = 77
12 x 7 = 84
```

We now have a program which can produce *any* multiplication table from 1 to 12. But there is nothing sacred[7] about the range 1 to 12. How can we *generalize* the program to produce *any* table in *any* range? We must let the user tell the program what type of table and what range he wants. And in the program, we will need to replace the numbers 1 and 12 by variables, (**start** and **finish**, say).

All these changes are reflected in Program P5.15 (next page).

---

[7] special, maybe, since that's what we all learnt in school

Program P5.15

```java
import java.util.*;
public class TimesTable1 {
   public static void main(String[] args) {
      Scanner in = new Scanner(System.in);
      System.out.printf("Type of table? ");
      int factor = in.nextInt();
      System.out.printf("From? ");
      int start = in.nextInt();
      System.out.printf("To? ");
      int finish = in.nextInt();
      System.out.printf("\n"); //print a blank line
      for (int m = start; m <= finish; m++)
         System.out.printf("%2d x %d = %2d\n", m, factor, m * factor);
   }
}
```

To cater for bigger numbers, we would need to increase the field width of 2 in the **printf** statement if we want the numbers to line up neatly. The following sample run produces a "6 times" table from 10 to 16.

```
Type of table? 6
From? 10
To? 16

10 x 6 = 60
11 x 6 = 66
12 x 6 = 72
13 x 6 = 78
14 x 6 = 84
15 x 6 = 90
16 x 6 = 96
```

Comment on Program P5.15

The program assumes that **start** is less than or equal to **finish**. What if this is not so? For example, suppose the user enters 20 for **start** and 15 for **finish**. The **for** statement becomes

```
for (int m = 20; m <= 15; m++)
```

m is set to 20; since this value is immediately bigger than the final value 15, the body is not executed at all and the program ends with nothing printed.

To cater for this possibility, we can let the program *validate* the values of **start** and **finish** to ensure that the 'From' value is less than or equal to the 'To' value. One way of doing this is:

```
       if (start > finish)
          System.out.printf("Invalid data: From value is bigger than To value\n");
       else {
          System.out.printf("\n");
          for (int m = start; m <= finish; m++)
             System.out.printf("%2d x %d = %2d\n", m, factor, m * factor);
       }
```

Validating data entered is yet another example of *defensive programming*. Also, it is better to print a message informing the user of the error rather than have the program do nothing. This makes the program more *user-friendly*.

5.12 Temperature conversion table

Some countries use the Celsius scale for measuring temperature while others use the Fahrenheit scale. Suppose we want to print a table of temperature conversions from Celsius to Fahrenheit. The table runs from 0°C to 100°C in steps of 10, thus:

```
Celsius   Fahrenheit

   0          32
  10          50
  20          68
  30          86
  40         104
  50         122
  60         140
  70         158
  80         176
  90         194
 100         212
```

For a Celsius temperature, C, the Fahrenheit equivalent is $32 + 9C/5$.

If we use **c** to hold the Celsius temperature, we can write a **for** statement to let **c** take on the values 0, 10, 20, ..., up to 100, with

   for (c = 0; c <= 100; c += 10)

Each time the loop is executed, **c** is incremented by 10. Using this, we write Program P5.16 (next page) to produce the table.

An interesting part of the program are the **printf** statements. In order to get the temperatures centred under the heading, we need to do some counting. Consider the heading

        Celsius   Fahrenheit

with the **C** in column 1 and 2 spaces between **s** and **F**.

Assume we want the Celsius temperatures lined up under **i** and the Fahrenheit temperatures lined up under **n** (see output above).

Program P5.16

```java
public class Temperature {
  public static void main(String[] args) {
    double c, f;
    System.out.printf("Celsius  Fahrenheit\n\n");
    for (c = 0; c <= 100; c += 10) {
      f = 32 + 9 * c / 5;
      System.out.printf("%5.0f %9.0f\n", c, f);
    }
  }
}
```

By counting, we find that **i** is in column 5 and **n** is in column 15.

From this, we can figure out that the value of **c** must be printed in a field width of 5 (the first 5 columns) and the value of **f** must be printed in the next 10 columns. We use a field width of 9 for **f** since there is already one space between **f** and **%**.

We print **c** and **f** without a decimal point using 0 as the number of decimal places in the format specification. If any temperature is not a whole number, the 0 specification will print it *rounded* to the nearest whole number, as in the table below.

As an exercise, re-write Program P5.16 so that it requests threes values for **start**, **finish** and **incr** and produces a conversion table with Celsius temperatures going from **start** to **finish** in steps of **incr**. Follow the ideas of the previous section for producing any multiplication table. For example, if **start** is 20, **finish** is 40 and **incr** is 2, the program should produce (with Fahrenheit temperatures rounded to the nearest whole number):

```
Celsius   Fahrenheit

   20        68
   22        72
   24        75
   26        79
   28        82
   30        86
   32        90
   34        93
   36        97
   38       100
   40       104
```

As another exercise, write a program which produces a table from Fahrenheit to Celsius. For a Fahrenheit temperature, F, the Celsius equivalent is 5(F - 32)/9.

5.13 The expressive power of for

In Java, the **for** statement can be used for a lot more than just counting the number of times a loop is executed. This is possible because <expr1>, <expr2> and <expr3> can be *any* expressions; they are not even required to be related in any way. So, for instance, <expr1> can be **j = 1**, <expr2> can test if **a** is equal to **b** and <expr3> can be **k++** or any other expression the programmer desires. The following is perfectly valid:

    for (j = 1; a == b; k++) <statement>

It is also possible to omit any of <expr1>, <expr2> or <expr3>. However, the semicolons *must* be included. Thus, to omit <expr3>, one can write

    for (<expr1>; <expr2>;) <statement>

In this case,

(1)   <expr1> is evaluated; then
(2)   <expr2> is evaluated. If it is **false**, execution continues after <statement>. If it is **true**, <statement> is executed and this step (2) is repeated.

This is equivalent to

    <expr1>;
    while (<expr2>) <statement>

If, in addition, we omit <expr1>, we will have

    for (; expr2 ;) <statement>   // note the semicolons

Now, <expr2> is evaluated. If it is **false**, execution continues after <statement>. If it is **true**, <statement> is executed, followed by another evaluation of <expr2>, and so on. The net effect is that <statement> is executed as long as <expr2> is true—the same effect achieved by

    while (<expr2>) <statement>

Most times, <expr1> will initialize some variable, <expr2> will test it and <expr3> will change it. But more is possible. For instance, the following is valid:

    for (lo = 1, hi = n; lo <= hi; lo++, hi--) <statement>

Here, <expr1> consists of *two* assignment statements separated by a *comma*; <expr3> consists of *two* expressions separated by a comma. This is very useful when two variables are related and we want to highlight the relationship. In this case, the relationship is captured in one place, the **for** statement. We can easily see how the variables are initialized and how they are changed.

This feature comes in very handy when dealing with arrays and strings. We will see examples on pages 195 and 231. For now, we leave you with a simple example of printing all pairs of integers which add up to a given integer, **n**.

The code is:

```
for (lo = 1, hi = n - 1; lo <= hi; lo++, hi--)
    System.out.printf("%2d %2d\n", lo, hi);
```

If **n** is 10, this code will print

```
 1  9
 2  8
 3  7
 4  6
 5  5
```

The variables **lo** and **hi** are initialized to the first pair. After a pair is printed, **lo** is *incremented* by 1 and **hi** is *decremented* by 1 to get the next pair. When **lo** passes **hi**, all pairs have been printed.

Exercises 5

1. What is an end-of-data marker? Give the other names for it.
2. On page 65, problem 7, write the program to read several sets of prices and discounts from a file. Choose an appropriate end-of-data marker. Also, print the number of items and the total amount the customer must pay.
3. On page 66, problem 9, write the program to process data for several customers from a file. Assume that the fixed charge and the rate per unit are the same for all customers and are given on the first line. This is followed by the data for the customers. Each set of data consists of two lines: a name on the first line and the meter readings on the second line. The 'name' **xxxx** ends the data. Print the information for the customers under a suitable heading. Also,
   - count how many customers were processed
   - print the total due to the electricity company
   - find the customer whose bill was the highest
4. On page 66, problem 12, write the program to process several sets of data from a file. Each set of data consists of two lines: a name on the first line and gross salary, deductions allowed and rate of tax on the second line. The 'name' **xxxx** ends the data. Also,
   - count how many persons were processed
   - print totals for gross salary, tax deducted and net pay
   - find the person who earned the highest net pay
5. On page 66, problem 16, write the program to convert several lengths. Choose an appropriate end-of-data marker.
6. On page 88, problem 1, write the program to read several sets of hours worked and cost of parts and, for each, print the charge for the job. Choose an appropriate end-of-data marker. (You cannot choose 0 since either hours or parts could be 0). Also, print the total charge for all jobs.
7. On pages 88-89, for problems 2, 3 and 9, write the programs to process several pairs of weights, lengths and times.

Writing programs using repetition logic

8. A contest was held for the promotion of SuperMarbles. Each contestant was required to guess the number of marbles in a jar. Write a program to determine the Grand Prize winner (ignoring the possibility of a tie) based on the following:

   The first line of data contains a single integer (**answer**, say) representing the actual number of marbles in the jar. Each subsequent line contains a contestant's ID number (an integer) and an integer representing that contestant's guess. The data is terminated by a line containing 0 only.

   The Grand Prize winner is that contestant who guesses closest to **answer** *without exceeding it*. There is no winner if all guesses are too big.

   Assume all data are valid. Print the number of contestants and the ID number of the winner, if any.

9. The manager of a hotel wants to calculate the cost of carpeting the rooms in the hotel. All the rooms are rectangular in shape. He has a file, **rooms.txt**, which contains data for the rooms. Each line of data consists of the room number, the length and breadth of the room (in metres), and the cost per square metre of the carpet for that room. For example, the data line:

       325   3.0   4.5   40.00

   means that room 325 is 3.0 metres by 4.5 metres, and the cost of the carpet for that room is $40.00 per square metre. The last line of the file contains 0 only, indicating the end of the data.

   Write a program to do the following, sending output to the file **rooms.out**:

   - print a suitable heading and under it, for each room, print the room number, the area of the room and the cost of the carpet for the room;
   - print the number of rooms processed;
   - print the total cost of carpeting all the rooms;
   - print the number of the room which will cost the most to carpet (ignore ties).

10. The price of an item is **p** dollars. Due to inflation, the price of the item is expected to increase by **r%** each year. For example, the price might be $79.50 and inflation might be 7.5%. Write a program which reads values for **p** and **r**, and, starting with year 1, prints a table consisting of year and year-end price. The table ends when the year-end price is at least twice the original price.

11. A fixed percentage of water is taken from a well each day. Request values for **W** and **P** where

    - **W** is the amount (in litres) of water in the well at the start of the first day
    - **P** is the percentage of the water in the well taken out each day

    Write a program to print the number of the day, the amount taken for that day and the amount remaining at the end of the day. The output should be terminated when 30 days have been printed or the amount remaining is less than 100 litres, whichever comes first. For example, if **W** = 1000 and **P** = 10, the output should start as follows:

Day	Amount Taken	Amount Remaining
1	100	900
2	90	810
3	81	729

12. You are given a file containing an unknown amount of numbers. Each number is one of the numbers 1 to 9. A number can appear zero or more times and can appear anywhere in the file. The number 0 indicates the end of the data. Some sample data are:

    5 3 7 7 7 4 3 3 2 2 2 6 7 4 7 7 2 2 9 6 6 6 6 6 8 5 5 3 7 9 9 9 0

    Write a program to read the data *once* and print the number which appears the most in consecutive positions and the number of times it appears. Ignore the possibility of a tie. For the above data, output should be 6 5.

13. Write a program to print the following 99 times:

    When you have nothing to say, it is a time to be silent

14. Write a program to print 8 copies of your favourite song.

15. Write a program to print a table of squares from 1 to 10. Each line of the table consists of a number and the square of that number.

16. Write a program to request a value for **n** and print a table of squares from 1 to **n**.

17. Write a program to request values for **first** and **last**, and print a table of squares from **first** to **last**.

18. Write a program to print 100 mailing labels for

    The Computer Store
    57 First Avenue
    San Fernando

19. Write a program to print a conversion table from miles to kilometres. The table ranges from 5 to 100 miles in steps of 5. (1 mile = 1.61 km).

20. Write a program which requests a user to enter an amount of money. The program prints the interest payable per year for rates of interest from 5% to 12% in steps of 0.5%.

21. Write a program to request a value for **n**; the user is then asked to enter **n** numbers, one at a time. The program calculates and prints the sum of the numbers. The following is a sample run:

    ```
    How many numbers? 3
    Enter a number? 12
    Enter a number? 25
    Enter a number? 18

    The sum of the 3 numbers is 55
    ```

22. Write a program to request an integer **n** from 1 to 9 and print a line of output consisting of ascending digits from 1 to **n** followed by descending digits from **n - 1** to 1. For example, if **n** = 5, print the line

    123454321

23. Solve problem 9, above, assuming that the first line of data contains the number of rooms (*n*, say) to carpet. This is followed by *n* lines of data, one line for each room.

24. Solve problem 11, above, but this time print the table for exactly 30 days. In other words, do not stop if the amount of water falls below 100 litres.

6 Working with characters

In this chapter, we will explain:

- some important features of character sets
- how to work with character constants and values
- how to declare character variables in Java
- how you can use characters in arithmetic expressions
- how to read, manipulate and print characters
- how to test for end-of-line
- how to test for end-of-file
- how to compare characters
- how to read characters from a file
- how to convert a number from character form to integer form

In Section 2.6, we introduced the idea of a character set. We also defined a character constant and its value. We also saw how Java represents certain characters using an *escape sequence*. And we learnt that **char** is one of Java's primitive types used for storing and working with characters.

6.1 Character constants and values

A character constant is a single character enclosed in single quotes such as **'A'**, **'+'** and **'5'**. Some characters cannot be represented like this because we cannot type them or because they play a special role in Java (e.g. ', \). For these, we use an escape sequence enclosed in single quotes. For example,

'\n'	newline character, code 10
'\f'	new page (formfeed) character, code 12
'\t'	tab character, code 9
'\''	single quote (quote, backslash, quote, quote), code 39
'\\'	backslash, code 92
'\0'	the *null* character, code 0

The *character value* of a character constant is the character represented, without the single quotes. Thus, the character value of **'T'** is **T** and the character value of '\\' is \.

A character constant has an *integer value* associated with it—the numeric code of the character represented. Thus, the integer value of **'T'** is 84 since the ASCII code for **T** is 84. The integer value of '\\' is 92 since the ASCII code for \ is 92. And the integer value of '\n' is 10 since the ASCII code for 'newline' is 10.

We could print the *character* value using the specification **%c** in **printf** and we could print the *integer* value using **%d**. For example, the statement

System.out.printf("Character: %c, Integer: %d\n", 'T', (int) 'T');

will print

Character: T, Integer: 84

Note that we must use the cast **(int)** to convert the character value to integer since **%d** expects an integer value. One could argue that **printf** should be smart enough to convert the character to integer (without the cast) to match with **%d** but that is not the case.

6.2 Characters in arithmetic expressions

Java allows us to use variables and constants of type **char** directly in arithmetic expressions. When we do, it uses the *integer value* of the character. For example, the statement

int n = 'A' + 3;

assigns 68 to **n** since the code for **'A'** is 65.

Similarly, we can assign an integer value to a **char** variable but, since an **int** is bigger than a **char**, we must use a cast[1], as in

char ch = (char) 68;

In this case, "the character whose code is 68" is assigned to **ch**; this character is **'D'**. If we print an integer using **%c** in **printf**, Java will interpret the integer as the code for some character and print the character. For example, if **n** = 68,

System.out.printf("Integer: %d, Character: %c\n", n, n);

will print

Integer: 68, Character: D

It seems strange that no cast is needed here to convert **n** to a character when a cast is usually needed to convert **int** to **char** but one was required above to convert a character to **int** when one is not normally needed. Such are the quirks of programming languages.

For a more useful example, consider the following:

int d = '5' - '0';

5 is assigned to **d** since the code for **'5'** is 53 and the code for **'0'** is 48.

---

[1] In this specific example, we can omit the cast since Java can determine that the value 68 can fit in a **char**. In general, if the value being assigned is a constant and it is small enough to fit in a **char**, the cast is not needed.

Take note that the code for a digit in character form is **not** the same as the value of the digit; for instance, the *code* for the character '5' is 53 but the value of the digit 5 is 5. Sometimes we know that a character variable contains a digit and we want to get the (integer) value of the digit.

The above statements show how we can get the value of the digit—we simply subtract the code for '0' from the code for the digit. It does not matter what the actual codes for the digits are; it matters only that the codes for 0 to 9 are consecutive. (Exercise: check this for yourself assuming a different set of code values for the digits).

In general, if **ch** contains a digit character ('0' to '9'), we can obtain the integer value of the digit with the statement

```
int d = ch - '0';
```

Suppose **ch** contains an uppercase letter and we want to convert it to its equivalent lowercase letter. For example, assume **ch** contains 'H' and we want to change it to 'h'. First we observe that the ASCII codes for 'A' to 'Z' range from 65 to 90 and the codes for 'a' to 'z' range from 97 to 122. We further observe that the *difference* between the codes for the two cases of a letter is always 32; for example,

```
'r' - 'R' = 114 - 82 = 32
```

Hence we can convert a letter from uppercase to lowercase by adding 32 to the uppercase code. This can be done with

```
ch = (char) (ch + 32); //cast needed to convert int to char
```

If **ch** contains 'H' (code 72), the above statement adds 32 to 72 giving 104; the "character whose code is 104" is assigned to **ch**, that is, 'h'. We have changed the value of **ch** from 'H' to 'h'. Conversely, to convert a letter from lowercase to uppercase, we *subtract* 32 from the lowercase code.

By the way, we do not really need to know the codes for the letters. All we need is the *difference* between the uppercase and lowercase codes. We can let Java tell us what the difference is by using 'a' - 'A', like this:

```
ch = (char) (ch + 'a' - 'A');
```

This works no matter what the actual codes for the letters are. It assumes, of course, that **ch** contains an uppercase letter and the difference between the uppercase and lowercase codes is the same for all letters.

6.3 Reading and printing characters

Many programs revolve around the idea of reading and writing one character at a time and developing the skill of writing such programs is a very important aspect of programming.

Java provides the method **System.in.read()** to read a *single* character from the standard input (the keyboard). It can be used as in

    int n = System.in.read();

To be precise, **read** returns the next byte in the data—to all intents and purposes, this is the next character. However, the value returned is an **int**—the integer code for the character. When there is no more input (we say when the 'end of file' is reached) **read** returns −1. Our programs can test for this value to detect when there is no more data.

Suppose the data typed by the user is:

Hello

When the above statement is executed, the first character **H** is read and its code 72 is stored in **n**. We can then use **n** in whatever way we like. Suppose we just want to print the first character read. We could print **n** but that would print **72**—not very useful. We can print the character corresponding to **n** using %c, thus:

    System.out.printf("The first character is %c\n", n);

This will print

    The first character is H

We could also assign the character to a **char** variable **ch** with

    ch = (char) n; // ch now contains 'H'

or even

    ch = (char) System.in.read(); // we don't really need n

and then print it with

    System.out.printf("The first character is %c\n", ch);

Finally, we don't even need **ch**. If all we want to do is print the first character in the data, we could do it with:

    System.out.printf("The first character is %c\n", System.in.read());

It is very important to note a big difference between reading a number and reading a character. When reading a number, the program will skip over any amount of whitespace until it finds the number. When reading a character, the *very next character* (whatever it is, even a space) is returned.

We now write a complete program, Program P6.1 (next page), which prompts for data and reads the first character. The character and its code are then printed.

For similar reasons as explained on page 108, we need **throws IOException** in the header for **main**. We also need the **import** statement since **IOException** is defined in **java.io**.

Working with characters

> **Program P6.1**
>
> ```
> import java.io.*;
> public class FirstChar {
>   public static void main(String[] args) throws IOException {
>   //read the first character in the data, print it and its code
>     System.out.printf("Type some data and press 'Enter'\n");
>     int n = System.in.read();
>     System.out.printf("\nThe first character is %c\n", n);
>     System.out.printf("Its code is %d\n", n);
>   }
> }
> ```

The following is a sample run:

```
Type some data and press 'Enter'
Hello

The first character is H
Its code is 72
```

A word of caution: we might be tempted to write

```
System.out.printf("The first character is %c \n", System.in.read());
System.out.printf("Its code is %d \n", System.in.read());  // wrong
```

But if we did, and assuming that **Hello** is typed as input, these statements will print:
```
The first character is H
Its code is 101
```

Why? In the first **printf**, **read** returns **H** which is printed. In the second **printf**, **read** returns the *next* character which is **e**; it is **e**'s code (101) that is printed.

As mentioned, **read** returns the integer value of the character read. What does it return when the user presses "Enter" or "Return" on the keyboard? On DOS or Windows, it actually returns two characters—a carriage return, **\r**, followed by a newline, **\n**; these have integer values 13 and 10, respectively. (On MacOS, it returns **\r** only. On Unix, it returns **\n** only). However, these characters are unprintable; if we try to print them, we won't see anything.

When program P6.1 is waiting for you to type data, if you press "Enter" or "Return" only, the first lines of output would be (on DOS/Windows or MacOS):
```
The first character is
Its code is 13
```

On Unix, it would print a blank line between these two lines and a code of 10. Why the blank line? Since **ch** contains **\n**, the statement

System.out.printf("\nThe first character is %c\n", n);

is effectively the same as (**%c** replaced by the character value of **n**)

System.out.printf("\nThe first character is \n\n");

The **\n** after **is** ends the first line and the last **\n** ends the second line, effectively printing a blank line. Note, however, that the code for **\n** is printed correctly.

In Program P6.1, we read just the first character. If we want to read and print the first 3 characters, we could do this with Program P6.2.

Program P6.2

```
import java.io.*;
public class First3Char {
   public static void main(String[] args) throws IOException {
   //read and print the first 3 character in the data
      System.out.printf("Type some data and press 'Enter'\n");
      for (int j = 1; j <= 3; j++) {
        int n = System.in.read();
        System.out.printf("Character %d is %c \n", j, n);
      }
   }
}
```

The following is a sample run of the program:

```
Type some data and press 'Enter'
Hi, how are you?
Character 1 is H
Character 2 is i
Character 3 is ,
```

If we want to read and print the first 20 characters, all we have to do is change 3 to 20 in the **for** statement.

Suppose the first part of the data line contains an arbitrary number of blanks. How do we find and print the first non-blank character? Since we do not know how many blanks to read, we cannot say something like "read 7 blanks, then the next character".

More likely, we need to say something like "as long as the character read is a blank, keep reading". We have the notion of doing something (reading a character) as long as some 'condition' is true; the condition here is whether the character is a blank. This can be expressed more concisely as follows:

Working with characters

> read a character
> while the character read is a blank
>   read the next character

Program P6.3 shows how to read the data and print the first non-blank character. (This code will be written more concisely later in this section).

```
                    Program P6.3
import java.io.*;
public class FirstNonBlank {
   public static void main(String[] args) throws IOException {
   //find and print the first non-blank character
      System.out.printf("Type some data and press 'Enter'\n");
      int n = System.in.read();
      while (n == ' ')           // as long as n is a blank
         n = System.in.read();   // get another character
      System.out.printf("The first non-blank is %c\n", n);
   }
}
```

The following is a sample run of the program (◊ denotes a blank):

```
Type some data and press 'Enter'
◊◊◊Hello
The first non-blank is H
```

The program will locate the first non-blank character regardless of how many blanks precede it.

Note that Java allows us to compare an **int**, **n**, with a character constant, ' '. The character is converted to an **int** and then the values are compared.

As a reminder of how the **while** statement works, consider the following portion of code from Program P6.3 with different comments:

> int n = System.in.read(); //executed once; gives n a value to be tested next
> while (n == ' ')
>   n = System.in.read();;   //executed as long as n is ' '

and suppose the data entered is (◊ denotes a space):

> ◊◊◊Hello

The code will execute as follows:

1. the first character is read and stored in **n**; it is a blank
2. the **while** condition is tested; it is **true**
3. the **while** body **n = System.in.read();** is executed and the second character is read and stored in **n**; it is a blank

139

4. the **while** condition is tested; it is **true**
5. the **while** body n = System.in.read(); is executed and the third character is read and stored in **n**; it is a blank
6. the **while** condition is tested; it is **true**
7. the **while** body n = System.in.read(); is executed and the fourth character is read and stored in **n**; it is **H**
8. the **while** condition is tested; it is **false**
9. control goes to **printf** which prints

   ```
   The first non-blank is H
   ```

What if **H** was the first character in the data? The code will execute as follows:

1. the first character is read and stored in **n**; it is **H**
2. the **while** condition is tested; it is **false**
3. control goes to **printf** which prints

   ```
   The first non-blank is H
   ```

It still works! If the **while** condition is **false** the first time it is tested, the body is not executed at all.

As another example, suppose we want to print all characters up to, but not including, the first blank. To do this, we could use Program P6.4.

```
                    Program P6.4
import java.io.*;
public class FirstNonBlanks {
   public static void main(String[] args) throws IOException {
   //print all characters before the first blank in the data
      System.out.printf("Type some data and press 'Enter' \n");
      int n = System.in.read();  //get the first character
      while (n != ' ') {    //as long as n is NOT a blank
         System.out.printf("%c \n", n); //print it
         n = System.in.read();   //get another character
      }
   }
}
```

The following is a sample run of the program:

```
Type some data and press 'Enter'
Way to go
W
a
y
```

Working with characters

The body of the **while** consists of two statements. These are enclosed by **{** and **}** to satisfy Java's rule that the **while** body must be a single statement or a block. Here, the body is executed as long as the character read is *not* a blank—we write the condition using **!=** (not equal to).

If the character is not a blank, it is printed and the next character read. If *that* is not a blank, it is printed and the next character read. If *that* is not a blank, it is printed and the next character read. And so on, until a blank character *is* read, making the **while** condition **false**, causing an *exit* from the loop.

We would be amiss if we didn't enlighten you about some of the expressive power in Java. For instance, in Program P6.3, we could have read the character **and** tested it in the **while** condition. We could have rewritten the following three lines:

```
n = System.in.read();
while (n == ' ')
   n = System.in.read();
```

as one line

```
while ((n = System.in.read()) == ' ') ; // get a character and test it
```

n = System.in.read() is an *assignment expression* whose value is the integer assigned to **n**, that is, the character read. This value is then tested to see if it is a blank. The brackets around **n = System.in.read()** are required since **==** has higher precedence than **=**. Without them, the condition would be interpreted as **n = (System.in.read() == ' ')**. This would attempt to assign the value of a condition (which is **false** or **true**) to the integer **n**; this assignment makes no sense and is not allowed by Java.

Now that we have moved the statement in the body into the condition, the body is empty; this is permitted in Java. The condition would now be executed repeatedly until it becomes **false**.

To give another example, in Program 6.4, the code

```
int n = System.in.read();        //get the first character
while (n != ' ') {        //as long as n is NOT a blank
  System.out.printf("%c \n", n); //print it
  n = System.in.read(); //get another character
}
```

could be re-coded as (assuming **n** is declared before the loop; Java does not allow it to be declared in the **while** condition)

```
while ((n = System.in.read()) != ' ')   // get a character
   System.out.printf("%c \n", n);       // print it if non-blank; repeat
```

Now that the body consists of just one statement, the braces are no longer required. Five lines have been reduced to two.

6.4 Counting characters

Program P6.3 prints the first non-blank character. Suppose we want to *count* how many blanks there were before the first non-blank. We could use an integer variable **numBlanks** to hold the count. Program P6.5 is the modified program for counting the leading blanks.

```
                          Program P6.5
import java.io.*;
public class CountBlanks {
   public static void main(String[] args) throws IOException {
   //find and print the first non-blank character in the data;
   // count the number of blanks before the first non-blank
     int n, numBlanks = 0;
     System.out.printf("Type some data and press 'Enter' \n");
     while ((n = System.in.read()) == ' ')      // repeat as long as n is blank
        numBlanks++;              // add 1 to numBlanks
     System.out.printf("The number of leading blanks is %d\n", numBlanks);
     System.out.printf("The first non-blank is %c\n", n);
   }
}
```

The following is a sample run of the program (◊ denotes a space):

```
Type some data and press 'Enter'
◊◊◊◊Hello
The number of leading blanks is 4
The first non-blank is H
```

Comments on Program P6.5:

- **numBlanks** is initialized to 0 *before* the **while** loop.
- **numBlanks** is incremented by 1 inside the loop so that **numBlanks** is incremented each time the loop body is executed. Since the loop body is executed when **n** contains a blank, the value of **numBlanks** is always the number of blanks read so far.
- When we exit the **while** loop, the value in **numBlanks** will be the number of blanks read. This value is then printed.
- Observe that if the first character in the data were non-blank, the **while** condition would be immediately **false** and control will go directly to the first **printf** statement with **numBlanks** having the value 0. The program will print, correctly:

    ```
    The number of leading blanks is 0
    ```

Working with characters

Counting characters in a line

Suppose we want to count the number of characters in a line of input. Now we must read characters until the end of the line. How does our program test for end-of-line? Recall that when the "Enter" or "Return" key is pressed by the user, two characters, \r and \n, are returned on DOS/Windows, \r is returned on MacOS and \n is returned on Unix. The following **while** condition reads a character and tests for \r (on Unix, you will have to test for \n; from now on, we will assume our programs are written for a DOS/Windows computer):

```
while ((n = System.in.read()) != '\r')
```

Program P6.6 reads a line of input and counts the number of characters in it, not counting the "end-of-line" character.

Program P6.6

```java
import java.io.*;
public class CountChars {
   public static void main(String[] args) throws IOException {
   //count the number of characters in the input line
      int n, numChars = 0;
      System.out.printf("Type some data and press 'Enter' \n");
      while ((n = System.in.read()) != '\r') // repeat as long as n is not \r
         numChars++;           // add 1 to numChars
      System.out.printf("The number of characters is %d\n", numChars);
   }
}
```

The main difference between this and Program P6.5 is that this one reads characters until the end of the line rather than until the first non-blank. A sample run is:

```
Type some data and press 'Enter'
One moment in time
The number of characters is 18
```

Note that on DOS/Windows, \n would not be read. This is fine here but, in another program, it may be necessary to read it before proceeding.

6.5 Counting blanks in a line of data

Suppose we want to count **all** the **blanks** in a line of data. We must still read characters until the end of the line is encountered. But now, for each character read, we must check whether it is a blank. If it is, the count is incremented. We would need two counters—one to count the number of characters in the line and the other to count the number of blanks. The logic could be expressed as:

```
set number of characters and number of blanks to 0
while we are not at the end-of-line
   read a character
   add 1 to number of characters
   if character is a blank then add 1 to number of blanks
endwhile
```

This logic is implemented as shown in Program P6.7.

```
                         Program P6.7
import java.io.*;
public class CountBlanks1 {
   public static void main(String[] args) throws IOException {
   //count the number of characters and blanks in the input line
      int n, numChars = 0, numBlanks = 0;
      System.out.printf("Type some data and press 'Enter' \n");
      while ((n = System.in.read()) != '\r') { // repeat as long as n is not \r
         numChars++;                   // add 1 to numChars
         if (n == ' ') numBlanks++;    // add 1 if n is blank
      }
      System.out.printf("The number of characters is %d\n", numChars);
      System.out.printf("The number of blanks is %d\n", numBlanks);
   }
}
```

A sample run is:

```
Type some data and press 'Enter'
One moment in time
The number of characters is 18
The number of blanks is 3
```

The **if** statement tests the condition **n == ' '**; if it is **true** (that is, **n** contains a blank), **numBlanks** is incremented by 1. If it is **false**, **numBlanks** is *not* incremented; control would normally go to the next statement within the loop but there is none (the **if** is the last statement). Therefore, control goes back to the top of the **while** loop, where another character is read and tested for \r.

6.6 Comparing characters

Characters can be compared using the relational operators ==, !=, <, <=, > and >=. We've compared the **int** variable **n** with a blank using **n == ' '** and **n != ' '**.

Let us now write a program to read a line of data and print the 'largest' character, that is, the character with the highest code. For instance, if the line consisted of

Working with characters

English words, the letter which comes latest in the alphabet would be printed. (Recall, though, that lowercase letters have higher codes than uppercase letters so that, for instance, **'g'** is greater than **'T'**).

'Finding the largest character' involves the following steps:

- Choose a variable to hold the largest value; we choose **bigChar**.
- Initialize **bigChar** to a very small value. The value chosen should be such that no matter what character is read, *its* value would be greater than this initial value. We initialize **bigChar** to 0.
- As each character (**n**, say) is read, it is compared with **bigChar**; if **n** is greater than **bigChar**, then we have a 'larger' character and **bigChar** is set to this new character.
- When all the characters have been read and checked, **bigChar** will contain the largest one.

These ideas are expressed in Program P6.8.

Program P6.8

```
import java.io.*;
public class LargestChar {
   public static void main(String[] args) throws IOException {
   //read a line of data and find the 'largest' character
     int n, bigChar = 0;
     System.out.printf("Type some data and press 'Enter' \n");
     while ((n = System.in.read()) != '\r')
        if (n > bigChar) bigChar = n; // is this character bigger?
     System.out.printf("\nThe largest character is %c\n", bigChar);
   }
}
```

The following is a sample run; **u** is printed since its code is the highest of all the characters typed.

Type some data and press 'Enter'
<u>Where The Mind Is Without Fear</u>

The largest character is u

6.7 Reading characters from a file

In our examples so far, we have read characters typed at the keyboard. In Section 5.7, we saw how to read data from a file using methods like **nextInt** and **nextDouble** from the **Scanner** class. Unfortunately, the **Scanner** class does not provide a method for reading characters. If we want to read characters from a file, **input.txt**, say, we must make a declaration such as

>FileReader in = new FileReader("input.txt");

The method, **read**, that we've been using is available in the **FileReader** class. We could read the next character from **input.txt** into an **int** variable (**n**, say) with

>n = in.read();

If there are no more characters to read, **read** returns -1. This is the reason why the value returned has to be stored in an **int**; we cannot store -1 in a **char**.

To illustrate, let us write a program which reads one line of data from a file, **input.txt**, and prints it on the screen. This is shown as Program P6.9.

```
                    Program P6.9
import java.io.*;
public class ReadFromFile1 {
   public static void main(String[] args) throws IOException {
      FileReader in = new FileReader("input.txt");
      int n;
      while ((n = in.read()) != '\r')
         System.out.printf("%c", n);
      System.out.printf("\n");
      in.close();
   }
}
```

The program reads one character at a time from the file and prints it on the screen. It does this until \r is read, indicating that the entire line has been read. On exit from the **while** loop, it prints \n to end the line on the screen.

Be careful, though. This program assumes that the line of data in the file is terminated by \r\n (generated when you press "Enter" or "Return"). However, if the line is not terminated by \r\n (the user did not press "Enter" or "Return"), the program will 'hang'—it will be caught in a loop from which it cannot get out (we say it will be caught in an *infinite loop*). Why?

Because the **while** condition ((n = in.read()) != '\r') will never become false (this happens when **ch** *is* '\r') since there is no \r to be read. But, as mentioned, when the end-of-file is reached, the value returned by **read** is -1. Knowing this, we could easily fix our problem by testing for \r *and* -1 in the **while** condition, thus:

>while ((n = in.read()) != '\r' && n != -1)

Even if \r\n is not present, **read** will return -1 when the end of the file is reached, and the condition **n != -1** would be **false**, causing an exit from the loop.

6.8 Writing characters to a file

In Section 5.8, we showed you how to send output to a file (**output.txt**, say) using

> PrintWriter out = new PrintWriter(new FileWriter("output.txt"));

Now, if we want to write a *character* (in **n**, say) to the file, we can do it with

> out.printf("%c", n);

Here, **n** can be **int** or **char** (or **short** or **byte**).

To illustrate writing to a file, we write Program P6.10 which copies the contents of the file, **input.txt**, to the file, **output.txt**.

Program P6.10

```java
import java.io.*;
public class CopyFile {
    public static void main(String[] args) throws IOException {
        FileReader in = new FileReader("input.txt");
        PrintWriter out = new PrintWriter(new FileWriter("output.txt"));
        int n;
        while ((n = in.read()) != -1)
            out.printf("%c", n);
        in.close();
        out.close();
    }
}
```

The program simply reads characters from **input.txt** and writes them to **output.txt** until the end of the file is reached. Note, for instance, that this will preserve the line structure since the characters **\r\n** (indicating the end of a line) in the input file are written 'as is' to the output file.

Example – echo the input, number the lines

Let us expand this example to read data from a file and write back the same data (*echo* the data) to another file with the lines numbered starting from 1.

The program would read the data and write it, thus:

```
1. First line of data
2. Second line of data
     etc.
```

This problem is a bit more difficult than those we have met so far. When faced with such a problem, it is best to tackle it a bit at a time, solving easier versions of the problem and working your way up to solving the complete problem. Since we already know how to echo the input, we need only figure out how to print the line numbers. A simplistic approach is based on the following outline:

```
set lineNo to 1
print lineNo
read a character, ch
while ch is not the end-of-file character
   print ch
   if ch is \r
      read and print the next character (\n)
      add 1 to lineNo
      print lineNo
   endif
   read a character, ch
endwhile
```

We can easily add the code that deals with the line numbers to Program P6.10 to get Program P6.11. Note that when we print the line number, we do not terminate the line with \n since the data must be written on the same line as the line number.

Program P6.11
```java
import java.io.*;
public class CopyFileNumberLines {
   public static void main(String[] args) throws IOException {
      FileReader in = new FileReader("input.txt");
      PrintWriter out = new PrintWriter(new FileWriter("output.txt"));
      int n, lineNo = 1;
      out.printf("%2d. ", lineNo);
      while ((n = in.read()) != -1) {
         out.printf("%c", n);
         if (n == '\r') {
            out.printf("%c", in.read()); //read and print \n
            lineNo++;
            out.printf("%2d. ", lineNo);
         }
      }
      in.close();
      out.close();
   }
}
```

Assuming that the input file contains
```
There was a little girl
  Who had a little curl
Right in the middle of her forehead
```

Program P6.11 will print:

Working with characters

```
1. There was a little girl
2.   Who had a little curl
3. Right in the middle of her forehead
4.
```

Almost, but not quite, correct! The little glitch is that we print an extra line number at the end. To see why, look at the **if** statement. When \r of the third data line is read, 1 would be added to **lineNo**, making it 4, which is printed by the next statement. This printing of an extra line number also holds if the input file is empty, since line number 1 would be printed in this case, but there is no such line.

Program P6.12 shows how to get around this problem. When run, it will number the lines without printing an extra line number.

Program P6.12

```java
import java.io.*;
public class CopyFileNumberLines1 {
  public static void main(String[] args) throws IOException {
    FileReader in = new FileReader("input.txt");
    PrintWriter out = new PrintWriter(new FileWriter("output.txt"));
    int n, lineNo = 0;
    boolean writeLineNo = true;
    while ((n = in.read()) != -1) {
      if (writeLineNo) {
        out.printf("%2d. ", ++lineNo);
        writeLineNo = false;
      }
      out.printf("%c", n);
      if (n == '\r') {
        out.printf("%c", in.read()); //read and print \n
        writeLineNo = true;
      }
    }
    in.close();
    out.close();
  }
}
```

We delay printing the line number until we are sure that there is at least one character on the line. We use a **boolean** variable **writeLineNo**, initially set to **true**. If we have a character to print and **writeLineNo** is **true**, the line number is printed and **writeLineNo** is set to **false**. When **writeLineNo** is **false**, all that happens is that the character just read is printed.

When \n is printed to end a line of output, **writeLineNo** is set to **true**. If it turns out that there *is* a character to print on the next line, the line number will be printed first since **writeLineNo** is **true**. If there are no more characters to print, nothing further is printed; in particular, the line number is not printed.

In the statement

> out.printf("%d. ", ++lineNo);

the expression **++lineNo** means that **lineNo** is incremented *first* before being printed. By comparison, if we had used **lineNo++**, then **lineNo** would be printed first and *then* incremented.

6.9 Converting digit characters to an integer

Let us consider how we can convert a sequence of digits into an integer. When we type the number 385, we are actually typing three individual characters: '3' then '8' then '5'. Inside the computer, the integer 385 is completely different from the three characters '3' '8' '5'. So when we *type* 385 and try to read it into an **int** variable, the computer has to convert this sequence of three characters into the *integer* 385.

To illustrate, the 8-bit ASCII codes for the characters '3', '8' and '5' are 00110011, 00111000 and 00110101, respectively. When typed to the screen or a file, the digits 385 are represented by

> 00110011 00111000 00110101

If, for example, an integer is stored using 16 bits, the *integer* 385 is represented by its binary equivalent

> 0000000110000001

Observe that the character representation is quite different from the integer representation. When we ask **nextInt** to read an integer that we type, it must convert the character representation to the integer representation. We now show how this is done.

The basic step requires us to convert a digit character into its equivalent integer value; for example, we must convert the character '5' (represented by 00110101) into the integer 5 (represented by 0000000000000101).

Assuming that the codes for the digits 0 to 9 are consecutive (as they are in ASCII and other character sets), this can be done as follows:

integer value of digit = code for digit character – code for character '0'

For example, in ASCII, the code for '5' is 53 and the code for '0' is 48. Subtracting 48 from 53 gives us the integer value (5) of the character '5'. Once we can convert individual digits, we can construct the value of the number as we read it from left to right, using the following algorithm:

Working with characters

```
set num to 0
get a character, ch
while ch is a digit character
   convert ch to the digit value, d = ch - '0'
   set num to num*10 + d
   get a character, ch
endwhile
num now contains the integer value
```

The sequence of characters 385 is converted as follows:

```
num = 0
get '3'; convert to 3
num = num*10 + 3 = 0*10 + 3; num is now 3
get '8'; convert to 8
num = num*10 + 8 = 3*10 + 8; num is now 38
get '5'; convert to 5
num = num*10 + 5 = 38*10 + 5; num is now 385
```

There are no more digits and the final value of **num** is 385.

Let us use this idea to write a program which reads data character by character until it finds an integer. It constructs and then prints the integer.

The program will have to read characters until it finds a digit, the first of the integer. Having found the first digit, it must construct the integer by reading characters as long as it keeps getting a digit. For example, if the data was

```
Number of items: 385, all in good condition
```

the program will read characters until it finds the first digit, 3. It will construct the integer using the 3 and then reading 8 and 5. When it reads the comma, it knows the integer has ended.

This outline can be expressed in pseudocode by

```
read a character, ch
while ch is not a digit do
   read a character, ch
endwhile
//at this point, ch contains a digit
while ch is a digit do
   use ch to build the integer
   read a character, ch
endwhile
print the integer
```

How do we test if the character in **ch** is a digit? We must test if

```
ch >= '0' && ch <= '9'
```

If this is true, we know that the character is between '0' and '9', inclusive. Conversely, to test if **ch** is *not* a digit, we can test if

ch < '0' || ch > '9'

Putting all these ideas together gives us Program P6.13.

Program P6.13

```
import java.io.*;
public class ReadInt {
  public static void main(String[] args) throws IOException {
    System.out.printf("Type data including a number and press Enter\n");
    int ch = System.in.read();
    // as long as the character is not a digit, keep reading
    while (ch < '0' || ch > '9') ch = System.in.read();
    // at this point, ch contains the first digit of the number
    int num = 0;
    while (ch >= '0' && ch <= '9') { // as long as we get a digit
      num = num * 10 + ch - '0';  // update num
      ch = System.in.read();
    }
    System.out.printf("Number is %d\n", num);
  }
}
```

A sample run is shown below:

```
Type data including a number and press Enter
hide the number &(%%)7085&*(&^ here
Number is 7085
```

This program will find the number, no matter where it is hidden in the line.

Exercises 6

1. Give the range of ASCII codes for (a) the digits (b) the uppercase letters (c) the lowercase letters.
2. How is the single quote represented as a character constant?
3. What is the character value of a character constant?
4. What is the numeric value of a character constant?
5. How is the expression **5 + 'T'** evaluated? What is its value?
6. What value is assigned to **n** by **int n = 7 + 't'**?
7. What character is stored in **ch** by **char ch = (char) (4 + 'n')**?
8. If **ch = '8'**, what value is assigned to **d** by **int d = ch - '0'**?

9. If **ch** contains any uppercase letter, explain how to change **ch** to the equivalent lowercase letter.
10. If **ch** contains any lowercase letter, explain how to change **ch** to the equivalent uppercase letter.
11. Write a program to request a line of data and print the first digit on the line.
12. Write a program to request a line of data and print the first letter on the line.
13. Write a program to request a line of data and print the number of digits and letters on the line.
14. Write a program to read a passage from a file and print how many times each vowel appears.
15. Modify Program P6.13 so that it will find negative integers as well.
16. Write a program which reads a file containing a Java program and outputs the program to another file with all the // comments removed.
17. Write a program to read the data, character by character, and store the next number (with or without a decimal point) in a **double** variable (**dv**, say). For example, given the data

    ```
    Mary works for $43.75 per hour
    ```

    your program should store 43.75 in **dv**.
18. In the programming language Pascal, comments can be enclosed by { and } or by (* and *). Write a program which reads a data file **input.pas** containing Pascal code and writes the code to a file **output.pas**, replacing each { with (* and each } with *). For example, the statements

    ```
    read(ch);          {get the first character}
    while ch = ' ' do  {as long as ch is a blank}
       read(ch);       {get another character}
    writeln('The first non-blank is ', ch);
    ```

    should be converted to

    ```
    read(ch);          (*get the first character*)
    while ch = ' ' do  (*as long as ch is a blank*)
       read(ch);       (*get another character*)
    writeln('The first non-blank is ', ch);
    ```

19. As in 18, but remove the comments altogether.
20. Someone has typed a letter in a file **letter.txt**, but does not always start the word after a period with a capital letter. Write a program to copy the file to another file **format.txt** so that all words after a period now begin with a capital letter. For example, the text

    Things are fine. we can see you now. let us know when is a good time.
    bye for now.

    must be re-written as

    Things are fine. We can see you now. Let us know when is a good time.
    Bye for now.

7 Methods

In this chapter, we will explain:

- why methods are important in programming
- how to write methods
- what happens when a method is called
- where methods are placed in a program
- some important concepts relating to methods using several examples

Java uses the term *method* to mean essentially the same as what other languages, like C, call *function*. In this book, we use the terms interchangeably.

So far, all our programs have consisted of a single method called **main**. However, we have used some predefined Java methods such as **printf**, **nextInt** and **read**. When we run a program, it starts executing with the first statement in **main** and ends when it reaches the last statement[1].

As we have seen, it is possible to write reasonably useful programs with only **main**. However, there are many limitations to this approach. The problem to be solved may be too complex to be solved with one method. We may need to break it up into subproblems and try to solve each of these individually. It would be impractical to solve all the subproblems in one method. It might be better to write a separate method to solve each subproblem.

Also, we may want to reuse the solution to common problems. It would be difficult to reuse a solution if it is part of the solution to a bigger problem. For example, if we need the highest common factor (HCF) of two numbers in several places, it would be best to write a method which works out the HCF of two given numbers; we call this method whenever we need to find the HCF of two numbers.

A well-written method performs some well-defined task; for example, skip a specified number of lines in the output or arrange some numbers in ascending order. However, quite often, a method also *returns a value*; for example, calculate the salary of a person and return the answer or play one turn of a game and return the score for that turn. The value returned is normally used at the point from which the method was called. It is usual to refer to a method that returns a value as a *function*; however, this is not a hard and fast rule.

We have used the function **nextInt** which returns the next *integer* in the input. And we have used **read** to return the next *character* in the input.

---

[1] It can also end if a **return** statement is executed.

Methods

We are now ready to learn how to write our own methods (called *user-defined* methods) and we will see several examples in the rest of this book.

7.1 skipLines

We have seen that we can use **\n** in a **printf** statement to print a blank line. For example, the statement

    System.out.printf("%d\n\n%d\n", a, b);

will print **a** on one line, skip one line and print **b** on the next line. We can usually skip any number of lines by writing the appropriate number of \n's in the **printf** statement.

Sometimes we may want to skip 3 lines, sometimes 2 lines, sometimes 5 lines, and so on. It would be nice if there was a statement we could use to skip any number of lines we want. For instance, to skip 3 lines, we should be able to write:

    skipLines(3);

and to skip 5 lines, we write:

    skipLines(5);

What we want is a *method* called **skipLines** which takes an *integer argument* (**n**, say) and skips **n** lines. In Java, we write this method as follows:

```
public static void skipLines(int n) {
  for (int j = 1; j <= n; j++)
    System.out.printf("\n");
}
```

Observe that the structure of the method is similar to the structure of **main**. It consists of a *header* (the first line, except **{**) followed by the *body* enclosed in braces. The word **void** indicates that the method does not return a value and **(int n)** defines **n** as an integer *parameter*. When the method is called, we must supply it with an integer value to match the parameter **n**.

This is the *definition* of the method **skipLines**. We *use* the method by *calling* it when we write a statement such as:

    skipLines(3);

in **main**[2]. We say that we *call* (or *invoke*) the method with the *argument*[3] 3. The "call" is executed as follows:

---

[2] A function can normally be called from any other function but, to focus our discussion, we will assume it is called from **main**.
[3] In this book, we use the term 'parameter' when referring to the *definition* of the function and the term 'argument' when the function is *called*. Others use the terms interchangeably

- The *value* of the argument is determined. In this case, it is just the constant 3 but, in general, it could be an expression.
- The value is copied to a temporary memory location. This location is passed to the method where it is labelled with the name of the parameter, **n**. In effect, the parameter variable **n** is set to the value of the argument. We can picture this as:

$$n \boxed{3}$$

- The body of the method is executed. In this case, since **n** is 3, the **for** loop becomes **for (int j = 1; j <= 3; j++)** and it prints \n three times.
- When the method is finished, the location containing the argument is discarded and control returns to **main** to the statement following **skipLines(3);**.

Note that we can get **skipLines** to print a different number of blank lines by supplying a different argument when we call it.

When the *value* of an argument is passed to a method, we say the argument is passed "by value". In Java, arguments are passed "by value".

7.2 A program with a method

We write Program P7.1 to show how **skipLines** fits into a complete program.

```
Program P7.1
public class TestMethod {
   public static void main(String[] args) {
      System.out.printf("Sing a song of sixpence\n");
      skipLines(2);
      System.out.printf("A pocket full of rye\n");
   }
   public static void skipLines(int n) {
      for (int j = 1; j <= n; j++)
         System.out.printf("\n");
   }
}
```

A Java program consists of one or more classes. A class, in turn, consists of data and methods for manipulating that data. Broadly speaking, some classes are written to perform some task (like playing a game) and some are written to provide templates for creating *objects*. In this book, we deal mainly with the first kind. In Chapter 10, we show how to create objects from a class definition.

Each class can consist of one or more methods. A method can be *static* (so-called class method) or it can be non-static (so-called *instance* method). An instance method works on *objects* of a class. In this book, we deal with static methods mainly. For this reason, our methods will be preceded by the words **public static**.

In terms of layout, the methods, including **main**, which make up a Java program can appear in any order. However, it is customary to place **main** first where the overall logic of the program can be easily seen. Having said that, some people prefer to place it as the last method.

We emphasize that this program is for illustrative purposes only since the output could be produced more easily with:

```
System.out.printf("Sing a song of sixpence\n\n\n");
System.out.printf("A pocket full of rye\n");
```

The method header

In our example, we used the header

```
public static void skipLines(int n)
```

In general, apart from **public static**, the method header consists of:

- a *type* (such as **void**, **int**, **double**, **char**), which specifies the type of value returned by the method. If no value is returned, we use the word **void**. The method **skipLines** does not return a value so we use **void**.
- the name we make up for the method, **skipLines** in the example.
- one or more parameters, called the *parameter list*, enclosed in brackets[4]; one parameter **n** of type **int** is used in the example.

The method header is followed by the left brace of the body.

Parameters are specified in the same way variables are declared. In fact, they really *are* declarations. The following are all valid examples of headers of **void** methods:

```
public static void sample1(int m, int n)  // 2 parameters

public static void sample2(double a, int n, char c) // 3 parameters

public static void sample3(double a, double b, int j, int k) // 4 parameters
```

Each parameter must be declared individually and two consecutive declarations are separated by a comma. For example, it is invalid to write

```
public static void sample1(int m, n)  // not valid; must write (int m, int n)
```

We will see examples of methods which return a value shortly.

How a method gets its data

A method is like a mini program. In the programs we have written, we have stated what data must be supplied to the program, what processing must take place and

---

[4] It is allowed to write a method without any parameters; in this case, the brackets alone are present, for example, **public static void printHeading()**.

what the output (results) should be. We must do the same when we write a method.

When we write a method header, we use the parameter list to specify what data must be supplied to the method when it is called. The list specifies *how many* data items, the *type* of the each item and the *order* in which they must be supplied.

For example, we wrote **skipLines** with an integer parameter **n**; this says that an integer value must be supplied to **skipLines** when it is called. When **skipLines** *is* called, the argument supplied becomes the specific value of **n** and the method is executed assuming that **n** has this value. In the call **skipLines(3)**, the argument 3 is the data that **skipLines** needs to perform its job.

It is worth emphasizing that **main** gets its data by using **nextInt** or **read**, among others, to read and store the data in variables. On the other hand, a method gets its data when it is called. The variables in the parameter list are set to the values of the corresponding arguments used in the call. For example, when we write the header

> public static void sample(int n, char c, double b)

we are saying that, when we call **sample**, we must do so with 3 arguments: the first must be an **int** value, the second a **char** value and the third a **double** value.

Assuming that **num** is **int**, **ch** is **char** and **x** is **double**, the following are all valid calls to **sample**:

> sample(25, 'T', 7.5);
> sample(num, 'A', x);
> sample(num, ch, 7); //an int argument can match a double parameter
> sample(num + 1, ch, x / 2.0);

If, when a method is called, the type of an argument is not the same as the corresponding parameter, Java tries to convert the argument to the required type. For example, in the call

> sample('A', 'C', 'E');

the numeric value of **'A'** (which is 65) is converted to the **int** value 65 and the parameter **n** is set to 65; the numeric value of **'E'** (which is 69) is converted to the **double** value 69.0 and the parameter **b** is set to 69.0.

In general, it is normally okay to convert from a 'smaller' type (like **char**) to a 'bigger' type (like **int** or **double**). But, for example, Java will complain about

> sample(num, 72, 'E'); // error - cannot convert int, 72, to char

since it will not automatically convert **int** to the 'smaller' type **char**.

If it is not possible to convert the argument to the required type, you will get a "type mismatch" error, as in the call

> sample(num, ch, true); // error - cannot convert boolean to double

You will also get an error if you do not supply the required number of arguments, as in

```
sample(num, x); // error - must have 3 arguments
```

7.3 max

Finding the larger of two values is something we need to do sometimes. If **a** and **b** are two numbers, we can set the variable **max** to the larger of the two with:

```
if (a > b) max = a;
else max = b;
```

If the numbers are equal, **max** will be set to **b** (the **else** part will be executed). We can, of course, write this statement every time we want to get the larger of two values. But this will become clumsy and awkward. It will be more convenient and readable if we can simply write something like

```
big = max(a, b);
```

or even

```
System.out.printf("The bigger is %d\n", max(a, b));
```

We can, if we write the function **max** as follows:

```
public static int max(int a, int b) {
   if (a > b) return a;
   return b;
}
```

The first line (except {) is the *function header*. It consists of **public static** followed by

- the word **int**, indicating that the function returns an integer value
- the name we make up for the function, **max** in the example
- one or more parameters, called the *parameter list*, enclosed in brackets; two parameters **a** and **b** of type **int** are used in the example

The *body* of the function is the part from { to }. Here, we use the **if** statement to determine the larger of **a** and **b**. If **a** is bigger, the function "returns" **a**; if not, it returns **b**.

In Java, a function "returns a value" by using the **return** statement. It consists of the word **return** followed by the value to be returned. The value is returned to the place at which the function was called.

To show how **max** fits into an overall program and how it can be used, we write Program P7.2 which reads pairs of integers and, for each pair, prints the larger of the two. The program ends when the user types 0 0.

Program P7.2

```java
import java.util.*;
public class MaxTest {
   public static void main(String[] args) {
      Scanner in = new Scanner(System.in);
      int n1, n2;
      System.out.printf("Enter two whole numbers: ");
      n1 = in.nextInt();
      n2 = in.nextInt();
      while (n1 != 0 || n2 != 0) {
         System.out.printf("The bigger is %d\n", max(n1, n2));
         System.out.printf("Enter two whole numbers: ");
         n1 = in.nextInt();
         n2 = in.nextInt();
      }
   } //end main

   private static int max(int a, int b) {
      if (a > b) return a;
      return b;
   } //end max
} //end class
```

The following is a sample run:

```
Enter two whole numbers: 24 33
The bigger is 33
Enter two whole numbers: 10 -13
The bigger is 10
Enter two whole numbers: -5 -8
The bigger is -5
Enter two whole numbers: 0 7
The bigger is 7
Enter two whole numbers: 0 0
```

For variety, we declare **max** as **private static**. When we declare a method as **private**, it is *known* only in the class in which it is declared. Any method from the class may call it but it cannot be called from any method outside the class.

The variables **n1** and **n2**, declared in **main**, are considered as belonging to **main**.

When the program is run, suppose **n1** is 24 and **n2** is 33. When the function is called with **max(n1, n2)** from within **printf**, the following occurs:

- The *values* of the arguments **n1** and **n2** are determined. These are 24 and 33, respectively.

- Each value is copied to a temporary memory location. These locations are passed to the function **max** where 24 is labelled with **a**, the first parameter, and 33 is labelled with **b**, the second parameter. We can picture this as:

   a | 24 | b | 33 |

- The **if** statement is executed; since **a** (24) is not greater than **b** (33), control goes to the statement **return b;** and 33 is returned as the value of the function. This value is returned to the place from which **max** was called (the **printf** statement).
- Just before the function returns, the locations containing the arguments are thrown away. The value returned by **max** (33, in our example) replaces the call to **max**. Thus, **max(n1, n2)** is replaced by 33 and **printf** prints

    ```
    The bigger is 33
    ```

When a function returns a value, it makes sense for this value to be used in a situation where a value is required. Above, we printed the value. We could also assign the value to a variable, as in

    big = max(n1, n2);

or use it as part of an expression, as in

    ans = 2 * max(n1, n2);

What does *not* make sense is to use it in a statement by itself, thus:

    max(n1, n2);   //a useless statement

Here, the value is not being used in any way, so the statement makes no sense at all. It is the same as if we had written a number on a line by itself, like this

    33;   //a useless statement

Think carefully when you call a function which returns a value. Be very clear in your mind what you intend to use the value for.

As written, **max** returns the larger of two integers. What if we want to find the larger of two **double** numbers? Could we use **max**? Unfortunately, no. If we call **max** with **double** values as arguments, we will get an error since Java will not let us assign a **double** value to an **int** parameter (bigger to smaller).

But if we call **max** with two character arguments, it would work by returning the larger of the two codes. For example, **max('A', 'C')** will return 67, the code for **C**.

On the other hand, if we wrote **max** with **double** parameters and **double** return type, it would work for both **double** and **int** arguments, since we can assign an **int** value to a **double** parameter without losing any information.

But we can do better since Java allows us to have two (or more) functions called **max** in the same class. Consider the following:

```java
private static double max(double a, double b) {
  if (a > b) return a;
  return b;
}
```

We can add this function to the class and it does not conflict with the other **max**. The reason is that the two functions have different *signatures*.

The method header defines what is called the *signature* of the method. The signature includes the method name and the parameter types (in order) but does not include the return type. If two methods have different names, they obviously have different signatures. If they have the same name but there is at least one difference in their parameter lists, they have different signatures. For example, the following all have different signatures:

```
public static int test()
public static int test(int a)
public static int test(double a)
public static int test(int a, int b)
public static int test(char c, boolean b)
public static int test(boolean b, char c)
```

The last two are different because the *order* of the parameters is different. In Java, we can use the *same* name for two *different* methods if they have different signatures. When we do this, we say we are *overloading* the name.

In the above example, when **test** is called, Java can figure out which of the 6 methods to invoke based on the arguments supplied. For instance, **test()** will invoke the first one, **test(3, 8)** will invoke the fourth one and **test(false, 'w')** will invoke the last one.

Note, however, that the following have the *same* signature:

```
public static int test(int a, char c)
public static boolean test(int b, char ch)
```

They are the same since the return type (**int** and **boolean**) play no part in the signature. Also, only the *type* of a parameter is relevant; the *name* is unimportant. In both cases, the signature is **test(int, char)**.

In passing, we note that the *visibility* of a method (whether it is **public** or **private**) plays no part in its signature.

In our example, the call **max(24, 33)** will invoke the **int** version while the calls **max(2.7, 5.1)** and **max(25, 4.0)** will invoke the **double** version.

7.4 Print the day

Let us write a program which requests a number from 1 to 7 and prints the name of the day of the week. For example, if the user enters 5, the program prints **Thursday**. Program P7.3 does the job using a series of **if...else** statements.

```
                    Program P7.3
    import java.util.*;
    public class PrintDay {
      public static void main(String[] args) {
        Scanner in = new Scanner(System.in);
        System.out.printf("Enter a day from 1 to 7: ");
        int d = in.nextInt();
        if (d == 1) System.out.printf("Sunday\n");
        else if (d == 2) System.out.printf("Monday\n");
        else if (d == 3) System.out.printf("Tuesday\n");
        else if (d == 4) System.out.printf("Wednesday\n");
        else if (d == 5) System.out.printf("Thursday\n");
        else if (d == 6) System.out.printf("Friday\n");
        else if (d == 7) System.out.printf("Saturday\n");
        else System.out.printf("Invalid day\n");
      }
    }
```

Now suppose that printing the name of a day of the week was a small part of a much larger program. We wouldn't want to clutter up **main** with this code nor would we want to re-write this code every time we needed to print the name of a day. It would be much nicer if we could write **printDay(n)** and get the appropriate name printed. We would be able to do this if we write a method **printDay** to do the job.

The first thing to ask is what information does **printDay** need to do its job. The answer is that it needs the number of the day. This immediately suggests that **printDay** must be written with the number of the day as a parameter. Apart from this, the body of the method will contain essentially the same code as Program P7.3. Also, **printDay** (shown on the next page) does not return a value so its "return type" is **void**.

When we write the method, we can use *any* variable name we want for the parameter. We never have to worry about *how* the method will be called. Many beginners mistakenly believe that if the method is called with **printDay(n)**, the parameter in the header must be **n**. But that cannot be true since it could be called with **printDay(4)** or **printDay(n)** or **printDay(j)** or even **printDay(n + 1)**. The choice is up to the calling method.

```java
public static void printDay(int d) {
    if (d == 1) System.out.printf("Sunday\n");
    else if (d == 2) System.out.printf("Monday\n");
    else if (d == 3) System.out.printf("Tuesday\n");
    else if (d == 4) System.out.printf("Wednesday\n");
    else if (d == 5) System.out.printf("Thursday\n");
    else if (d == 6) System.out.printf("Friday\n");
    else if (d == 7) System.out.printf("Saturday\n");
    else System.out.printf("Invalid day\n");
}
```

All we need to know is that *whatever* the *value* of the argument, *that* value will be assigned to **d** (or whatever variable we happen to use as the parameter) and the method will be executed assuming the parameter (**d**, in our case) has that value.

We now re-write Program P7.3 as P7.4 to illustrate how the method fits into an overall program and how it can be used.

Program P7.4
```java
import java.util.*;
public class PrintDay1 {
   public static void main(String[] args) {
      Scanner in = new Scanner(System.in);
      System.out.printf("Enter a day from 1 to 7: ");
      int n = in.nextInt();
      printDay(n);
   }
   public static void printDay(int d) {
      if (d == 1) System.out.printf("Sunday\n");
      else if (d == 2) System.out.printf("Monday\n");
      else if (d == 3) System.out.printf("Tuesday\n");
      else if (d == 4) System.out.printf("Wednesday\n");
      else if (d == 5) System.out.printf("Thursday\n");
      else if (d == 6) System.out.printf("Friday\n");
      else if (d == 7) System.out.printf("Saturday\n");
      else System.out.printf("Invalid day\n");
   }
} //end class
```

Now that we have delegated the printing to a method, notice how **main** is much less cluttered. We use **n** in **main** to show it can be different from the parameter, **d**.

As with all Java programs, execution begins with the first statement in **main**. This prompts the user for a number and the program goes on to print the name of the day by calling **printDay**.

A sample run is:

```
Enter a day from 1 to 7: 4
wednesday
```

In **main**, suppose **n** has the value 4. The call **printDay(n)** is executed as follows:

- The *value* of the argument **n** is determined. It is 4.
- The value 4 is copied to a temporary memory location. This location is passed to the method **printDay** where it is labelled with the name of the parameter, **d**. In effect, **d** is set to the value of the argument.
- The body of the method is executed. In this case, since **d** is 4, the statement **System.out.printf("Wednesday\n")** will be executed.
- After printing **Wednesday**, the method is finished. The location containing the argument is discarded and control returns to **main** to the statement following the call **printDay(n)**. In this case, there are no more statements so the program ends.

7.5 Highest Common Factor

In Chapter 5, we wrote Program P5.2 (page 97) which read two numbers and found their highest common factor (HCF). You should refresh your memory by taking a look at the program.

It would be nice if, whenever we want to find the HCF of two numbers (**m** and **n**, say), we could make a function call **hcf(m, n)** to get the answer. For instance, the call **hcf(42, 24)** would return the answer 6. To be able to do this, we write the function as shown below.

```java
public static int hcf(int m, int n) {
//returns the hcf of m and n
   while (n != 0) {
      int r = m % n;
      m = n;
      n = r;
   }
   return m;
}
```

The logic for finding the HCF is the same as used in P5.2. The difference here is that values for **m** and **n** will be passed to the function when it is called. In P5.2, we prompted the user to enter values for **m** and **n** and fetched them using **nextInt**.

Suppose the function is called with **hcf(42, 24)**. The following occurs:

- Each of the arguments is copied to a temporary memory location. These locations are passed to the function **hcf** where 42 is labelled with **m**, the first parameter, and 24 is labelled with **n**, the second parameter, like this:

  m | 42 | n | 24 |

- The **while** loop is executed, working out the HCF. On exit from the loop, the HCF is stored in **m**, which will contain 6 at this time. This is the value returned by the function to the place from where it was called.

- Just before the function returns, the locations containing the arguments are thrown away; control then returns to the place from where the call was made.

Program P7.5 tests the function by reading pairs of numbers and printing the HCF of each pair.

```
Program P7.5
import java.util.*;
public class HCF1 {
  public static void main(String[] args) {
    Scanner in = new Scanner(System.in);
    System.out.printf("Enter two positive numbers: ");
    int a = in.nextInt();
    int b = in.nextInt();
    while (a > 0 && b > 0) {
      System.out.printf("The HCF is %d\n", hcf(a, b));
      System.out.printf("Enter two positive numbers: ");
      a = in.nextInt();
      b = in.nextInt();
    }
  } //end main

  public static int hcf(int m, int n) {
  //returns the hcf of m and n
    while (n != 0) {
      int r = m % n;
      m = n;
      n = r;
    }
    return m;
  } //end hcf
} //end class
```

The call to **hcf** is made in the **printf** statement. The program stops if either number is less than or equal to 0. A sample run is:

```
Enter two positive numbers: 42 24
The HCF is 6
Enter two positive numbers: 32 512
The HCF is 32
Enter two positive numbers: 100 31
The HCF is 1
Enter two positive numbers: 84 36
The HCF is 12
Enter two positive numbers: 0 0
```

We emphasize again that even though the function is written with parameters called **m** and **n**, it can be called with any two integer values—constants, variables or expressions. In particular, it does not *have* to be called with variables named **m** and **n**. In our program, we called it with **a** and **b**.

Using HCF to find LCM

A common task in arithmetic is to find the lowest common multiple (LCM) of two numbers. For example, the LCM of 8 and 6 is 24 since 24 is the smallest number which can divide both 8 and 6 exactly.

If we know the HCF of the two numbers, we can find the LCM by multiplying the numbers and dividing by their HCF. Given that the HCF of 8 and 6 is 2, we can find their LCM by working out $\frac{8 \times 6}{2}$ = 24. In general,

$$LCM(m, n) = (m \times n) / HCF(m, n)$$

Knowing this, we can easily write a function **lcm** which, given two arguments **m** and **n**, returns the LCM of **m** and **n**.

```
//returns the lcm of m and n
public static int lcm(int m, int n) {
   return (m * n) / hcf(m, n);
}
```

We leave it as an exercise for you to write a program to test **lcm**. Remember to include the function **hcf** in your program. You may place **hcf** before or after **lcm**.

7.6 factorial

So far, we have written several functions which illustrate various concepts you need to know in writing and using functions. We now write another one and discuss it in detail, reinforcing some of the concepts we have met thus far and introducing new ones.

Before we write the function, let us first write a program which reads an integer *n* and prints *n*! (*n* factorial) where

$0! = 1$
$n! = n(n-1)(n-2)\ldots 1$ for $n > 0$

For example, $5! = 5.4.3.2.1 = 120$.

The program will be based on the following algorithm:

```
set nfac to 1
read a number, n
for j = 2 to n do
   nfac = nfac * j
endfor
print nfac
```

Dry run the algorithm with a value of 3 for **n** and convince yourself that it will print 6, the value of 3!. Check also that it produces the correct answer when **n** is 0 or 1 (hint: the **for** loop is not executed when **n** is 0 or 1).

The algorithm does not validate the value of **n**. For instance, **n** should not be negative since factorial is not defined for negative numbers. As a matter of interest, what would the algorithm print if **n** is negative? (Hint: the **for** loop is not executed). To keep matters simple, our Program P7.6 does not validate **n**.

Program P7.6

```java
import java.util.*;
public class Factorial {
   public static void main(String[] args) {
      Scanner in = new Scanner(System.in);
      int nfac = 1;
      System.out.printf("Enter a positive whole number: ");
      int n = in.nextInt();
      for (int j = 2; j <= n; j++)
         nfac = nfac * j;
      System.out.printf("%d! = %d\n", n, nfac);
   }
}
```

A sample run of this program is:

```
Enter a positive whole number: 4
4! = 24
```

We now consider the problem of writing a function (which we will call **factorial**) which, given an integer n, calculates and returns the value of $n!$. Since $n!$ is an integer, the "return type" of the function is **int**.

We first write the function header. It is

```
public static int factorial(int n)
```

It is interesting to note that the function header is all the information we need in order to use the function correctly. Ignoring for the moment what the rest of **factorial** might look like, we can use it as follows:

```
System.out.printf("5! = %d\n", factorial(5));
```

or

```
int num = in.nextInt();
System.out.printf("%d! = %d\n", num,factorial(num));
```

In the latter case, if **num** is 4, **printf** prints:

```
4! = 24
```

The call **factorial(num)** returns the value 24 directly to the **printf** statement.

Following the logic of Program P7.6, we write the function **factorial** as follows:

```
public static int factorial(int n) {
   int nfac = 1;
   for (int j = 2; j <= n; j++)
      nfac = nfac * j;
   return nfac;
}
```

It is worthwhile comparing Program P7.6 and the function:

- The program prompts for and reads a value for **n**; the function gets a value for **n** when the function is called, as in **factorial(4)**. It is *wrong* to attempt to read a value for **n** in this function.
- In addition to **n**, both the program and the function need the variables **nfac** and **j** to express their logic.
- The *logic* for calculating a factorial is the same for both program and function.
- The program prints the answer (in **nfac**); the function *returns* the answer (in **nfac**) to the calling function. The answer is returned to the point at which **factorial** was called.

Other comments on **factorial**

- Variables declared within a function are said to be *local to the function*. Thus, **nfac** and **j** are *local* variables; **nfac** is used to hold the factorial and **j** is used as the **for** loop variable which takes on the values from 2 to **n**. When **factorial** is called, storage is allocated to **nfac** and **j**. These variables are used to work out the factorial. Just before the function returns, **nfac** and **j** are discarded.
- You should verify that the function works properly if **n** is 0 or 1 (that is, it returns 1).

We now take a detailed look at what happens when **factorial** is called (from **main**, say). Consider the statements (**m** and **fac** are **int**):

```
m = 3;
fac = factorial(m);
```

The second statement is executed as follows:

- The *value* of the argument **m** is determined; it is 3.
- This value is *copied* to a temporary memory location and *this* location is passed to the function. The function labels it with the name of the parameter, **n**. The net effect is as if execution of the function began with the statement

    ```
    n = 3;
    ```

    In programming terminology, we say that the argument **m** is passed "by value". The *value* of the argument is copied to a temporary location and it is this temporary location that is passed to the function. The function has *no access* whatsoever to the *original* argument. In this example, **factorial** has no access to **m** and, hence, cannot affect it in any way.
- After **n** is assigned the value 3, execution of **factorial** proceeds as described above. Just before the function returns, the storage location occupied by **n** is discarded. In effect, the parameter **n** is treated like a local variable except that it is initialized to the value of the argument supplied.
- The value returned by the function is the last value stored in **nfac**. In this example, the last value assigned to **nfac** is 6. Therefore, the value 6 is returned to the place from which the call **factorial(3)** was made.
- The value 6 returned by **factorial** is assigned to **fac**.
- Execution continues with the next statement, if any.

Using factorial

We illustrate how **factorial** can be used by writing a complete Program P7.7 (next page) which prints n! for n = 0, 1, 2, 3, 4, 5, 6 and 7.

When run, this program prints the following:

```
n     n!
0      1
1      1
2      2
3      6
4     24
5    120
6    720
7   5040
```

Program P7.7

```java
import java.util.*;
public class FactorialTest {
  public static void main(String[] args) {
    Scanner in = new Scanner(System.in);
    System.out.printf(" n    n!\n\n");
    for (int n = 0; n <= 7; n++)
      System.out.printf("%2d %5d\n", n, factorial(n));
  }
  public static int factorial(int n) {
    int nfac = 1;
    for (int j = 2; j <= n; j++)
      nfac = nfac * j;
    return nfac;
  }
} //end class
```

As you can see, the value of factorial increases very quickly. Even 8! is 40320, which is too big to fit in a 16-bit integer (largest value which can be stored is 32767). As an exercise, experiment with **n** to find out the first number for which the factorial is too big to fit in a **short** or **int**. Hint: nonsense output will be printed.

When **main** is executed,

- **printf** prints a heading
- The **for** loop is executed with **n** assuming the values 0, 1, 2, 3, 4, 5, 6, 7. For each value of **n**, **factorial** is called with **n** as its argument. The factorial is calculated and returned to the place in **printf** from where it was called.

We have deliberately used a variable called **n** in **main** to illustrate that this **n** does not (and cannot) conflict with the parameter **n** of **factorial**. Suppose **n** in **main** is stored in memory location 865 and has the value 3. The call **factorial(n)** stores the *value* of **n**, i.e. 3, in a temporary location (472, say) and this temporary location is passed to **factorial** where it is known as **n**. This is illustrated by:

We now have *two* locations called **n**. While in **factorial**, **n** refers to location 472; when in **main**, **n** refers to location 865; **factorial** has no access whatsoever to location 865.

It does not happen here, but if **factorial** were to change the value of **n**, it is the value in location 472 that would be changed; the value in location 865 would not be affected. When **factorial** finishes, location 472 is discarded—*that* **n** no longer exists.

From another point of view, **factorial** is oblivious to the actual argument that was used to call it since it sees only the argument's value, not how it was derived.

We used **n** in **main** as a loop variable to illustrate the point above. However, we could have used any variable. In particular, we could have used **j** and there would be no conflict with the local variable **j** of the function **factorial**. While in **factorial**, **j** refers to the local variable; when in main, **j** refers to the **j** declared in **main**.

An example – combinations

Suppose there are 7 people on a committee. How many subcommittees of 3 people can be formed? The answer is denoted by $^7C_3$ where

$$^7C_3 = \frac{7!}{4!\,3!} = 35$$

We say there are 35 *combinations* of 7 objects taken 3 at a time. In general, ^nC_r denotes the number of combinations of *n* objects taken *r* at a time and is given by the formula:

$$^nC_r = \frac{n!}{(n-r)!\,r!}$$

Using **factorial**, we can write a function, **combinations**, which, given **n** and **r**, returns the number of combinations of **n** objects taken **r** at a time. Here it is:

```
public static int combinations(int n, int r) {
   return factorial(n) / (factorial(n-r) * factorial(r));
}
```

The body consists of one **return** statement with 3 calls to **factorial**.

We note, in passing, that this is perhaps the easiest, but not the most efficient, way to evaluate ^nC_r. For instance, if we were calculating $^7C_3$ by hand, we would use:

$$\frac{7.6.5}{3.2.1} \text{ rather than } \frac{7.6.5.4.3.2.1}{4.3.2.1.3.2.1}$$

that the function uses. As an exercise, write an efficient function for evaluating combinations.

To show the functions **factorial** and **combinations** in a complete program and to show how they may be used, we write a program to read values for **n** and **r** and print the number of combinations we can get from *n* objects taken *r* at a time.

Program P7.8 (next page) shows how it's done.

Program P7.8

```java
import java.util.*;
public class Combinations {
   public static void main(String[] args) {
      Scanner in = new Scanner(System.in);

      int n, r, nCr;
      System.out.printf("Enter values for n and r: ");
      n = in.nextInt();
      r = in.nextInt();
      while (n != 0) {
         nCr = combinations(n, r);
         if (nCr == 1)
            System.out.printf("There is 1 combination of %d objects taken " +
                       "%d at a time\n\n", n, r);
         else
            System.out.printf("There are %d combinations of %d objects " +
                       "taken %d at a time\n\n", nCr, n, r);
         System.out.printf("Enter values for n and r: ");
         n = in.nextInt();
         r = in.nextInt();
      } //end while
   } //end main

   public static int factorial(int n) {
      int nfac = 1;
      for (int j = 2; j <= n; j++)
         nfac = nfac * j;
      return nfac;
   } //end factorial

   public static int combinations(int n, int r) {
      return factorial(n) / (factorial(n-r) * factorial(r));
   }
} //end class
```

The program reads values for **n** and **r** and prints the number of combinations. This is done until a value of 0 is entered for **n**. A sample run is shown on the next page.

Observe the use of **if...else** to get the program to "speak" correct English. In the statement, also note how a long string is broken into two pieces and each piece is put on one line. We use **+** to indicate that they must be joined. Recall that, in Java, the opening and closing quotes of a string constant must be on the same line. When the program is compiled, the pieces will be joined together and stored in memory as one string.

```
Enter values for n and r: 7 3
There are 35 combinations of 7 objects taken 3 at a time
Enter values for n and r: 5 2
There are 10 combinations of 5 objects taken 2 at a time
Enter values for n and r: 6 6
There is 1 combination of 6 objects taken 6 at a time
Enter values for n and r: 3 5
There are 0 combinations of 3 objects taken 5 at a time
Enter values for n and r: 0 0
```

7.7 An example – job charge

In Program 4.5 (page 82), we read the number of hours worked and the cost of parts and calculated the cost for a job. Let us write a function which, given the hours worked and cost of parts, returns the cost for the job. When we say that a function is *given* some data, that immediately implies that such data should be defined as parameters of the function. The function is shown below.

```
final static double ChargePerHour = 100;
final static double MinJobCost = 150;

public static double calcJobCost(double hours, double parts) {
   double jobCharge = hours * ChargePerHour + parts;
   if (jobCharge < MinJobCost) return MinJobCost;
   return jobCharge;
}
```

The logic of the function is the same as that of the program. Here, the parameter list indicates what data would be given to the function when it is called. Also, we must specify the return type of the function; it is **double** since the job cost is a **double** value.

When the function is called, as in

> jobCost = calcJobCost(1.5, 87.50);

the parameter **hours** is set to 1.5 and **parts** is set to 87.50; the body of the function is then executed using *these* values for **hours** and **parts**.

As an exercise, write a complete program to read several values for hours worked and cost of parts and, for each pair, print the cost of the job.

Methods

7.8 An example – calculating pay

In Program P4.6 (page 84), we read values for **hours** and **rate**, and calculated net pay. All the code was written in **main**. We now write a function which, *given* values for **hours** and **rate**, returns the value of net pay calculated as described on page 78. The function is shown below.

```
final static int MaxRegularHours = 40;
final static double OvertimeFactor = 1.5;
public static double calcNetPay(double hours, double rate) {
    if (hours <= MaxRegularHours) return hours * rate;
    return MaxRegularHours * rate +
            (hours - MaxRegularHours) * rate * OvertimeFactor;
}
```

If the condition **hours <= MaxRegularHours** is **true**, the first **return** is executed; if it is **false**, the second **return** is executed. Note that there is no need for **else**. If the first **return** is taken, we exit the function and the second **return** cannot be executed.

If we want to find out the net pay of someone who worked for 50 hours at $12.00 per hour, all we have to do is call **calcNetPay(50, 12.00)**.

As an exercise, write a complete program to read several values for a name, hours worked and rate of pay and, for each person, print the net pay received. Hint: study Program P5.8 on page 114.

7.9 An example – finding the sum of exact divisors

Let us write a function to return the sum of the exact divisors of a given integer. We assume the divisors include 1 but not the given number. For example, the exact divisors of 50 are 1, 2, 5, 10 and 25. Their sum is 43. The function is shown below:

```
//returns the sum of the exact divisors of n
public static int sumDivisors(int n) {
    int sumDiv = 1;
    for (int j = 2; j <= n / 2; j++)
        if (n % j == 0) sumDiv += j;
    return sumDiv;
}
```

- **sumDiv** is used to hold the sum of the exact divisors; it is set to 1 since 1 is always an exact divisor.

- Other possible divisors are 2, 3, 4 and so on up to n/2. The **for** loop checks each of these in turn.
- If **j** is an exact divisor of **n** then the remainder when **n** is divided by **j** is 0, that is, **n % j** is 0. If this is so, **j** is added to **sumDiv**.
- The last statement returns the value of **sumDiv** to the place from which **sumDivisors** is called.

In the next example, we will see how **sumDivisors** may be used.

Classifying numbers as deficient, perfect or abundant

Positive integers can be classified based on the sum of their exact divisors. If n is an integer and s is the sum of its exact divisors (including 1 but not n) then:

- if **s < n**, **n** is *deficient*; e.g. 15 (divisors 1, 3, 5; sum 9)
- if **s = n**, **n** is *perfect*; e.g. 28 (divisors 1, 2, 4, 7, 14; sum 28)
- if **s > n**, **n** is *abundant*; e.g. 12 (divisors 1, 2, 3, 4, 6; sum 16)

Let us write Program P7.9 to read several numbers and, for each, print whether it is deficient, perfect or abundant.

Program P7.9

```java
import java.util.*;
public class ClassifyNumber {
   public static void main(String[] args) {
      Scanner in = new Scanner(System.in);
      System.out.printf("Enter a number: ");
      int num = in.nextInt();
      while (num != 0) {
         int sum = sumDivisors(num);
         if (sum < num) System.out.printf("Deficient\n\n");
         else if (sum == num) System.out.printf("Perfect\n\n");
         else System.out.printf("Abundant\n\n");
         System.out.printf("Enter a number: ");
         num = in.nextInt();
      }
   } //end main

   //returns the sum of the exact divisors of n
   public static int sumDivisors(int n) {
      int sumDiv = 1;
      for (int j = 2; j <= n / 2; j++)
         if (n % j == 0) sumDiv += j;
      return sumDiv;
   } //end sumDivisors
} //end class
```

The following is a sample run of Program P7.9:

```
Enter a number: 15
Deficient

Enter a number: 12
Abundant

Enter a number: 28
Perfect

Enter a number: 0
```

Note that we call **sumDivisors** once for each number and store the result in **sum**. We use **sum** when we need the "sum of divisors" rather than re-calculate it each time.

As an exercise, write a program to find all the perfect numbers less than 10,000.

7.10 Some character functions

In this Section, we write several functions relating to characters.

Perhaps the simplest is a function which takes a character as argument; it returns **true** if the character is a digit and **false** if it is not. This description suggests that we must write a function which takes a **char** argument and returns a **boolean** value. We will call it **isDigit**. Here it is:

```
public static boolean isDigit(char ch) {
   return ch >= '0' && ch <= '9';
}
```

The Boolean expression **(ch >= '0' && ch <= '9')** is **true** if **ch** lies between **'0'** and **'9'**, inclusive; that is, if **ch** contains a digit. Hence, if **ch** contains a digit, the function returns **true**; if **ch** does not contain a digit, it returns **false**.

We *could* have written the body of the function as

```
if (ch >= '0' && ch <= '9') return true;
return false;
```

but the single **return** statement used above is the preferred way.

Similarly, we can write the function **isUpperCase** which returns **true** if its argument is an uppercase letter and **false** if it's not, thus:

```
public static boolean isUpperCase(char ch) {
   return ch >= 'A' && ch <= 'Z';
}
```

and the function **isLowerCase** which returns **true** if its argument is a lowercase letter and **false** if it's not, thus:

```
public static boolean isLowerCase(char ch) {
   return ch >= 'a' && ch <= 'z';
}
```

If we wish to know if the character is a letter (either uppercase or lowercase), we can write **isLetter** which uses **isUpperCase** and **isLowerCase**, thus:

```
public static boolean isLetter(char ch) {
   return isUpperCase(ch) || isLowerCase(ch);
}
```

Example – position of a letter in the alphabet

Let us write a function which, given a character, returns 0 if it is not a letter of the English alphabet; otherwise, it returns the position—an integer value—of the letter in the alphabet. The function should work if the character is either an uppercase or a lowercase letter. For example, given **'Y'** or **'y'**, the function should return 25.

The function takes a **char** argument and returns an **int** value. Using the functions **isUpperCase** and **isLowerCase**, we write the function (which we call **position**) as follows:

```
public static int position(char ch) {
   if (isUpperCase(ch)) return ch - 'A' + 1;
   if (isLowerCase(ch)) return ch - 'a' + 1;
   return 0;
}
```

We use **isUpperCase** and **isLowerCase** to establish what kind of character we have. If it is neither, control goes to the last statement and we return 0.

If we have an uppercase letter, we find the *distance* between the letter and **A** by subtracting the code for **A** from the code for the letter. For example, the distance between **A** and **A** is 0 and the distance between **A** and **F** is 5. Adding 1 gives the position of the letter in the alphabet. Here, adding 1 gives us 1 for **A** and 6 for **F**.

If we have a lowercase letter, we find the *distance* between the letter and **a** by subtracting the code for **a** from the code for the letter. For example, the distance between **a** and **b** is 1 and the distance between **a** and **z** is 25. Adding 1 gives the position of the letter in the alphabet. Here, adding 1 gives us 2 for **b** and 26 for **z**.

To illustrate how the function may be used, we write Program P7.10 which reads a line of input; for each character on the line, it prints 0 if it is not a letter and its position in the alphabet if it is a letter.

Program P7.10

```java
import java.io.*;
public class LetterPosition {
   public static void main(String[] args) throws IOException {
      int c;
      System.out.printf("Type anything and press 'Enter'\n");
      while ((c = System.in.read()) != '\r')
         System.out.printf("%c  %d\n", c, position((char) c));
   }
   public static boolean isUpperCase(char ch) {
      return ch >= 'A' && ch <= 'Z';
   }
   public static boolean isLowerCase(char ch) {
      return ch >= 'a' && ch <= 'z';
   }
   public static int position(char ch) {
      if (isUpperCase(ch)) return ch - 'A' + 1;
      if (isLowerCase(ch)) return ch - 'a' + 1;
      return 0;
   }
} //end class
```

A sample run is:

```
Type some letters and non-letters and press "Enter"
FaT($hY&f
F   6
a   1
T   20
(   0
$   0
h   8
Y   25
&   0
f   6
```

Note that **c** is declared as **int** because **read** returns an **int** value. However, since the argument to **position** is a **char**, when we call **position**, we must convert **c** to **char**. This we do with a cast, **(char) c**. Without the cast, Java will complain that it cannot match the **char** parameter with an **int** argument.

We have written the functions **isDigit**, **isUpperCase**, **isLowerCase** and **isLetter** to illustrate basic concepts about character functions. However, Java provides several predefined functions, with the same names, for working with characters. They belong to the Java class **Character** and, to use them, we must write, for example, **Character.isDigit(ch)** where **ch** can be any character value.

As an exercise, rewrite P7.10 using the **Character** functions.

7.11 Example – fetch the next integer

On page 152, we wrote P6.13 which read the data character by character, built and stored the next integer found in a variable, and finally printed the integer.

We now write a *function*, **getInt**, which reads the data character by character and *returns* the next integer found. The function takes no arguments but the brackets must still be written after the name. The code is essentially the same as in P6.13, except that we use the predefined function **Character.isDigit**. Here is **getInt**:

```java
public static int getInt() throws IOException {
    char ch = (char) System.in.read();
    // as long as the character is not a digit, keep reading
    while (!Character.isDigit(ch)) ch = (char) System.in.read();
    // at this point, ch contains the first digit of the number
    int num = 0;
    while (Character.isDigit(ch)) { // as long as we get a digit
        num = num * 10 + ch - '0';  // update num
        ch = (char) System.in.read();
    }
    return num;
} //end getInt
```

Since **getInt** calls **read**, we need **throws IOException** in the header. And, for variety, we have chosen to store the next character read in a **char** variable, **ch**. But since **read** returns an **int**, we must use a cast to assign it to **ch**.

Note that
> while (ch < '0' || ch > '9')

of P6.13 is replaced by
> while (!Character.isDigit(ch))

and
> while (ch >= '0' && ch <= '9')

is replaced by
> while (Character.isDigit(ch))

We believe this makes the program a little more readable.

The function needs the variables **ch** and **num** to do its job; **ch** holds the next character in the data and **num** holds the number constructed so far. We declare them within the function, making them local variables. This way, they will not conflict with any variables with the same names declared anywhere else in the program. This makes the function *self-contained*—it does not depend on variables declared elsewhere.

The function can be used as in

    int id = getInt();

This fetches the next positive integer from the input, regardless of how many and what kind of characters come before it, and stores it in **id**. Recall that **nextInt** works only if the next integer is preceded by zero or more *whitespace* characters. Our **getInt** is more general.

We test it by rewriting Program P4.2 (page 74) which requests two lengths given in metres and centimetres and finds the sum. We observed then that the data must be entered with digits only. If, for instance, we had typed 3m 75cm we would have gotten an error since 3m is not a valid integer constant. With **getInt**, we *will* be able to enter the data in the form 3m 75cm.

The **main** method of the new program is shown below. It is identical with P4.2 with **in.nextInt()** replaced by **getInt()**. Also, since we use **read** in **getInt**, we must use **import java.io.*;**.

```
import java.io.*;
public class SumOfLengths2 {
  //find the sum of two lengths given in metres and cm
  public static void main(String[] args) throws IOException {
    int m1, cm1, m2, cm2, mSum, cmSum;
    System.out.printf("Enter first length: ");
    m1 = getInt();
    cm1 = getInt();
    System.out.printf("Enter second length: ");
    m2 = getInt();
    cm2 = getInt();
    mSum = m1 + m2;  //add the metres
    cmSum = cm1 + cm2;  //add the centimetres
    if (cmSum >= 100) {
      cmSum = cmSum - 100;
      mSum = mSum + 1;
    }
    System.out.printf("\nSum is %dm %dcm\n", mSum, cmSum);
  } //end main
  //the code for getInt (previous page) goes here
} //end class
```

A sample run is

```
Enter first length: 3m 75cm
Enter second length: 5m 50cm
Sum is 9m 25cm
```

You are encouraged to:

- modify **getInt** so that it works for negative integers;
- write a function **getDouble** which returns the next floating-point number in the input. It should work even if the next number does not contain a decimal point.

Exercises 7

1. Explain why methods/functions are important in writing a program.
2. Given the function header

    public static void test(int n)

    explain carefully what happens when the call **test(5)** is made.
3. Given the function header

    public static double fun(int n)

    explain carefully what happens when the following statement is executed:

    System.out.printf("The answer is %f\n", fun(9));
4. Given the function header

    public static void test(int m, int n, double x)

    say whether each of the following calls is valid or invalid. If invalid, state why.

    test(1, 2, 3);
    test(-1, 0.0, 3.5);
    test(7, 2);
    test(14, '7', 3.14);
5. Write a function **sqr** which, given an integer **n**, returns n^2.
6. Write a function **isEven** which, given an integer **n**, returns **true** if **n** is even and **false** if **n** is odd.
7. Write a function **isOdd** which, given an integer **n**, returns **true** if **n** is odd and **false** if **n** is even.
8. Write a function **isPerfectSquare** which, given an integer **n**, returns **true** if **n** is a perfect square (e.g. 25, 81) and **false** if it is not. Use only elementary arithmetic operations. Hint: try numbers starting at 1. Compare the number times itself with **n**.
9. Write a function **isVowel** which, given a character **c**, returns **true** if **c** is a vowel and **false** if it is not.
10. Write a function which, given an integer **n**, returns the sum $1 + 2 + ... + n$.
11. Write a function which, given an integer **n**, returns the sum $1^2 + 2^2 + ... + n^2$.
12. Write a function which, given integer values for **month** and **year**, returns the number of days in the month. See problem 6 on page 88.

13. Using Program P4.8 (page 87) as a guide, write a function which, given three integer values representing the sides of a triangle, returns:
    - **0** if the values cannot be the sides of any triangle. This is so if any value is negative or zero, or if the length of any side is greater than or equal to the sum of the other two;
    - **1** if the triangle is scalene (all sides different);
    - **2** if the triangle is isosceles (two sides equal).
    - **3** if the triangle is equilateral (three sides equal);

14. Write a function which, given three integer values representing the sides of a triangle, returns **true** if the triangle is right-angled and **false** if it is not. The sides are given in any order.

15. Write a function **power** which, given a **double** value **x** and an integer **n**, returns x^n.

16. Write a function **numLength** which, given an integer **n**, returns the number of digits in the integer. For example, given **309**, the function returns **3**.

17. Write a function **max3** which, given 3 integers, returns the biggest.

18. Write a function **isPrime** which, given an integer **n**, returns **true** if **n** is a prime number and **false** if it is not. A prime number is an integer > 1 which is divisible only by 1 and itself.

    Using **isPrime**, write a program to prompt for an even number **n** greater than **4** and print all pairs of prime numbers which add up to **n**. Print an appropriate message if **n** is not valid. For example, if **n** is 22, your program should print

    ```
     3 19
     5 17
    11 11
    ```

19. You are required to generate a sequence of integers from a given positive integer *n*, as follows. If *n* is even, divide it by 2. If *n* is odd, multiply it by 3 and add 1. Repeat this process with the new value of *n*, stopping when *n* = 1. For example, if *n* is 13, the following sequence will be generated:

    13 40 20 10 5 16 8 4 2 1

    Write a function which, given *n*, returns the *length* of the sequence generated, including *n* and 1. For *n* = 13, your function should return **10**.

    Using the function, write a program to read two integers *m* and *n* (*m* < *n*), and print the maximum sequence length for the numbers between *m* and *n*, inclusive. Also print the number which gives the maximum length. For example, if *m* = 1 and *n* = 10, your program should print

    9 generates the longest sequence of length 20

20. We can code the 52 playing cards using the numbers 1 to 52. We can assign 1 to the Ace of Spades, 2 to the Two of Spades and so on, up to 13 to the King of Spades. We can then assign 14 to the Ace of Hearts, 15 to the Two of Hearts and so on, up to 26 to the King of Hearts. Similarly, we can assign the numbers 27-39 to Diamonds and 40-52 to Clubs.

    Write a function which, given integers **rank** and **suit**, returns the code for that card. Assume **rank** is a number from **1** to **13** with **1** meaning **Ace** and **13** meaning **King**; **suit** is **1**, **2**, **3** or **4** representing Spades, Hearts, Diamonds and Clubs, respectively.

8 Working with arrays

In this chapter, we will explain:

- what is an array and how to declare one
- how to store values in an array
- how to read a known number of values into an array using a **for** loop
- how to process elements of an array using a **for** loop
- how to read an unknown number of values into an array using a **while** loop
- how to extract a required element from an array with a subscript
- how to find the sum of numbers stored in an array
- how to find the average of numbers stored in an array
- how to use an array to keep several counts
- how to pass an array as an argument to a function
- how to find the largest and smallest values in an array
- how to search an array using sequential search and binary search
- how to sort an array using selection sort and insertion sort
- how to read and store an unknown amount of numbers in an array
- how to merge two sorted lists to create one sorted list

The variables we have been using so far (such as **ch**, **n**, **sum**) are normally called *simple* variables. At any given time, a simple variable can be used to store *one* item of data, for instance, one number or one character. Of course, the value stored in the variable can be changed, if we wish. However, there are many situations in which we wish to store a group of related items and to be able to refer to them by a common name. The *array variable* allows us to do this.

For example, suppose we wish to store a list of 60 scores made by students in a test. We can do this by inventing 60 different **int** variables and storing one score in one variable. But it would be quite tedious, cumbersome, unwieldy and time-consuming to write code to manipulate these 60 variables. (Think of how you would assign values to these 60 variables.) And what if we needed to deal with 200 scores?

A better way is to use an *array* to store the 60 scores. We can think of this array as having 60 'locations'—we use one location to store one *element*, in this case, one score. To refer to a particular score, we use a *subscript*. For example, if **score** is the name of the array, then **score[5]** refers to the score in position 5—here 5 is used as a subscript. It is written inside the *square* brackets, **[** and **]**.

In general, an array can be used to store a list of values of the *same type*; for instance, we speak of an array of integers, an array of characters, an array of strings or an array of floating-point numbers. As you will see, using an array allows us to work with a list in a simple, systematic way, regardless of its size. We can process all or some items using a simple loop. We can also do things like search for an item in the list or sort the list in ascending or descending order.

8.1 Declaring an array

Before an array can be used, it must be *declared*. For example, the statement

    int[] score;

declares that **score** is an '**int** array' or an 'array of **int**s' or an 'array of integers'. In Java, the square brackets after the type **int** denotes an array. If we pronounce [] as 'array', then the declaration reads '**int** array **score**'. The declaration could have been written as:

    int score[];

with the square brackets written after the array name. Some people prefer this form since it reminds them that **score** is an array. Others prefer the first form since all the 'type' information is in one place. For the most part, we will use the first form in this book.

As written, the statement only creates an array variable **score**; it does *not* create or allocate storage for the actual array. This can be done using **new**, as in:

    score = new int[60];

As you would expect, both the declaration and creation of the array can be combined into one, thus:

    int[] score = new int[60];

This creates **60 int** variables which can be referred to collectively by the *array variable* **score**. To refer to a specific one of these variables, we use a *subscript* written in square brackets after the array name. In Java, a subscript is an integer value which starts at 0. In this example,

    score[0] refers to the 1st score;
    score[1] refers to the 2nd score;
    score[2] refers to the 3rd score;

    .
    .

    score[58] refers to the 59th score;
    score[59] refers to the 60th score;

As you can see, array subscripting is a bit awkward in Java; it would be much nicer (and logical) if **score[j]** were to refer to the jth score. We will see how to get around this shortly.

It is an error to try to refer to an element that is outside the range of subscripts allowed. If you do, you will get an "array subscript" error[1]. For example, you cannot refer to **score[-1]**, **score[60]** or **score[99]** since they do not exist.

A subscript can be written using a constant (like 25), a variable (like **n**) or an expression (like **j + 1**). The *value* of the subscript determines which element is being referred to.

In our example, *each element* of the array is an **int** and can be used in any way that an ordinary **int** variable can. In particular, a value can be stored in it, its value can be printed and it can be compared with another **int**.

We could picture **score** as in Figure 8.1.

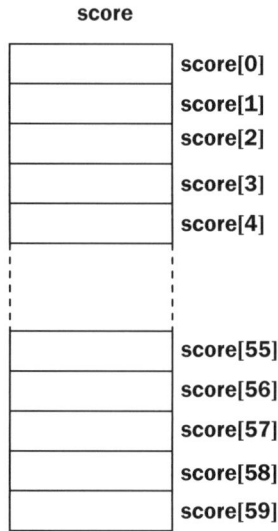

Figure 8.1: The declaration int[] score = new int[60];

When an array is created using **new**, its elements are given default initial values as follows:

- numeric (**short, byte, int, long, float, double**) elements are set to 0;
- **boolean** elements are set to **false**;
- **char** elements are set to '**\0**';

Even though Java does the initialization for you, it is not good programming practice to rely on default initial values set by a compiler. It is always best to initialize your variables explicitly, if only in the interest of clarity and transparency.

To give another example, suppose we need to store the item numbers (integers) and prices (floating-point numbers) of 100 items. We can use one array (**item**,

---

[1] More specifically, an **ArrayIndexOutOfBoundsException** is thrown

say) to hold the item numbers and another array (**price**, say) to hold the prices. These can be declared with:

```
int[] item = new int[100];
double[] price = new double[100];
```

The elements of **item** range from **item[0]** to **item[99]** and the elements of **price** range from **price[0]** to **price[99]**. When we store values in these arrays (see next), we will ensure that

price[0] holds the price of **item[0]**;
price[1] holds the price of **item[1]**;

and, in general,

price[j] holds the price of **item[j]**.

In passing, note that the size of an array can be specified using any integer expression, as long as the value can be determined when the declaration is executed. For instance, if **j** is 8 when the statement:

```
int[] num = new int[j * 2 + 9];
```

is executed, it is equivalent to:

```
int[] num = new int[25];
```

8.2 Storing values in an array

Consider the array, **score**. If we wish, we could set selected elements to specific values, as follows:

```
score[3] = 56;
score[7] = 81;
```

But what if we wish to set the 60 locations to 60 scores? Would we have to write 60 statements such as:

```
score[0] = 45;
score[1] = 63;
score[2] = 39;
    .
    .
score[59] = 78;
```

This is certainly one way of doing the job, but it is very tedious, time-consuming and inflexible. A neater way is to let the subscript be a *variable* rather than a *constant*. For example, **score[j]** can be used to refer to the score in location j; which score is meant depends on the value of j. If the value of j is 47, then **score[j]** refers to **score[47]**, the score in location 47.

Note that **score[j]** can be used to refer to another score simply by changing the value of **j**, but, at any one time, **score[j]** refers to one specific score, determined by the current value of **j**.

Suppose the 60 scores are stored in a file **scores.txt**. The following code will read the 60 scores and store them in the array **score**:

```
Scanner in = new Scanner(new FileReader("scores.txt"));
for (int j = 0; j < 60; j++)
   score[j] = in.nextInt();
```

Suppose the file **scores.txt** begins with the following data:

```
45   63   39  ...
```

The **for** loop is executed with the value of **j** ranging from 0 to 59:

- when **j** is 0, the first score, **45**, is read and stored in **score[0]**;
- when **j** is 1, the second score, **63**, is read and stored in **score[1]**;
- when **j** is 2, the third score, **39**, is read and stored in **score[2]**;

and so on, up to

- when **j** is 59, the 60th score is read and stored in **score[59]**.

Note that this method is much more concise than writing 60 assignment statements. We are using one statement

```
score[j] = in.nextInt();
```

to store the scores in 60 different locations. This is achieved by varying the value of the subscript, **j**. This method is also more flexible. If we had to deal with 200 scores, say, we only need to change 60 to 200 in the declaration of **score** and in the **for** statement (and supply the 200 scores in the data file). The previous method would require us to write 200 assignment statements.

If we wish to print the scores as they are read, we could write the **for** loop as:

```
for (int j = 0; j < 60; j++) {
   score[j] = in.nextInt();
   System.out.printf("%d\n", score[j]);
}
```

On the other hand, if we wish to print the scores *after* they are read and stored in the array, we could write *another* **for** loop:

```
for (j = 0; j < 60; j++)
   System.out.printf("%d\n", score[j]);
```

We have used the same loop variable **j** that was used to read the scores. But it is not required that we do so. Any other loop variable would have the same effect. For instance, we could have written:

```
for (int x = 0; x < 60; x++)
    System.out.printf("%d\n", score[x]);
```

What is important is the *value* of the subscript, *not the variable* that is used as the subscript.

We often need to set all elements of a numeric array to 0. This may be necessary, for instance, if we are going to use them to hold totals, or as counters. For example, to set the 60 elements of **score** to 0, we could write:

```
for (int j = 0; j < 60; j++)
    score[j] = 0;
```

The **for** loop is executed 60 times, with **j** taking on the values 0 to 59:

- the first time through the loop, **j** is 0, so **score[0]** is set to 0;
- the second time through the loop, **j** is 1, so **score[1]** is set to 0;

and so on, until

- the 60th time through the loop, **j** is 59, so **score[59]** is set to 0.

If we want to set the elements to a different value (-1, say), we could write:

```
for (int j = 0; j < 60; j++)
    score[j] = -1;
```

It should be noted that even though we have declared **score** to be of size 60, it is not required that we use all the elements. For example, suppose we want to set just the first 20 elements of **score** to 1, we could do this with:

```
for (int j = 0; j < 20; j++)
    score[j] = 1;
```

This sets elements **score[0]**, **score[1]**, **score[2]**, up to **score[19]** to 1. Elements **score[20]** to **score[59]** remain with their initial value of 0.

About not using element 0

As we have seen, starting from element 0 can be a bit awkward and unnatural when we have to say things like "the third element is stored in location 2"; the subscript is "out of sync" with the position of the element. It would be much more sensible and logical to say "the first element is stored in location 1" or "the fifth element is stored in location 5".

For situations like these, it is better to ignore element 0 and pretend that the subscripts start from 1. However, you will have to declare the *size* of your array to be one more than you actually need. For instance, if we want to cater for 60 scores, we will have to declare **score** as

```
int[] score = new int[61];
```

This creates elements **score[0]** to **score[60]**. We can ignore **score[0]** and use only **score[1]** to **score[60]**. Having to declare an extra element is a small price to pay for being able to work with our problem in a more natural and logical manner.

There are times when it is better to work with an array from position 0. But, for those times when it is not, we will *declare* our array size to be one more than required and ignore the element in position 0.

Suppose we want to cater for **n** scores. A good way to do this is as follows:

```
int[] score = new int[n + 1];
```

We can now work with elements **score[1]** to **score[n]**.

8.3 Example – finding average and differences from average

Consider the problem of finding the average of a set of numbers (integers) and the amount by which each number differs from the average. In order to find the average, we need to know all the numbers. We saw in Section 5.2, page 99, how to find the average by reading and storing one number at a time. Each new number read replaced the previous one. At the end, we could calculate the average but we've lost all the numbers.

Now, if we also want to know how much each number differs from the average, we would need to store the original numbers so that they are available after the average is calculated. We will store them in an array. The program will be based on the following assumptions:

- no more than 100 numbers will be supplied; this information is needed to declare the size of the array;
- the numbers will be terminated by 0; it is assumed that 0 is not one of the numbers.

The following shows how we want the program to work:

```
Enter up to 100 numbers (end with 0)
2 7 5 3 0

Numbers entered: 4
Sum of numbers: 17

The average is 4.25

Numbers and differences from average
    2   -2.25
    7    2.75
    5    0.75
    3   -1.25
```

Program P8.2 shows how to write the program to work like this.

Program P8.2

```java
import java.util.*;
public class AvgDiff {
   final static int MaxNum = 100;
   public static void main(String[] args) {
   //find average and difference from average
      Scanner in = new Scanner(System.in);
      int[]num = new int[MaxNum];
      double sum = 0;
      int n = 0;
      System.out.printf("Enter up to %d numbers (end with 0)\n", MaxNum);
      int a = in.nextInt();
      while (a != 0) {
         sum += a;
         num[n++] = a;  //store in location n, then add 1 to n
         a = in.nextInt();
      }
      if (n == 0) System.out.printf("No numbers entered\n");
      else {
         System.out.printf("\nNumbers entered: %d\n", n);
         System.out.printf("Sum of numbers: %1.0f\n\n", sum);
         double average = sum / n;
         System.out.printf("The average is %3.2f\n", average);
         System.out.printf("\nNumbers and differences from average\n");
         for (a = 0; a < n; a++)
            System.out.printf("%4d %6.2f\n", num[a], num[a] - average);
      } //end if
   } //end main
} //end class
```

Points to note about Program P8.2:

- We set the symbolic constant **MaxNum** to 100; we use it to declare the array and in the prompt for numbers. This makes the program easy to modify if we change our mind and wish to cater for a different amount of numbers.
- We enter the **while** loop when the number read is not 0. Inside the loop, we add it to the sum, store it in the array and count it. Each time we reach the end of the loop, the value of **n** is the amount of numbers stored in the array so far.
- On exit from the **while** loop, we test **n**. If it is still 0, then no numbers were supplied and there's nothing else to do. The program does not make the mistake of trying to divide by **n** if it is 0. If **n** is positive, we confidently divide the sum by it to find the average.

- The **for** loop 'steps through' the array, printing the numbers and their differences from the average. Here, **n** is the number of elements of the array that were actually used, not necessarily the entire array. The elements used are **num[0]** to **num[n-1]**.
- The program works out the sum of the numbers as they are read. If we need to find the sum of the first **n** elements *after* they have been stored in the array, we can do this with:

    sum = 0;
    for(int j = 0; j < n; j++) sum += num[j];

Program P8.2 does the basics. But what if the user entered more than 100 numbers? Recall that, as declared, the elements of **num** range from **num[0]** to **num[99]**.

Now suppose that **n** is 100, meaning that 100 numbers have already been stored in the array. If another one is entered, and it is not 0, the program will enter the **while** loop and attempt to execute the statement

   num[n++] = a;

Since **n** is 100, this is now the same as **num[100] = a**. But there is no element **num[100]**—you will get an "array subscript" error. When you start working with arrays, you must be very careful that your program logic does not take you outside the range of subscripts. If it does, your program will crash.

To cater for this possibility, we could write the **while** condition as

   while (a != 0 && n < MaxNum) { ...

If **n** is equal to **MaxNum** (100), it means we have already stored 100 values in the array and there is no room for any more. In this case, the loop condition will be **false**, the loop will not be entered and the program will not try to store another value in the array.

This is another example of *defensive programming*, of trying to make our programs immune to outside forces. Now there is no way for a user action to cause our program to crash by exceeding the bounds of the array.

8.4 Example – letter frequency count

Let us write a program which counts the frequency of each letter in the input. The program will treat an uppercase letter and its lowercase equivalent as the same letter; for example, **E** and **e** increment the same counter.

In Program P7.10 on page 179, we wrote a function, **position**, which, given a character, returns 0 if the character is not a letter; if it is a letter, it returns its position in the alphabet. We will use **position** to solve this problem. However, we will rewrite it using the **Character** functions **isUpperCase** and **isLowerCase**.

To solve this problem, we need 26 counters, one for each letter of the alphabet. We need a counter for **a**s and **A**s, one for **b**s and **B**s, one for **c**s and **C**s, and so on. We *could* declare 26 variables called **a**, **b**, **c**, ..., up to **z**; **a** holds the count for **a**s and **A**s, **b** holds the count for **b**s and **B**s, and so on. And, in our program, we could write statements of the form (assuming **ch** contains the next character):

```
if (ch == 'a' || ch == 'A') a++;
else if (ch == 'b' || ch == 'B') b++;
else if (ch == 'c' || ch == 'C') c++;
else if ...
```

This gets tiresome very quickly. And we will have similar problems when we have to print the results. Having to work with 26 variables for such a small problem is neither suitable nor convenient. As we will see, an array lets us solve this problem much more easily.

We will need an **int** array with 26 elements to hold the count for each letter of the alphabet. Since it is more natural to use element 1 (rather than element 0) to hold the count for **a**s and **A**s, element 2 (rather than element 1) to hold the count for **b**s and **B**s, and so on, we will declare the array **letterCount** as

```
int[] letterCount = new int[27];
```

We will ignore **letterCount[0]** and use

- **letterCount[1]** to hold the count for **a**s and **A**s
- **letterCount[2]** to hold the count for **b**s and **B**s
- **letterCount[3]** to hold the count for **c**s and **C**s
    etc.
- **letterCount[26]** to hold the count for **z**s and **Z**s

When a character is read into an **int**, **ch**, we will call the function **position**, as in

```
n = position((char) ch);
```

If **n** is greater than 0, we know that **ch** contains a letter and **n** is the position in the alphabet of that letter. For example, if **ch** contains **Y**, then **n** is 25, since **Y** is the 25th letter of the alphabet. If we add 1 to **letterCount[n]**, we are adding 1 to the count for the letter that **ch** contains. Here, if we add 1 to **letterCount[25]**, we are adding 1 to the count for **Y**. This is accomplished by

```
if (n > 0) ++letterCount[n];
```

The complete program is shown as Program P8.3 (next page).

It reads data from the file **passage.txt** and sends output to the file **output.txt**. You may wish to remind yourself how this is done by looking at page 147.

Take a look at the **printf** statement that prints one line of the output:

```
out.printf("%4c %8d\n", 'a' + n - 1, letterCount[n]);
```

Program P8.3

```java
import java.io.*;
public class LetterFreq {
  public static void main(String[] args) throws IOException {
    int n, ch;
    int[] letterCount = new int[27];
    FileReader in = new FileReader("passage.txt");
    PrintWriter out = new PrintWriter(new FileWriter("output.txt"));
    for (n = 1; n <= 26; n++) letterCount[n] = 0;  //set counts to 0
    while ((ch = in.read()) != -1) {
      n = position((char) ch);
      if (n > 0) ++letterCount[n];
    }
    //print the results
    out.printf("Letter  Frequency\n\n");
    for (n = 1; n <= 26; n++)
      out.printf("%4c %8d\n", 'a' + n - 1, letterCount[n]);
    in.close();
    out.close();
  } //end main
  public static int position(char ch) {
    if (Character.isUpperCase(ch)) return ch - 'A' + 1;
    if (Character.isLowerCase(ch)) return ch - 'a' + 1;
    return 0;
  } //end position
} //end class
```

This prints a (lowercase) letter followed by its count. Let us see how. The code for **'a'** is 97. When **n** is 1,

$$\text{'a'} + n - 1$$

is evaluated as 97+1-1, which is 97; when 97 is printed with **%c**, it is interpreted as a character, so **a** is printed. When **n** is 2,

$$\text{'a'} + n - 1$$

is evaluated as 97+2-1, which is 98; when 98 is printed with **%c**, it is interpreted as a character, so **b** is printed. When **n** is 3,

$$\text{'a'} + n - 1$$

is evaluated as 97+3-1, which is 99; when 99 is printed with **%c**, it is interpreted as a character, so **c** is printed.. And so on. As **n** takes on the values from 1 to 26,

$$\text{'a'} + n - 1$$

will take on the codes for the letters from 'a' to 'z'.

As a matter of interest, we could have used the special form of the **for** statement described on page 129 to achieve the same result. Here it is:

```
for (ch = 'a', n = 1; n <= 26; ch++, n++)
    out.printf("%4c %8d\n", ch, letterCount[n]);
```

The loop is still executed with **n** going from 1 to 26. But, in sync with **n**, it is also executed with **ch** going from **'a'** to **'z'**. Note the use of **ch++** to move on to the next character.

If **passage.txt** contains

> The quick brown fox jumps over the lazy dog.
> If the quick brown fox jumped over the lazy dog then
> Why did the quick brown fox jump over the lazy dog?

the program sends the following output to the file, **output.txt**.

```
Letter  Frequency
   a        3
   b        3
   c        3
   d        6
   e       11
   f        4
   g        3
   h        8
   i        5
   j        3
   k        3
   l        3
   m        3
   n        4
   o       12
   p        3
   q        3
   r        6
   s        1
   t        7
   u        6
   v        3
   w        4
   x        3
   y        4
   z        3
```

8.5 Passing an array as an argument to a method/function

In Chapter 7, we saw how arguments are passed to methods. In Java, arguments are passed "by value". When an argument is passed "by value", a temporary location is created with the value of the argument, and this temporary location is passed to the method. The method never has access to the original argument.

In Java, *an array name denotes the address of its first element*. We say the array name contains a *reference* to the array elements. When we use an array name as an argument to a method, the *address* of the first element is passed to the method which, therefore, has access to the array. We say that an array is passed *by reference*.

We now take a closer look at some issues involved in writing methods/functions with array arguments.

We will write a function, **sumList**, which returns the sum of the integers in an array passed to the function. For example, if the array contains

3	8	1	5	7
0	1	2	3	4

the function should return 24.

We *could* write the function header like this:

> public static int sumList(int[] num)

The array argument is written just like an array declaration.

Now, suppose **score** is declared in **main** as

> int[] score = new int[10];

and we make the call **sumList(score)**. We can simply think that, in the function, **score** is known by the name **num**; any reference to **num** is a reference to the original argument **score**.

The more precise explanation is this: since the name **score** denotes the address of **score[0]**, *this* address is passed to the function where it becomes the address of the first element of **num**, **num[0]**.

The function is free to to assume any size it wishes for **num**. Obviously, this can land us in trouble if we attempt to process array elements which do not exist. In this case, for example, if we try to process **num[10]**, we will get an "array subscript" error or, more precisely, an **ArrayIndexOutOfBoundsException** will be thrown, since **num[10]**, this is, **score[10]**, does not exist.

For this reason, it is good programming practice to 'tell' the function how many elements to process. We do this using another argument, as in:

> public static int sumList(int[] num, int n)

Now the calling function can tell **sumList** how many elements to process by supplying a value for **n**. Using the declaration of **score**, above, the call **sumList(score, 10)** tells the function to process the first 10 elements of **score** (the whole array). But, and herein lies the advantage of this approach, we could also make a call such as **sumList(score, 5)** to get the function to process the first 5 elements of **score**.

Using *this* function header, we write **sumList** as follows:

```
public static int sumList(int[] num, int n) {
    int sum = 0;
    for (int j = 0; j < n; j++) sum += num[j];
    return sum;
}
```

The function 'steps through' the array, from **num[0]** to **num[n - 1]**, using a **for** loop. Each time through the loop, it adds one element to **sum**. On exit from the loop, the value of **sum** is returned as the value of the function.

The construct

for (j = 0; j < n; j++)

is typical for processing the first **n** elements of an array.

To use the function, consider the following code in **main**:

```
int score[10];
for (int j = 0; j < 5; j++) score[j] = in.nextInt();
System.out.printf("Sum of scores is %d\n", sumList(score, 5));
```

The **for** loop reads 5 values into the array. Suppose the values read into **score** are:

score

3	8	1	5	7
0	1	2	3	4

In **printf**, the call **sumList(score, 5)** will get the function to return the sum of the first 5 elements of **score**, that is, 24. You should gather by now that, to find the sum of the first 3 elements, say, we can call **sumList(score, 3)**.

8.6 Finding the largest number in an array

Let us consider the problem of finding the largest of a set of values stored in an array. The *principle* of finding the largest is the same as we discussed in Section 5.5, page 102. Suppose the integer array **num** contains the following values:

num

25	72	17	43	84	14	61
0	1	2	3	4	5	6

We can easily see that the largest number is 84 and that it is in location 4. But how does a program determine this? One approach is as follows:

- Assume that the first element (the one in position 0) is the largest; we do this by setting **big** to 0. As we step through the array, we will use **big** to hold the

position of the largest number encountered so far; **num[big]** will refer to the actual number.
- Next, starting at position 1, we look at the number in each successive position, up to 6, and compare the number with the one in position **big**.
- The first time, we compare **num[1]** with **num[0]**; since **num[1]**, 72, is larger than **num[0]**, 25, we update **big** to 1. This means that the largest number so far is in position 1.
- Next, we compare **num[2]**, 17, with **num[big]** (that is, **num[1]**), 72; since **num[2]** is smaller than **num[1]**, we go on to the next number, leaving **big** at 1.
- Next, we compare **num[3]**, 43, with **num[big]** (that is, **num[1]**), 72; since **num[3]** is smaller than **num[1]**, we go on to the next number, leaving **big** at 1.
- Next, we compare **num[4]**, 84, with **num[big]** (that is, **num[1]**), 72; since **num[4]** is larger than **num[1]**, we update **big** to 4. This means that the largest number so far is in position 4.
- Next, we compare **num[5]**, 14, with **num[big]** (that is, **num[4]**), 84; since **num[5]** is smaller than **num[4]**, we go on to the next number, leaving **big** at 4.
- Next, we compare **num[6]**, 61, with **num[big]** (that is, **num[4]**), 84; since **num[6]** is smaller than **num[4]**, we go on to the next number, leaving **big** at 4.
- Since there is no next number, the process ends with the value of **big** being 4, the *position* of the largest number. The actual number is denoted by **num[big]**; since **big** is 4, this is **num[4]**, which is 84.

We can express the process just described by the following pseudocode:

```
big = 0
for j = 1 to 6
   if num[j] > num[big] then big = j
endfor
print "Largest is ", num[big], " in position ", big
```

We will now write a function, **getLargest**, to find the largest value in an array. To be general, we will specify which *portion* of the array to search for the value. This is important since, most times, we declare an array to be of some maximum size (100, say) but do not always put 100 values in the array.

When we *declare* the array to be of size 100, we are *catering* for 100 values. But, at any time, the array may have less than this amount. We use another variable (**n**, say) to tell us how many values are currently stored in the array. For example, if **n** is 36, it means that values are stored in elements 0 to 35 of the array.

So when we are finding the largest, we must specify which elements of the array to search. We will write the function such that it takes three arguments—the array **num**, and two integers **lo** and **hi**—and returns the *position* of the largest number from **num[lo]** to **num[hi]**, inclusive. It is up to the caller to ensure that **lo** and **hi** are within the range of subscripts declared for the array. For instance, the call

- **getLargest(score, 0, 6)** will return the position of the largest number from **score[0]** to **score[6]**; and the call
- **getLargest(mark, 10, 20)** will return the position of the largest number from **mark[10]** to **mark[20]**.

Here is the function, **getLargest**:

```
public static int getLargest(int[] num, int lo, int hi) {
  int big = lo;
  for (int j = lo + 1; j <= hi; j++)
    if (num[j] > num[big]) big = j;
  return big;
}
```

The function assumes the largest number is in position **lo**, the first one, by setting **big** to **lo**. In turn, it compares the numbers in locations **lo + 1** up to **hi** with the one in location **big**. If a bigger one is found, **big** is updated to *its* location.

8.7 Finding the smallest number in an array

The function, **getLargest**, could be easily modified to find the *smallest* value in an array. Simply change **big** to **small**, say, and replace **>** by **<**, giving:

```
public static int getSmallest(int[] num, int lo, int hi) {
  int small = lo;
  for (int j = lo + 1; j <= hi; j++)
    if (num[j] < num[small]) small = j;
  return small;
}
```

This function returns the location of the smallest element from **num[lo]** to **num[hi]**, inclusive. On page 209, we will show you how to use this function to arrange a set of numbers in ascending order.

We have shown how to find the largest and smallest values in an integer array. The procedure is exactly the same for arrays of other types such as **double**, **char** or **float**. The only change which has to be made is in the declaration of the arrays. Keep in mind that when we compare two characters, the 'larger' one is the one with the higher numeric code.

8.8 Example – a voting problem

We now illustrate how to use some of the ideas just discussed to solve the following problem.

Problem: In an election, there are seven candidates. Each voter is allowed one vote for the candidate of his/her choice. The vote is recorded as a number from 1 to 7. The number of voters is unknown beforehand but the votes are terminated by a vote of 0. Any vote which is not a number from 1 to 7 is an invalid (spoilt) vote. A file, **votes.txt**, contains the names of the candidates. The first name is considered as candidate 1, the second as candidate 2, and so on. The names are followed by the votes. Write a program to read the data and evaluate the results of the election. Print all output to the file, **results.txt**.

Your output should specify the total number of votes, the number of valid votes and the number of spoilt votes. This is followed by the votes obtained by each candidate and the winner(s) of the election.

Given the following data:

```
Victor Taylor
Denise Duncan
Kamal Ramdhan
Michael Ali
Anisa Sawh
Carol Khan
Gary Owen

3 1 2 5 4 3 5 3 5 3 2 8 1 6 7 7 3 5
6 9 3 4 7 1 2 4 5 5 1 4 0
```

your program should send the following output to **results.txt**:

```
    Invalid vote: 8
    Invalid vote: 9

    Number of voters: 30
    Number of valid votes: 28
    Number of spoilt votes: 2

    Candidate           Score

    Victor Taylor         4
    Denise Duncan         3
    Kamal Ramdhan         6
    Michael Ali           4
    Anisa Sawh            6
    Carol Khan            2
    Gary Owen             3

    The winner(s):
    Kamal Ramdhan
    Anisa Sawh
```

Working with arrays

We need to store the names of the 7 candidates and the votes obtained by each. We will use an **int** array for the votes. In order to work naturally with candidates 1 to 7, we will write the declaration

```
int[] vote = new int[8];
```

and use **vote[1]** to **vote[7]** for counting the votes for the candidates; **vote[j]** will hold the count for candidate **j**. We will not use **vote[0]**.

But what kind of array can we use for the names? We will need an "array of **String**s". We will use the declaration

```
String[] name = new String[8];
```

We will store the candidates' names in **name[1]** to **name[7]**. We will store the name of candidate **j** in **name[j]**; **name[0]** will not be used.

To make the program flexible, we will define the symbolic constant:

```
final static int MaxCandidates = 7;
```

and, in **main**, use the declarations

```
String[] name = new String[MaxCandidates + 1];
int[] vote = new int[MaxCandidates + 1];
```

One of the first things the program must do is read the names and set the vote counts to 0. We will write a method **initialize** to do this. As explained on page 57, we will read a candidate's name using **nextLine**. Here is the function:

```
public static void initialize(Scanner in, String[] name, int[] vote) {
  for (int j = 1; j <= MaxCandidates; j++) {
    name[j] = in.nextLine();
    vote[j] = 0;
  }
} //end initialize
```

To make the method flexible, we pass **in** as the first argument. Data will be read from whatever **in** is connected to. If it's connected to a file, it will read from the file; if it's connected to the standard input, it will read from the keyboard. For similar reasons, we will pass **out** to **printResults** (next page).

Next, we must read and process the votes. Processing vote **v** involves checking that it is valid. If it is, we want to add 1 to the score for candidate **v**. We will read and process the votes with the following:

```
        v = in.nextInt();
        while (v != 0) {
          if (v < 1 || v > MaxCandidates) {
            out.printf("Invalid vote: %d\n", v);
            ++spoiltVotes;
          }
          else {
            ++vote[v];
            ++validVotes;
          }
          v = in.nextInt();
        }
```

The key statement here is

```
        ++vote[v];
```

This is a clever way of using the vote **v** as a subscript to add 1 for the right candidate. For example, if **v** is 3, we have a vote for candidate 3, **Kamal Ramdhan**. We wish to add 1 to the vote count for candidate 3. This count is stored in **vote[3]**. When **v** is 3, the statement becomes

```
        ++vote[3];
```

which adds 1 to **vote[3]**. The beauty is that the *same* statement will add 1 for *any* of the candidates, depending on the value of **v**. This illustrates some of the power of using arrays. It doesn't matter whether there are 7 candidates or 700; the one statement will work for all.

Now that we know how to read and process the votes, it remains only to determine the winner(s) and print the results. We will delegate this task to the method **printResults**.

Using the sample data, the array **vote** will contain the following values after all the votes have been tallied (remember we are not using **vote[0]**).

vote

4	3	6	4	6	2	3
1	2	3	4	5	6	7

To find the winner, we must first find the largest value in the array. To do this, we will call **getLargest** (page 199) with

```
        int win = getLargest(vote, 1, MaxCandidates);
```

which will set **win** to the *subscript* of the largest value from **vote[1]** to **vote[7]** (since **MaxCandidates** is 7). In our example, **win** will be set to 3 since the largest value, 6, is in position 3. (6 is also in position 5 but the way the code is written, it will return the first position which contains the largest, if there is more than one).

Now that we know the largest value is in **vote[win]**, we can 'step through' the array, looking for those candidates with that value. This way, we will find all the candidates (1 or more) with the highest vote and declare them as winners.

The details are given in the method **printResults** shown as part of Program P8.4, our solution to the voting problem posed at the beginning of this section.

Program P8.4

```java
import java.util.*;
import java.io.*;
public class Voting {
  final static int MaxCandidates = 7;

  public static void main(String[] args) throws IOException {
    Scanner in = new Scanner(new FileReader("votes.txt"));
    PrintWriter out = new PrintWriter(new FileWriter("results.txt"));
    String[] name = new String[MaxCandidates + 1];
    int[] vote = new int[MaxCandidates + 1];
    int v, validVotes = 0, spoiltVotes = 0;

    initialize(in, name, vote);
    v = in.nextInt();
    while (v != 0) {
      if (v < 1 || v > MaxCandidates) {
        out.printf("Invalid vote: %d\n", v);
        ++spoiltVotes;
      }
      else {
        ++vote[v];
        ++validVotes;
      }
      v = in.nextInt();
    } //end while

    printResults(out, name, vote, validVotes, spoiltVotes);

    in.close();
    out.close();
  } // end main

  public static void initialize(Scanner in, String[] name, int[] vote) {
    for (int j = 1; j <= MaxCandidates; j++) {
      name[j] = in.nextLine();
      vote[j] = 0;
    }
  } //end initialize
```

```
    public static int getLargest(int[] num, int lo, int hi) {
       int big = lo;
       for (int j = lo + 1; j <= hi; j++)
          if (num[j] > num[big]) big = j;
       return big;
    } //end getLargest

    public static void printResults(PrintWriter out, String[] name,
                                    int[] vote, int valid, int spoilt) {
       out.printf("\nNumber of voters: %d\n", valid + spoilt);
       out.printf("Number of valid votes: %d\n", valid);
       out.printf("Number of spoilt votes: %d\n", spoilt);
       out.printf("\nCandidate     Score\n\n");

       for (int j = 1; j <= MaxCandidates; j++)
          out.printf("%-15s %3d\n", name[j], vote[j]);

       out.printf("\nThe winner(s)\n");
       int win = getLargest(vote, 1, MaxCandidates);
       int winningVote = vote[win];
       for (int j = 1; j <= MaxCandidates; j++)
          if (vote[j] == winningVote) out.printf("%s\n", name[j]);
    } //printResults
} //end class
```

8.9 Searching an array – sequential search

In many cases, an array is used for storing a list of information. Having stored the information, it may be required to find a given item in the list. For example, an array may be used to store a list of the names of 50 people. It may then be required to find the position in the list at which a given name (**Inga**, say) is stored.

We need to develop a technique for searching the elements of an array for a given one. Since it is possible that the given item is not in the array, our technique must also be able to determine this. The *technique* for searching for an item is the same regardless of the *type* of elements in the array. We will use an integer array to illustrate the technique called *sequential search*.

Consider the array **num** of 7 integers:

num

35	17	48	25	61	12	42
0	1	2	3	4	5	6

We wish to determine if the number 61 is stored. In search terminology, 61 is called the *search key* or, simply, the *key*. The search proceeds as follows:

- compare 61 with the 1st number, **num[0]**, which is 35; they do not match so we move on to the next number;
- compare 61 with the 2nd number, **num[1]**, which is 17; they do not match so we move on to the next number;
- compare 61 with the 3rd number, **num[2]**, which is 48; they do not match so we move on to the next number;
- compare 61 with the 4th number, **num[3]**, which is 25; they do not match so we move on to the next number;
- compare 61 with the 5th number, **num[4]**, which is 61; they match, so the search stops and we conclude that the key is in position 4.

But what if we were looking for 32? In this case, we will compare 32 with all the numbers in the array and none of them will match. We conclude that 32 is not in the array.

Assuming the array contains **n** numbers, we can express the above logic as follows:

```
for j = 0 to n - 1
  if (key == num[j]) then key found, exit the loop
endfor
if j < n then key found in position j
else key not found
```

This is a situation where we *may* want to exit the loop before we have looked at all elements in the array. On the other hand, we may have to look at all the elements before we can conclude that the key is not there.

If we find the key, we exit the loop and **j** will be less than **n**. If we exit the loop because **j** becomes **n**, then the key is not in the array.

Let us express this technique in a function **search** which, given an **int** array **num**, an integer **key**, and two integers **lo** and **hi**, searches for **key** from **num[lo]** to **num[hi]**. If found, the function returns the position in the array. If not found, it returns -1. For example, the statement

```
int n = search(num, 61, 0, 6);
```

will search **num[0]** to **num[6]** for 61. It will find it in position 4 and return 4, which is stored in **n**. The call **search(num, 32, 0, 6)** will return -1 since 32 is not stored in the array. Here is the function, **search**:

```
public static int search(int[] num, int key, int lo, int hi) {
  for (int j = lo; j <= hi; j++)
    if (key == num[j]) return j;
  return -1;
}
```

We first set **j** to **lo** to start the search from that position. The **for** loop 'steps through' the elements of the array until it finds the key or **j** passes **hi**.

To give an example of how a search may be used, consider the voting problem of the last section. After the votes have been tallied, our arrays **name** and **vote** look like this (remember we are not using **name[0]** and **vote[0]**):

	name	vote
1	Victor Taylor	4
2	Denise Duncan	3
3	Kamal Ramdhan	6
4	Michael Ali	4
5	Anisa Sawh	6
6	Carol Khan	2
7	Gary Owen	3

Suppose we want to know how many votes **Carol Khan** received. We would have to search for her name in the **name** array. When we find it (in position 6), we can retrieve her votes from **vote[6]**. In general, if a name is in position **n**, the number of votes received will be in **vote[n]**.

We modify our **search** function to look for a name in the **name** array. Here it is:

```
//search for key from name[lo] to name[hi]
public static int search(String[] name, String key, int lo, int hi) {
    for (int j = lo; j <= hi; j++)
        if (key.equals(name[j])) return j;
    return -1;
}
```

Recall that, if **s1** and **s2** are strings, we compare them using **s1.equals(s2)**.

We can use this function as follows:

```
int n = search(name, "Carol Khan", 1, 7);
if (n > 0) System.out.printf("%s received %d vote(s)\n", name[n], vote[n]);
else System.out.printf("Name not found\n");
```

Using our sample data, search will return 6 which will be stored in **n**. Since 6 > 0, the code will print

Carol Khan received 2 vote(s)

8.10 Sorting an array – selection sort

Consider the voting program again. On page 200, we printed the results in the order in which the names were given. But suppose we want to print the results in alphabetical order by name or in order by votes received, with the winner(s) first. We would have to rearrange the names or the votes in the order we want. We say we would have to *sort* the names in *ascending* order or *sort* the votes in *descending* order.

Sorting is the process by which a set of values are arranged in ascending or descending order. There are many reasons to sort. Sometimes we sort in order to produce more readable output (for example, to produce an alphabetical listing). A teacher may need to sort her students in order by name or by average score. If we have a large set of values and we want to identify duplicates, we can do so by sorting; the repeated values will come together in the sorted list.

There are many ways to sort. We will discuss a method known as *selection sort*.

Consider the following array:

num

57	48	79	65	15	33	52
0	1	2	3	4	5	6

Sorting **num** in ascending order using selection sort proceeds as follows:

1st pass
- Find the smallest number in positions 0 to 6; the smallest is 15, found in position 4.
- Interchange the numbers in positions 0 and 4. This gives us:

num

15	48	79	65	57	33	52
0	1	2	3	4	5	6

2nd pass
- Find the smallest number in positions 1 to 6; the smallest is 33, found in position 5.
- Interchange the numbers in positions 1 and 5. This gives us:

num

15	33	79	65	57	48	52
0	1	2	3	4	5	6

3rd pass
- Find the smallest number in positions 2 to 6; the smallest is 48, found in position 5.
- Interchange the numbers in positions 2 and 5. This gives us:

num

15	33	48	65	57	79	52
0	1	2	3	4	5	6

4th pass

- Find the smallest number in positions 3 to 6; the smallest is 52, found in position 6.
- Interchange the numbers in positions 3 and 6. This gives us:

num

15	33	48	52	57	79	65
0	1	2	3	4	5	6

5th pass

- Find the smallest number in positions 4 to 6; the smallest is 57, found in position 4.
- Interchange the numbers in positions 4 and 4. This gives us:

num

15	33	48	52	57	79	65
0	1	2	3	4	5	6

6th pass

- Find the smallest number in positions 5 to 6; the smallest is 65, found in position 6.
- Interchange the numbers in positions 5 and 6. This gives us:

num

15	33	48	52	57	65	79
0	1	2	3	4	5	6

and the array is now completely sorted.

If we let **j** go from 0 to 5, on each pass, we find the smallest number from positions **j** to 6. If the smallest number is in position **s**, we interchange the numbers in positions **j** and **s**. For an array of size **n**, we make **n - 1** passes. In our example, we sorted 7 numbers in 6 passes. The following is an outline of the algorithm:

```
for j = 0 to n - 2
    s = position of smallest number from num[j] to num[n-1]
    swap num[j] and num[s]
endfor
```

On page 199, we wrote a function to return the position of the smallest number in an integer array. Take a look at it again if you are not sure how it works.

We will need a method which swaps two elements in an integer array. Here it is:

Working with arrays

```
//swap elements num[i] and num[j]
public static void swap(int[] num, int i, int j) {
   int hold = num[i];
   num[i] = num[j];
   num[j] = hold;
}
```

With **getSmallest** and **swap**, we can code the algorithm, above, as a method, **selectionSort**.

```
//sort list[lo] to list[hi] in ascending order
public static void selectionSort(int[] list, int lo, int hi) {
   for (int j = lo; j < hi; j++) {
      int s = getSmallest(list, j, hi);
      swap(list, j, s);
   }
}
```

To emphasize that we can use any names for our parameters, we write the method to sort an integer array called **list**. To make it general, we also tell the method which *portion* of the array to sort by specifying subscripts **lo** and **hi**. Instead of the loop going from 0 to **n - 2** as in the algorithm, it now goes from **lo** to **hi - 1**, just a minor change for greater flexibility.

We write Program P8.5 to test whether **selectionSort** works properly. Only **main** is shown in the box on the next page. To complete the program, you just add the code for **selectionSort**, **getSmallest** and **swap**.

The program requests up to 10 numbers (since the array is declared to be of size 10), stores them in the array **num**, calls **selectionSort**, then prints the sorted list.

The following is a sample run of the program:

```
Type up to 10 numbers followed by 0
57 48 79 65 15 33 52 0

The sorted numbers are
15 33 48 52 57 65 79
```

Comments on Program P8.5:

The program illustrates how to read and store an unknown amount of values in an array. The program caters for up to 10 numbers but must work if fewer numbers are supplied. We use **n** to subscript the array and to count the numbers. Initially, **n** is 0. The following describes what happens with the sample data:

Program P8.5
```java
import java.util.*;
public class TestSort {
  public static void main(String[] args) {
    Scanner in = new Scanner(System.in);
    int[] num = new int[10];
    System.out.printf("Type up to 10 numbers followed by 0\n");
    int n = 0;
    int v = in.nextInt();
    while (v != 0) {
      num[n++] = v;
      v = in.nextInt();
    }

    //n numbers are stored from num[0] to num[n-1]
    selectionSort(num, 0, n-1);
    System.out.printf("\nThe sorted numbers are\n");
    for (v = 0; v < n; v++) System.out.printf("%d ", num[v]);
    System.out.printf("\n");
  } //end main

  // selectionSort, getSmallest and swap go here
} //end class
```

- the 1st number, 57, is read; it is not 0 so we enter the **while** loop. We store 57 in **num[0]** then add 1 to **n**, making it 1; 1 number has been read and **n** is 1.
- the 2nd number, 48, is read; it is not 0 so we enter the **while** loop. We store 48 in **num[1]** then add 1 to **n**, making it 2; 2 numbers have been read and **n** is 2.
- the 3rd number, 79, is read; it is not 0 so we enter the **while** loop. We store 79 in **num[2]** then add 1 to **n**, making it 3; 3 numbers have been read and **n** is 3.
- the 4th number, 65, is read; it is not 0 so we enter the **while** loop. We store 65 in **num[3]** then add 1 to **n**, making it 4; 4 numbers have been read and **n** is 4.
- the 5th number, 15, is read; it is not 0 so we enter the **while** loop. We store 15 in **num[4]** then add 1 to **n**, making it 5; 5 numbers have been read and **n** is 5.
- the 6th number, 33, is read; it is not 0 so we enter the **while** loop. We store 33 in **num[5]** then add 1 to **n**, making it 6; 6 numbers have been read and **n** is 6.
- the 7th number, 52, is read; it is not 0 so we enter the **while** loop. We store 52 in **num[6]** then add 1 to **n**, making it 7; 7 numbers have been read and **n** is 7.
- the 8th number, 0, is read; it *is* 0 so we exit the **while** loop with **num** like this:

num

57	48	79	65	15	33	52
0	1	2	3	4	5	6

Working with arrays

At any stage, the value of **n** indicates how many numbers have been stored up to that point. At the end, **n** is 7 and 7 numbers have been stored in the array. The rest of the program can assume that **n** gives the number of values actually stored in the array; the values are stored from **num[0]** to **num[n-1]**.

For example, the call

selectionSort(num, 0, n-1);

is a request to sort **num[0]** to **num[n-1]** but, since **n** is 7, it is a request to sort **num[0]** to **num[6]**.

We use **v** to hold the numbers as they are read. Later, we use it as the **for** loop variable.

As written, the program will crash if the user enters more than 10 numbers before typing 0. When the 11th number is read, an attempt will be made to store it in **num[10]**, which does not exist, giving an "array subscript" error.

We can handle this by changing the **while** condition to

while (v != 0 && n < 10)

Now, if **n** reaches 10, the loop is not entered (since 10 is not less than 10) and no attempt will be made to store the 11th number. Indeed, all numbers after the 10th one will be ignored.

As usual, it is best to use a symbolic constant (**MaxNum**, say) set to 10, and use **MaxNum**, rather than the constant 10, throughout the program.

We have sorted an array in *ascending* order. We can sort **num[0]** to **num[n-1]** in *descending* order with the following algorithm:

for j = 0 to n - 2
    b = position of biggest number from num[j] to num[n-1]
    swap num[j] and num[b]
endfor

We urge you to try Exercises 13 and 14 to print the results of the voting problem (page 200) in ascending order by name and descending order by votes received.

8.11 Sorting an array - insertion sort

Consider the same array as before:

num

57	48	79	65	15	33	52
0	1	2	3	4	5	6

Now, think of the numbers as cards on a table and picked up one at a time in the order in which they appear in the array. Thus, we first pick up 57, then 48, then

79, and so on, until we pick up 52. However, as we pick up each new number, we add it to our hand in such a way that the numbers in our hand are all sorted.

When we pick up 57, we have just one number in our hand. We consider one number to be sorted.

When we pick up 48, we add it in front of 57 so our hand contains

    48 57

When we pick up 79, we place it after 57 so our hand contains

    48 57 79

When we pick up 65, we place it after 57 so our hand contains

    48 57 65 79

At this stage, four numbers have been picked up and our hand contains them in sorted order.

When we pick up 15, we place it before 48 so our hand contains

    15 48 57 65 79

When we pick up 33, we place it after 15 so our hand contains

    15 33 48 57 65 79

Finally, when we pick up 52, we place it after 48 so our hand contains

    15 33 48 52 57 65 79

The numbers have been sorted in ascending order.

The method described illustrates the idea behind *insertion sort*. The numbers in the array will be processed one at a time, from left to right. This is equivalent to picking up the numbers from the table, one at a time. Since the first number, by itself, is sorted, we will process the numbers in the array starting from the second.

When we come to process **num[j]**, we can assume that **num[0]** to **num[j-1]** are sorted. We then attempt to insert **num[j]** among **num[0]** to **num[j-1]** so that **num[0]** to **num[j]** are sorted. We will then go on to process **num[j+1]**. When we do so, our assumption that **num[0]** to **num[j]** are sorted will be true.

Sorting **num** in ascending order using insertion sort proceeds as follows:

1st pass
- Process **num[1]**, that is, 48. This involves placing 48 so that the first two numbers are sorted; **num[0]** and **num[1]** now contain

    num

48	57
0	1

    and the rest of the array remains unchanged.

2nd pass

- Process **num[2]**, that is, 79. This involves placing 79 so that the first three numbers are sorted; **num[0]** to **num[2]** now contain

  num
48	57	79
0	1	2

  and the rest of the array remains unchanged.

3rd pass

- Process **num[3]**, that is, 65. This involves placing 65 so that the first four numbers are sorted; **num[0]** to **num[3]** now contain

  num
48	57	65	79
0	1	2	3

  and the rest of the array remains unchanged.

4th pass

- Process **num[4]**, that is, 15. This involves placing 15 so that the first five numbers are sorted. To simplify the explanation, think of 15 as being taken out and stored in a simple variable (**key**, say) leaving a 'hole' in **num[4]**. We can picture this as follows:

  key   num
  | 15 | | 48 | 57 | 65 | 79 | | 33 | 52 |
  |----| |----|----|----|----|----|----|----|
           | 0 | 1 | 2 | 3 | 4 | 5 | 6 |

  The insertion of 15 in its correct position proceeds as follows:

- Compare 15 with 79; it is smaller so move 79 to location 4, leaving location 3 free. This gives:

  key   num
  | 15 | | 48 | 57 | 65 | | 79 | 33 | 52 |
  |----| |----|----|----|----|----|----|----|
           | 0 | 1 | 2 | 3 | 4 | 5 | 6 |

- Compare 15 with 65; it is smaller so move 65 to location 3, leaving location 2 free. This gives:

  key   num
  | 15 | | 48 | 57 | | 65 | 79 | 33 | 52 |
  |----| |----|----|----|----|----|----|----|
           | 0 | 1 | 2 | 3 | 4 | 5 | 6 |

- Compare 15 with 57; it is smaller so move 57 to location 2, leaving location 1 free. This gives:

key	num						
15	48		57	65	79	33	52
	0	1	2	3	4	5	6

- Compare 15 with 48; it is smaller so move 48 to location 1, leaving location 0 free. This gives:

key	num						
15		48	57	65	79	33	52
	0	1	2	3	4	5	6

- There are no more numbers to compare with 15 so it is inserted in location 0, giving

key	num						
15	15	48	57	65	79	33	52
	0	1	2	3	4	5	6

- We can express the logic of placing 15 by saying that as long as **key** is less than **num[k]**, for some **k**, we move **num[k]** to position **num[k + 1]** and move on to consider **num[k - 1]**, providing it exists. It won't exist when **k** is actually 0. In this case, the process stops and **key** is inserted in position 0.

5th pass

- Process **num[5]**, that is, 33. This involves placing 33 so that the first six numbers are sorted. This is done as follows:
- Store 33 in **key**, leaving location 5 free;
- Compare 33 with 79; it is smaller so move 79 to location 5, leaving location 4 free;
- Compare 33 with 65; it is smaller so move 65 to location 4, leaving location 3 free;
- Compare 33 with 57; it is smaller so move 57 to location 3, leaving location 2 free;
- Compare 33 with 48; it is smaller so move 48 to location 2, leaving location 1 free;
- Compare 33 with 15; it is bigger; insert 33 in location 1. This gives:

key	num						
33	15	33	48	57	65	79	52
	0	1	2	3	4	5	6

- We can express the logic of placing 33 by saying that as long as **key** is less than **num[k]**, for some **k**, we move **num[k]** to position **num[k + 1]** and move on to consider **num[k - 1]**, providing it exists. If **key** is greater than or equal to **num[k]** for some **k**, then key is inserted in position **k + 1**. Here, 33 is greater than **num[0]** and so is inserted into **num[1]**.

Working with arrays

6th pass
- Process **num[6]**, that is, 52. This involves placing 52 so that the first seven (all) numbers are sorted. This is done as follows:
- Store 52 in **key**, leaving location 6 free;
- Compare 52 with 79; it is smaller so move 79 to location 6, leaving location 5 free;
- Compare 52 with 65; it is smaller so move 65 to location 5, leaving location 4 free;
- Compare 52 with 57; it is smaller so move 57 to location 4, leaving location 3 free;
- Compare 52 with 48; it is bigger; insert 52 in location 3. This gives:

key
52

num						
15	33	48	52	57	65	79
0	1	2	3	4	5	6

The array is now completely sorted.

The following is an outline to sort the first **n** elements of an array, **num**, using insertion sort:

```
for j = 1 to n - 1 do
   insert num[j] among num[0] to num[j-1] so that
   num[0] to num[j] are sorted
endfor
```

Using this outline, we write the method **insertionSort** using the parameter **list**.

```
public static void insertionSort(int[] list, int n) {
//sort list[0] to list[n-1] in ascending order
  int j, k, key;
  for (j = 1; j < n; j++) {
    key = list[j];
    k = j - 1; //start comparing with previous item
    while (k >= 0 && key < list[k]) {
      list[k + 1] = list[k];
      --k;
    }
    list[k + 1] = key;
  }
} //end insertionSort
```

The **while** statement is at the heart of the sort. It states that as long as we are within the array (**k >= 0**) and the current number (**key**) is less than the one in the array (**key < list[k]**), we move **list[k]** to the right (**list[k + 1] = list[k]**) and move on to the next number on the left (**--k**).

215

We exit the **while** loop if **k** is equal to -1 or if **key** is greater than or equal to **list[k]**, for some **k**. In either case, **key** is inserted into **list[k + 1]**.

If **k** is -1, it means that the current number is smaller than all the previous numbers in the list and must be inserted in **list[0]**. But **list[k + 1]** *is* **list[0]** when **k** is -1, so **key** is inserted correctly in this case.

The method sorts in ascending order. To sort in descending order, all we have to do is change < to > in the **while** condition, thus:

    while (k >= 0 && key > list[k])

Now, a key moves to the left if it is *bigger*.

Program P8.5 can be used to test **insertionSort**. We just replace the call to **selectionSort** with **insertionSort(num, n);** and add the method, above, to P8.5.

We could easily generalize **insertionSort** to sort a *portion* of a list. To illustrate, we re-write **insertionSort** to sort **list[lo]** to **list[hi]** where **lo** and **hi** are passed as arguments to the function.

Since element **lo** is the first one, we start processing elements from **lo + 1** until element **hi**. This is reflected in the **for** statement. Also now, the lowest subscript is **lo**, rather than 0. This is reflected in the **while** condition **k >= lo**. Everything else remains the same as before.

```
public static void insertionSort(int[] list, int lo, int hi) {
//sort list[lo] to list[hi] in ascending order
   int j, k, key;
   for (j = lo + 1; j <= hi; j++) {
      key = list[j];
      k = j - 1; //start comparing with previous item
      while (k >= lo && key < list[k]) {
         list[k + 1] = list[k];
         --k;
      }
      list[k + 1] = key;
   }
}
```

8.12 Inserting an element in place

Insertion sort uses the idea of adding a new element to an already sorted list so that the list remains sorted. We can treat this as a problem in its own right (nothing to do with insertion sort). Specifically, given a sorted list of items from **list[m]** to **list[n]**, we want to add a new item (**newItem**, say) to the list so that **list[m]** to **list[n + 1]** are sorted.

Adding a new item increases the size of the list by 1. We assume that the array has room to hold the new item. We write the function **insertInPlace** to solve this problem.

```
public static void insertInPlace(int newItem, int[] list, int m, int n) {
//list[m] to list[n] are sorted
//insert newItem so that list[m] to list[n+1] are sorted
  int k = n;
  while (k >= m && newItem < list[k]) {
    list[k + 1] = list[k];
    --k;
  }
  list[k + 1] = newItem;
} //end insertInPlace
```

Using **insertInPlace**, we can re-write **insertionSort**, above, as follows:

```
public static void insertionSort(int list[], int lo, int hi) {
//sort list[lo] to list[hi] in ascending order
  for (int j = lo + 1; j <= hi; j++)
    insertInPlace(list[j], list, lo, j - 1);
}
```

8.13 Binary search

Binary search is a very fast method for searching a list of items for a given one, *providing the list is sorted* (either ascending or descending). To illustrate the method, consider a list of 13 numbers, sorted in ascending order.

num

17	24	31	39	44	49	56	66	72	78	83	89	96
0	1	2	3	4	5	6	7	8	9	10	11	12

Suppose we wish to search for 66. The search proceeds as follows:

- First, we find the middle item in the list. This is 56 in position 6. We compare 66 with 56. Since 66 is bigger, we know that if 66 is in the list at all, it *must* be *after* position 6, since the numbers are in ascending order. In our next step, we confine our search to locations 7 to 12.

- Next, we find the middle item from locations 7 to 12. In this case, we can choose either item 9 or item 10. The algorithm we will write will choose item 9, that is, 78.

  We compare 66 with 78. Since 66 is smaller, we know that if 66 is in the list at all, it *must* be *before* position 9, since the numbers are in ascending order. In our next step, we confine our search to locations 7 to 8.

- Next, we find the middle item from locations 7 to 8. In this case, we can choose either item 7 or item 8. The algorithm we will write will choose item 7, that is, 66.

  We compare 66 with 66. Since they are the same, our search ends successfully, finding the required item in position 7.

Suppose we were searching for 70. The search will proceed as above until we compare 70 with 66 (in location 7).

- Since 70 is bigger, we know that if 70 is in the list at all, it *must* be *after* position 7, since the numbers are in ascending order. In our next step, we confine our search to locations 8 to 8. This is just one location.
- We compare 70 with item 8, that is, 72. Since 70 is smaller, we know that if 70 is in the list at all, it *must* be *before* position 8. Since it can't be after position 7 *and* before position 8, we conclude that it is not in the list.

At each stage of the search, we confine our search to some portion of the list. Let us use the variables **lo** and **hi** as the subscripts which define this portion. In other words, our search will be confined to **num[lo]** to **num[hi]**.

Initially, we want to search the entire list so that we will set **lo** to 0 and **hi** to 12, in this example.

How do we find the subscript of the middle item? We will use the calculation

$$mid = (lo + hi) / 2;$$

Since integer division will be performed, the fraction, if any, is discarded. For example when **lo** is 0 and **hi** is 12, **mid** becomes 6; when **lo** is 7 and **hi** is 12, **mid** becomes 9; and when **lo** is 7 and **hi** is 8, **mid** becomes 7.

As long as **lo** is less than or equal to **hi**, they define a non-empty portion of the list to be searched. When **lo** is equal to **hi**, they define a single item to be searched. If **lo** ever gets bigger than **hi**, it means we have searched the entire list and the item was not found.

Based on these ideas, we can now write a function **binarySearch**. To be more general, we will write it so that the calling routine can specify which portion of the array it wants the search to look for the item.

Thus, the function must be given the item to be searched for (**key**), the array (**list**), the start position of the search (**lo**) and the end position of the search (**hi**). For example, to search for the number 66 in the array **num**, above, we can issue the call **binarySearch(66, num, 0, 12)**.

The function must tell us the result of the search. If the item is found, the function will return its location. If not found, it will return -1.

Working with arrays

```
public static int binarySearch(int key, int[] list, int lo, int hi) {
//search for key from list[lo] to list[hi]
//if found, return its location; otherwise, return -1
  while (lo <= hi) {
    int mid = (lo + hi) / 2;
    if (key == list[mid]) return mid; // found
    if (key < list[mid]) hi = mid - 1;
    else lo = mid + 1;
  }
  return -1; //lo and hi have crossed; key not found
}
```

If **item** contains a number to be searched for, we can write code as follows:

```
int ans = binarySearch(item, num, 0, 12);
if (ans == -1) System.out.printf("%d not found\n", item);
else System.out.printf("%d found in location %d\n", item, ans);
```

If we wish to search for **item** from locations **i** to **j**, we can write

```
int ans = binarySearch(item, num, i, j);
```

Program P8.6 can be used to test **binarySearch**.

Program P8.6
```
public class TestBinSearch {
  public static void main(String[] args) {
    int[] num = {17, 24, 31, 39, 44, 49, 56, 66, 72, 78, 83, 89, 96};
    int n = binarySearch(66, num, 0, 12);
    System.out.printf("%d\n", n);     //will print 7; 66 in pos. 7
    n = binarySearch(66, num, 0, 6);
    System.out.printf("%d\n", n);     //will print -1; 66 not in 0 to 6
    n = binarySearch(70, num, 0, 12);
    System.out.printf("%d\n", n);     //will print -1; 70 not in list
    n = binarySearch(89, num, 5, 12);
    System.out.printf("%d\n", n);     //will print 11; 89 in pos. 11
  } //end main
  // binarySearch goes here
} //end class
```

The program shows how we can declare an integer array, **num**, *and* initialize it in one statement. Java will determine the size of the array from the number of elements we supply. The elements must be constants separated by commas and enclosed by { and }. The program makes several calls to **binarySearch** and, for each one, prints the value returned.

8.14 Merging ordered lists

Merging is the process by which two or more sorted lists are combined into one sorted list. For example, given two lists of numbers, **A** and **B**, as follows:

    A: 21 28 35 40 61 75

    B: 16 25 47 54

they can be combined into one sorted list, **C**:

    C: 16 21 25 28 35 40 47 54 61 75

C contains all the numbers from **A** and **B**. How can the merge be performed?

One way to think about it is to imagine that the numbers in the given lists are stored on cards, one per card, and the cards are placed face up on a table, with the smallest at the top. We can imagine the lists **A** and **B** as follows:

    21   16
    28   25
    35   47
    40   54
    61
    75

We look at the top two cards, 21 and 16. The smaller, 16, is removed and placed in **C**. This exposes the number 25.

The top two cards are now 21 and 25. The smaller, 21, is removed and added to **C** which now contains 16 21. This exposes the number 28.

The top two cards are now 28 and 25. The smaller, 25, is removed and added to **C** which now contains 16 21 25. This exposes the number 47.

The top two cards are now 28 and 47. The smaller, 28, is removed and added to **C** which now contains 16 21 25 28. This exposes the number 35.

The top two cards are now 35 and 47. The smaller, 35, is removed and added to **C** which now contains 16 21 25 28 35. This exposes the number 40.

The top two cards are now 40 and 47. The smaller, 40, is removed and added to **C** which now contains 16 21 25 28 35 40. This exposes the number 61.

The top two cards are now 61 and 47. The smaller, 47, is removed and added to **C** which now contains 16 21 25 28 35 40 47. This exposes the number 54.

The top two cards are now 61 and 54. The smaller, 54, is removed and added to **C** which now contains 16 21 25 28 35 40 47 54. The list **B** has no more numbers.

We copy the remaining elements (61 75) of **A** to **C**, which now contains:

    16 21 25 28 35 40 47 54 61 75

and the merge is completed.

At each step of the merge, we compare the smallest remaining number of **A** with the smallest remaining number of **B**. The smaller of these is added to **C**. If the smaller comes from **A**, we move on to the next number in **A**; if the smaller comes from **B**, we move on to the next number in **B**.

This is repeated until all the numbers in either **A** or **B** have been used. If all the numbers in **A** have been used, we add the remaining numbers from **B** to **C**. If all the numbers in **B** have been used, we add the remaining numbers from **A** to **C**.

We can express the logic of the merge as follows:

```
while (at least one number remains in both A and B) {
  if (smallest in A < smallest in B)
    add smallest in A to C
    move on to next number in A
  else
    add smallest in B to C
    move on to next number in B
  endif
}
if (A has ended) add remaining numbers in B to C
else add remaining numbers in A to C
```

Implementing the merge

Assume that an array **A** contains m numbers stored in **A[0]** to **A[m-1]** and an array **B** contains n numbers stored in **B[0]** to **B[n-1]**. Assume that the numbers are stored in ascending order. We wish to merge the numbers in **A** and **B** into another array **C** such that **C[0]** to **C[m+n-1]** contains all the numbers in **A** and **B** sorted in ascending order.

We use integer variables **i**, **j** and **k** to subscript the arrays **A**, **B** and **C**, respectively. "Moving on to the next position" in an array can be done by adding 1 to the subscript variable. We implement the merge with the function, **merge**, shown in Program P8.7 (next page). The function takes the arguments **A**, **m**, **B**, **n** and **C**, performs the merge and returns the number of elements, **m + n**, in **C**.

P8.7 also shows a simple **main** function which tests **merge**. It sets up arrays **A** and **B**, calls **merge** and prints **C**. When run, the program prints:

    16 21 25 28 35 40 47 54 61 75

Program P8.7

```java
public class TestMerge {
  public static void main(String[] args) {
    int[] A = {21, 28, 35, 40, 61, 75}; //size 6
    int[] B = {16, 25, 47, 54};         //size 4
    int[] C = new int[20];    //enough to hold all the elements
    int n = merge(A, 6, B, 4, C);
    for (int j = 0; j < n; j++) System.out.printf("%d ", C[j]);
    System.out.printf("\n");
  } //end main

  public static int merge(int[] A, int m, int[] B, int n, int[] C) {
    int i = 0; //i points to the first (smallest) number in A
    int j = 0; //j points to the first (smallest) number in B
    int k = -1; //k will be incremented before storing a number in C[k]
    while (i < m && j < n) {
      if (A[i] < B[j]) C[++k] = A[i++];
      else C[++k] = B[j++];
    }
    if (i == m) ///copy B[j] to B[n-1] to C
      for ( ; j < n; j++) C[++k] = B[j];
    else // j == n, copy A[i] to A[m-1] to C
      for ( ; i < m; i++) C[++k] = A[i];
    return m + n;
  } //end merge
} //end class
```

As a matter of interest, we can also implement **merge** as follows:

```java
public static int merge(int[] A, int m, int[] B, int n, int[] C) {
  int i = 0; //i points to the first (smallest) number in A
  int j = 0; //j points to the first (smallest) number in B
  int k = -1; //k will be incremented before storing a number in C[k]
  while (i < m || j < n) {
    if (i == m) C[++k] = B[j++];
    else if (j == n) C[++k] = A[i++];
    else if (A[i] < B[j]) C[++k] = A[i++];
    else C[++k] = B[j++];
  }
  return m + n;
}
```

Working with arrays

The **while** loop expresses the following logic: as long as there is at least one element to process in either **A** *or* **B**, we enter the loop. If we are finished with **A** (**i == m**), copy an element from **B** to **C**. If we are finished with **B** (**j == n**), copy an element from **A** to **C**. Otherwise, copy the smaller of **A[i]** and **B[j]** to **C**. Each time we copy an element from an array, we add 1 to the subscript for that array.

While the previous version implements the merge in a straightforward way, it seems reasonable to say that this version is a bit neater.

Exercises 8

1. Explain the difference between a simple variable and an array variable.
2. Write array declarations for each of the following: (a) a floating-point array of size 25 (b) an integer array of size 50 (c) a character array of size 32.
3. What is a subscript? Name 3 ways in which we can write a subscript.
4. What values are stored in an array when it is first declared?
5. Name 2 ways in which we can store a value in an array element.
6. You have declared an array of size 500. Is it required that you store values in all elements of the array?
7. Write a function which, given a number from **1** to **12**, returns the name of the month. For example, given **8**, it returns **August**. Return the empty string if the number given is not valid.
8. Write code to read 200 names from a file and store them in an array.
9. An array **num** is of size **100**. You are given two values **i** and **j**, with $0 \leq i < j \leq 99$. Write code to find the average of the numbers from **num[i]** to **num[j]**.
10. Write a function which, given an array of arbitrary characters, returns the number of consonants in the array.
11. Modify the letter frequency count program (page 194) to count the number of non-letters as well. Make sure you do not count the end-of-line characters.
12. Write a function which, given an array of integers and an integer **n**, reverses the first **n** elements of the array.
13. In the voting problem of Section 8.8, print the results in alphabetical order by candidate name. Hint: in sorting the **name** array, when you move a name, make sure and move the corresponding item in the **vote** array. You may need to look ahead to page 250 to see how to sort a **String** array.
14. In the voting problem of Section 8.8, print the results in descending order by candidate score.
15. Write a program to read names and phone numbers into two arrays. Request a name and print the person's phone number. Use at least one function.
16. Write a function to sort a **double** array in *ascending* order using selection sort. Do the sort by finding the *largest* number on each pass.

17. The number 27472 is said to be *palindromic* since it reads the same forwards or backwards. Write a function which, given an integer **n**, returns **1** if **n** is palindromic and **0** if it is not.

18. Write a program to find out, for a class of students, the number of families with 1, 2, 3, ... up to 8 or more children. The data consists of the number of children in each pupil's family, terminated by a **0**. (Why is **0** a good value to use?)

19. The *median* of a set of n numbers (not necessarily distinct) is obtained by arranging the numbers in order and taking the number in the middle. If n is odd, there is a unique middle number. If n is even, then the average of the two middle values is the median. Write a program to read a set of n positive integers (assume $n < 100$) and print their median; n is not given but **0** indicates the end of the data.

20. The *mode* of a set of n numbers is the number which appears most frequently. For example, the mode of 7 3 8 5 7 3 1 3 4 8 9 is 3. Write a program to read a set of n positive integers (assume $n < 100$) and print their mode; n is not given but **0** indicates the end of the data.

21. There are 500 light bulbs (numbered 1 to 500) arranged in a row. Initially, they are all OFF. Starting with bulb 2, all even numbered bulbs are turned ON. Next, starting with bulb 3, and visiting every third bulb, it is turned ON if it is OFF, and it is turned OFF if it is ON. This procedure is repeated for every fourth bulb, then every fifth bulb, and so on up to the 500th bulb. Write a program to determine which bulbs are OFF at the end of the above exercise. Is there anything special about the bulbs that are OFF? Can you explain why?

22. The prime numbers from 1 to 2500 can be obtained as follows. From a list of the numbers 1 to 2500, cross out all multiples of 2 (but not 2 itself). Then, find the next number (**n**, say) that is not crossed out and cross out all multiples of **n** (but not including **n**). Repeat this last step provided that **n** has not exceeded 50 (the square root of 2500). The numbers remaining in the list (except 1) are prime. Write a program which uses this method to print all primes from 1 to 2500. Store your output in a file called **primes.out**. This method is called the *Sieve of Eratosthenes*, named after the Greek mathematician, geographer and philosopher.

23. A multiple-choice examination consists of twenty questions. Each question has five choices, labelled **A**, **B**, **C**, **D** and **E**. The first line of data contains the correct answers to the twenty questions in the first 20 *consecutive* character positions, for example:

BECDCBAADEBACBAEDDBE

Each subsequent line contains the answers for a candidate. Data on a line consists of a candidate number (an integer), followed by one or more spaces, followed by the twenty answers given by the candidate in the next twenty *consecutive* character positions. An **X** is used if a candidate did not answer a particular question. You may assume all data are valid and stored in a file **exam.dat**. A sample line is:

4325   BECDCBAXDEBACCAEDXBE

There are at most 100 candidates. A line containing a "candidate number" **0** only indicates the end of the data.

Points for a question are awarded as follows:– correct answer: 4 points; wrong answer: -1 point; no answer: 0 points

Write a program to process the data and print a report consisting of candidate number and the points obtained by him/her, *in ascending order by candidate number*. Also, print the average number of points gained by the candidates.

24. The children's game of 'count-out' is played as follows: n children (numbered 1 to n) are arranged in a circle. A sentence consisting of m words[2] is used to eliminate one child at a time until one child is left. Starting at child 1, the children are counted from 1 to m and the mth child is eliminated. Starting with the child after the one just eliminated, the children are again counted from 1 to m and the mth child eliminated. This is repeated until one child is left. Counting is done circularly and eliminated children are not counted. Write a program to read values for n (assumed <= 100) and m (> 0) and print the number of the last remaining child.

25. An array **chosen** contains **n** distinct integers arranged in no particular order. Another array **winners** contains **m** distinct integers arranged in *ascending* order. Write efficient code to determine how many of the numbers in **chosen** appear in **winners**.

26. **A** is an array sorted in descending order. **B** is an array sorted in descending order. Merge **A** and **B** into **C** so that **C** is in *descending* order.

27. **A** is an array sorted in descending order. **B** is an array sorted in descending order. Merge **A** and **B** into **C** so that **C** is in *ascending* order.

28. **A** is an array sorted in ascending order. **B** is an array sorted in descending order. Merge **A** and **B** into **C** so that **C** is in *ascending* order.

29. An array **A** contains integers that first increase in value and then decrease in value, for example,

17	24	31	39	44	49	36	29	20	18	13
0	1	2	3	4	5	6	7	8	9	10

It is unknown at which point the numbers start to decrease. Write efficient code to code to copy the numbers in **A** to another array **B** so that **B** is sorted in ascending order. Your code must take advantage of the way the numbers are arranged in **A**.

30. An integer array **num** is filled with **n** numbers in arbitrary order. Write code to find and print all pairs from **num** which add up to a given number, **y**.

31. An integer array **num** is filled with **n** numbers in arbitrary order. Write code to find and print all pairs of positions such that each pair contains identical values.

---

[2] For example, "eenie meenie mynie mo, sorry, child, you've got to go"; m = 10

9 Strings

In this chapter, we will explain:

- how to create a string implicitly
- how to create a string explicitly
- what is meant by *immutable* string
- how to compare strings for equality
- how to tell if one string is 'greater' or 'less' than another
- how to use several **String** methods
- how to determine if a string is a palindrome
- how to work with an array of strings
- how to use the **do...while** statement
- how to convert between character arrays and strings
- how to remove all occurrences of a given character from a string
- how to write a method for reading strings in a flexible manner
- how to write a (Geography) quiz program
- how a **String** is passed as an argument to a method
- how to search a **String** array
- how to sort a **String** array
- how to write a program to do a frequency count of words in a passage

So far, we have used strings extensively in our programs, mainly as arguments to **printf**. On page 44, we introduced the notion of a string constant and, on page 57, we showed how a program can read a string. We now look at some other issues pertaining to strings.

A *string constant* (or, simply, *string*) is a sequence of 0 or more characters enclosed in double quotation marks. Examples are: "Hello", "123", "M. Ali", "What the @%^&*!", "Welcome to Java". Two consecutive double quotes "" denote the *empty string*—a string with zero characters. In Java, the opening and closing quotes must be on the same line; a string cannot extend over more than one line.

In Java, a string is an *object* which belongs to the class **String** (uppercase **S**). In general, an object consists of *data* and *methods*. For a string, the data are the characters in the string and the methods are provided for manipulating the string. For example, the method **equals** allows you to test if two strings are the same.

9.1 Creating strings

When we write a statement such as:

    System.out.printf("Welcome");

we create the string **"Welcome"** *implicitly*. Java stores the string somewhere in memory and uses a *reference* to the string (the string's address) in **printf**. Since we do not know what this address is, we have no direct control over the string. Strings we create implicitly are sometimes called *transient* strings.

We can create a string *explicitly* by declaring a **String** variable and assigning a string to it, as in:

    String str;   // declare the variable
    str = "Welcome";   // assign a string to it

The first statement declares a **String** (object) variable called **str**. This means that **str** can assume a value which is a memory address—the address where the actual string is stored. The second statement stores the characters **Welcome** somewhere in memory (at location **3029**, say) and stores **3029** in **str**. This can be depicted as follows:

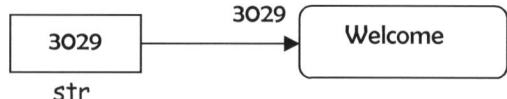

As usual, the two statements can be combined into one:

    String str = "Welcome";

We can print **str** as in:

    System.out.printf("%s to Java\n", str);

which will print:

    Welcome to Java

Now suppose we write:

    str = "Hello";

we might be tempted to think that this changes the string in memory from **Welcome** to **Hello** (since this is what happens with primitive types). But this is not so. Some new storage is found (at location 3224, say) and **Hello** is stored *there*. This *new* address is stored in **str**; the old address is lost so we can no longer access **Welcome**. The situation in memory is shown on the top of the next page.

The value of the string *reference* has changed, not the string itself. In fact, in Java, a **String** object is *read only*, or *immutable*—it can never be changed. A statement which *appears* to change a string actually creates a *new* string with the new contents and changes the *reference* to point to the new string.

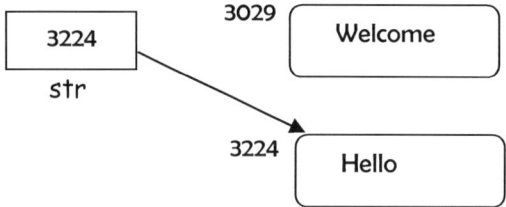

As another example, consider:

    str += " tiger";   // str = str + " tiger"

The **+** operator, when applied to strings, concatenates them (joins them together). The statement creates a new string **Hello tiger** and sets **str** to point to it. The old string **Hello** is still in memory but we have lost access to it. If we need the old string, we could write:

    String str1 = str;   // save the old string
    str += " tiger";   // create the new one

Now we can still access the old string with **str1**.

For the most part, when we are using strings, the distinction between a **String** variable containing a reference to a string as opposed to the string itself is not too important. When it does not matter, we will speak as if a **String** variable contains the string itself. We will say, for instance, 'The value of **str** is **Hello**' when, in reality, it is the memory address where **Hello** is stored.

Java also lets us create a string using **new**. The statement

    String s = new String();

is exactly the same as

    String s = "";

The statement

    String s = new String("Welcome");

is exactly the same as

    String s = "Welcome";

As you can see, using **new** is a bit more cumbersome than simple assignment; we would hardly ever use it to create a string from a literal. However, it is quite useful for creating a string from a character array. We will see how on page 237.

9.2 Some useful String methods

The **String** class contains a large number of methods for manipulating strings. We have already seen that **s1.equals(s2)** returns **true** if two strings **s1** and **s2** contain exactly the same characters. We describe some other commonly used ones. The examples are based on the following declarations:

Strings

```
String s, s1, s2, s3, s4, s5, s6;
s3 = "red";
s4 = "Red";
s5 = "";                          // empty string
s6 = "Red, red wine";
```

First, note that characters in a string are numbered starting at 0. If a string contains **n** characters, the *positions* in the string range from 0 to **n-1**. If any **String** method attempts to access a string position outside this range, a **StringIndexOutOfBoundsException** is thrown (see **charAt** below for an example). This normally indicates some error in program logic.

- **s.length()** returns an integer value—the number of characters in **s**. For example, **s3.length()** returns 3 and **s5.length()** returns 0.
- **s1.equalsIgnoreCase(s2)** returns **true** if **s1** and **s2** are the same, treating upper and lowercase letters as being equal and **false**, otherwise. For example, **s3.equals(s4)** is **false** but **s3.equalsIgnoreCase(s4)** is **true**.
- **s.charAt(n)** returns the character at position **n**. The expression **s.charAt(0)** returns the first character; **s.charAt(1)** returns the second character, and so on. For example, **s3.charAt(2)** returns **d** and **s6.charAt(9)** returns **w** (remember that a space counts as any other character). If **n** is less than 0 or bigger than **s.length() - 1**, an error occurs and a **StringIndexOutOfBoundsException** is thrown. The following bit of code counts the number of **A**s in a string **s**.

    ```
    int a = 0;
    for (int j = 0; j < s.length(); j++)
      if (s.charAt(j) == 'A') a++;
    System.out.printf("Number of As = %d\n", a);
    ```

    If **s** is the string **"A Little At A Time"**, the code will print

    ```
    Number of As = 3
    ```

- **s1.compareTo(s2)** is an **int** function which compares the strings **s1** and **s2**. The comparison is done character by character using the ordering of the Unicode (think ASCII, for our purposes) character set to decide if one character is 'less' than another. If the two strings are identical, the function returns 0. If they are not, and one is not a substring of the other, then they must differ at some first character position (**f**, say). The function returns

    ```
    s1.charAt(f) - s2.charAt(f)
    ```

    If **s1.charAt(f)** is less than **s2.charAt(f)**, the function returns a negative value. If **s1.charAt(f)** is greater than **s2.charAt(f)**, the function returns a positive value. For example, **"red".compareTo("Red")** returns 32, the difference between lowercase **r** (114) and uppercase **R** (82). Conversely, **"Red".compareTo("red")** returns -32. The call **"bed".compareTo("Red")** returns 16 indicating that **bed** is 'greater' than **Red**; this is so since lowercase letters have higher codes than uppercase ones (the code for **b** is 98).

If **s1** is a proper substring of **s2**, then **s1.compareTo(s2)** returns the *negative* number **s1.length() - s2.length()**, indicating that **s1** is 'less' than **s2**. If **s2** is a proper substring of **s1**, then **s1.compareTo(s2)** returns the positive number **s1.length() - s2.length()**, indicating that **s1** is 'greater' than **s2**. For example, **"be".compareTo("beach")** returns -3 and **"beach".compareTo("be")** returns 3.

For the most part, when we are comparing strings, we just need to know if the value returned by **s1.compareTo(s2)** is negative (**s1** is less than **s2**), zero (**s1** is equal to **s2**) or positive (**s1** is greater than **s2**); the specific value is not usually important. We will show how to use **compareTo** to perform a binary search on a list of strings on page 250.

- **s1.compareToIgnoreCase(s2)** is the same as **compareTo** except that an upper-case letter is considered equal to its equivalent lowercase letter; **N** is the same as **n**. For example, **s3.compareToIgnoreCase(s4)** returns 0.

9.3 Example – palindrome

Consider the problem of determining if a given string is a *palindrome* (the same when spelt forwards or backwards). Examples of palindromes (ignoring case, punctuation and spaces) are:

> civic
> Racecar
> Madam, I'm Adam.
> A man, a plan, a canal, Panama.

If all the letters were of the same case (upper or lower) and the string (**word**, say) contained no spaces or punctuation marks, we could solve the problem as follows:

> compare the first and last letters
> if they are different, the string is not a palindrome
> if they are the same, compare the second and second to last letters
> if they are different, the string is not a palindrome
> if they are the same, compare the third and third to last letters

and so on; we continue until we find a non-matching pair (and it's not a palindrome) or there are no more pairs to compare (and it is a palindrome). We can express this logic in pseudocode as follows:

> set lo to 0
> set hi to length(word) - 1
> while lo < hi do //while there are more pairs to compare
>   if word.charAt(lo) != word.charAt(hi) then return false //no palindrome
>   //the letters match, move on to the next pair
>   lo = lo + 1
>   hi = hi - 1
> endwhile
> return true // all pairs match, it is a palindrome

The **while** loop compares pairs of letters; if it finds a non-matching pair, it immediately returns **false**. If all pairs match, it will exit in the normal way when **lo** is no longer less than **hi**. In this case, it returns **true**.

The function **palindrome** is shown in Program P9.1 which tests it by reading several words and printing whether or not each is a palindrome.

```
                         Program P9.1
import java.util.*;
public class Palindrome {
   public static void main(String[] args) {
      Scanner in = new Scanner(System.in);
      System.out.printf("Type a word. (To stop, press 'Enter' only): ");
      String aWord = in.nextLine();
      while (!aWord.equals("")) {
         if (palindrome(aWord)) System.out.printf("is a palindrome\n");
         else System.out.printf("is not a palindrome\n");
         System.out.printf("Type a word. (To stop, press 'Enter' only): ");
         aWord = in.nextLine();
      }
   } //end main

   public static boolean palindrome(String word) {
      int lo = 0;
      int hi = word.length() - 1;
      while (lo < hi)
         if (word.charAt(lo++) != word.charAt(hi--)) return false;
      return true;
   } //end palindrome
} //end class
```

In the function, we use the single statement

```
if (word.charAt(lo++) != word.charAt(hi--) return false;
```

to express all the logic of the body of the **while** loop in the above algorithm. Since we use **++** and **--** as suffixes, **lo** and **hi** are changed *after* **word.charAt(lo)** is compared with **word.charAt(hi)**. We could, of course, have expressed it as:

```
if (word.charAt(lo) != word.charAt(hi) return false;
lo++;
hi--;
```

And, using **for**, we could express the entire body of palindrome with:

```
for (int lo = 0, int hi = word.length() - 1; lo < hi; lo++, hi--)
   if (word.charAt(lo) != word.charAt(hi)) return false;
return true;
```

The program prompts the user to type a word and tells her if it is a palindrome. It then prompts for another word. To stop, the user must press "Enter" only. When she does this, the empty string is stored in **aWord**. The **while** condition checks for this by comparing **aWord** with "" (two consecutive double quotes denote the empty string). The following is a sample run of Program P9.1:

```
Type a word. (To stop, press "Enter" only): racecar
is a palindrome
Type a word. (To stop, press "Enter" only): race car
is not a palindrome
Type a word. (To stop, press "Enter" only): Racecar
is not a palindrome
Type a word. (To stop, press "Enter" only): DEIFIED
is a palindrome
Type a word. (To stop, press "Enter" only):
```

Note that **race car** is not a palindrome because **'e'** is not the same as **' '** and **Racecar** is not a palindrome because **'R'** is not the same as **'r'**. We will fix this shortly.

A better palindrome function

The function we wrote works for one-word palindromes with all uppercase or all lowercase letters. We now tackle the more difficult problem of checking words or phrases which may contain uppercase letters, lowercase letters, spaces and punctuation marks. To illustrate our approach, consider the phrase:

> Madam, I'm Adam

We will convert all the letters to one case (lower, say) and remove all spaces and non-letters, giving

> madamimadam

We can now use the function we wrote in P9.1 to test if *this* is a palindrome.

Let us write a function **lettersOnlyLower** which, given a string **phrase**, converts all letters to lowercase and removes all spaces and non-letters. The function returns the converted string. Here it is:

```java
public static String lettersOnlyLower(String phrase) {
    String word = "";
    for (int j = 0; j < phrase.length(); j++)
        if (Character.isLetter(phrase.charAt(j)))
            word = word + phrase.charAt(j);
    return word.toLowerCase();
}
```

The **for** loop looks at each character of **phrase**, in turn. If it is a letter, it is added to **word**; if it is not a letter, it is ignored. At the end, **word** is converted to lowercase, using the predefined function **toLowerCase** from the **String** class. This function converts all the uppercase letters to lowercase, leaving all the other characters, if any, unchanged.

Putting everything together, we get Program P9.2 which tests our new function, **letterOnlyLower**. The program prompts the user for a phrase and tells her whether or not it is a palindrome. We also print the converted phrase to show you how the function works.

```
                         Program P9.2
import java.util.*;
public class Palindrome1 {
  public static void main(String[] args) {
    Scanner in = new Scanner(System.in);
    System.out.printf("Type a word. (To stop, press 'Enter' only): ");
    String aWord = in.nextLine();
    while (!aWord.equals("")) {
      aWord = lettersOnlyLower(aWord);
      System.out.printf("Converted to: %s\n", aWord);
      if (palindrome(aWord)) System.out.printf("is a palindrome\n");
      else System.out.printf("is not a palindrome\n");
      System.out.printf("Type a word. (To stop, press 'Enter' only): ");
      aWord = in.nextLine();
    }
  } //end main

  public static boolean palindrome(String word) {
    int lo = 0;
    int hi = word.length() - 1;
    while (lo < hi)
      if (word.charAt(lo++) != word.charAt(hi--)) return false;
    return true;
  } //end palindrome

  public static String lettersOnlyLower(String phrase) {
    String word = "";
    for (int j = 0; j < phrase.length(); j++)
      if (Character.isLetter(phrase.charAt(j)))
        word = word + phrase.charAt(j);
    return word.toLowerCase();
  } //end lettersOnlyLower
} //end class
```

A sample run is shown on the next page.

```
Type a phrase. (To stop, press "Enter" only): Madam I'm Adam
Converted to: madamimadam
is a palindrome
Type a phrase. (To stop, press "Enter" only): Flo, gin is a sin. I golf.
Converted to: floginisasinigolf
is a palindrome
Type a phrase. (To stop, press "Enter" only): Never odd or even.
Converted to: neveroddoreven
is a palindrome
Type a phrase. (To stop, press "Enter" only): Thermostat
Converted to: thermostat
is not a palindrome
Type a phrase. (To stop, press "Enter" only): Pull up if I pull up.
Converted to: pullupifipullup
is a palindrome
Type a phrase. (To stop, press "Enter" only):
```

9.4 Array of strings – name of the day revisited

In Program P7.4, page 164, we wrote a method **printDay** which printed the name of a day, given the number of the day. We will now write a function **nameOfDay** which, given the number of a day, returns the name of the day. For example,

    String today = nameOfDay(6);

will store **Friday** in **today**.

We show how to write **nameOfDay** using an array to store the names of the days. Suppose we have an array **day** as follows (**day[0]** is not used and is not shown):

day

Sunday	day[1]
Monday	day[2]
Tuesday	day[3]
Wednesday	day[4]
Thursday	day[5]
Friday	day[6]
Saturday	day[7]

If **d** contains a value from 1 to 7, then **day[d]** contains the name of the day corresponding to **d**. For instance, if **d** is 3, **day[d]** contains **Tuesday**.

We can declare the array **day** and initialize it with the names of the days using:

    String day[8] = {"", "Sunday", "Monday", "Tuesday", "Wednesday",
                    "Thursday", "Friday", "Saturday"};

The strings to be placed in the array are enclosed by **{** and **}** and separated by commas with no comma after the last one. The first string, the null string, is placed in **day[0]**, the second in **day[1]**, the third in **day[2]**, and so on.

The complete function, **nameOfDay**, is shown in Program P9.3 in which **main** is used simply to test the function.

```
Program P9.3
import java.util.*;
public class PrintDay2 {
   public static void main(String[] args) {
      Scanner in = new Scanner(System.in);
      System.out.printf("Enter a day from 1 to 7: ");
      int n = in.nextInt();
      System.out.printf("%s\n", nameOfDay(n));
   } //end main

   public static String nameOfDay(int n) {
      String[] day = {"", "Sunday", "Monday", "Tuesday", "Wednesday",
                          "Thursday", "Friday", "Saturday"};
      if (n < 1 || n > 7) return "Invalid day";
      return day[n];
   } //end nameOfDay
} //end class
```

Note that, in **main**, **n** is not really necessary. The last two statements could be written as:

```
System.out.printf("%s\n", nameOfDay(in.nextInt()));
```

The do...while *statement*

As written, if the user enters a number outside the range 1 to 7, the program simply prints **Invalid day** and stops. We can write the code so that as long as the user enters an invalid number, the program will ask him to enter another number. We will express the logic using a **do...while** statement. The format of the statement is:

```
do
   <statement>
while (<condition>);
```

The words **do** and **while**, and the brackets are required; <**statement**> is a single statement which is almost always a compound statement or block (statements within braces); <**condition**> is a Boolean expression (either **true** or **false**).

<statement> is executed as long as <condition> is **true**. It is important to realize that <statement> is executed and *then* **condition** is tested; thus <statement> is *always* executed at least once. (In the normal **while** statement, the body will *not* be executed if <condition> is **false** the first time.)

We can now express the logic for entering the number of the day as:

```
int n;
do {
   System.out.printf("Enter a day from 1 to 7: ");
   n = in.nextInt();
} while (n < 1 || n > 7);
```

The loop is executed as long as **n** is less than **1 or n** is greater than **7**; it is exited only when a value between 1 and 7, inclusive, is entered. Note that **n** is declared before the **do..while**. If we had put it inside the block as in:

```
int n = in.nextInt();
```

then its 'scope' would be limited to the block; it would be unknown after the right brace and, as such, would be unknown in the **while** condition and any subsequent statements.

9.5 Strings and character arrays

Much of the work that we need to do with strings in Java can be done with **String** objects. But because **String**s are immutable, some operations are not as efficient as they could be. Java provides the **StringBuffer** class for working with mutable strings but a simple character array can be more flexible and easier to use.

Consider the following statement from **lettersOnlyLower** on page 232:

```
word = word + phrase.charAt(j);
```

Suppose **phrase** contains **Red Rum, Sir, Is Murder**. Each time this statement is executed, one letter is added to **word**. At the end, **word** contains the string (more precisely, the address of the string) **RedRumSirIsMurder**.

This works but is not very efficient. Because strings in Java are immutable, each execution creates a *new* string with one more letter and **word** is set to point to the new string. In our example, at the end, **word** would be pointing to **RedRumSirIsMurder** (length 17). However, there would be 16 strings in memory—**R, Re, Red, RedR**, and so on, up to **RedRumSirIsMurde**—with nothing pointing to them. They would all be 'garbage collected' eventually by the system but it seems like a lot of work for such a simple problem.

We now show how to write the function more efficiently using a character array. Here is the function:

```
public static String lettersOnlyLower(String phrase) {
  char[] word = phrase.toCharArray();
  int n = 0; //used to index word
  for (int j = 0; j < phrase.length(); j++)
    if (Character.isLetter(phrase.charAt(j)))
      word[n++] = phrase.charAt(j);
  return new String(word, 0, n).toLowerCase();
}
```

The method **toCharArray**, when applied to a string, returns a **char** array containing the characters of the string. The size of the array is the same as the length of the string. For example, if **phrase** contains the string **"Top Spot"**, the statement

    char[] word = phrase.toCharArray();

would create:

word

T	o	p		S	p	o	t
0	1	2	3	4	5	6	7

We could now manipulate the array **word** in any way that an array can.

In this example, it is not important that **word** be initialized to anything special. In particular, it does not need to be initialized to the characters of **phrase**. All that matters is that **word** is large enough to hold the converted string. The statement sets its size to the same as the length of the string.

On each pass through the loop, one letter is stored in the array, **word**. No new strings are created so this operation is simple and efficient. When the **for** loop finishes execution, we will have:

word

T	o	p	S	p	o	t	t
0	1	2	3	4	5	6	7

and the value of **n** will be 7, meaning that 7 letters have been stored in **word**.

The expression **new String(word, 0, n)** creates a string of **n** characters starting with the character in **word[0]**. Here, it creates the string **TopSpot**. This is then converted to lowercase, giving **topspot**, the value returned by the function.

In general, if **chArr** is a **char** array, the expression

    new String(chArr, start, n)

creates a string of n characters starting with the character in **chArr[start]**. If either **start** or **n** goes outside the bounds of the array, an **IndexOutOfBoundsException** would be thrown. For example, if **chArr** is as follows:

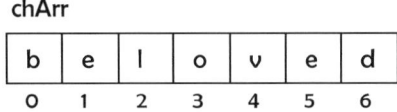

the statement

> String s = new String(chArr, 2, 4);

sets **s** to a string of length 4, starting at position 2, that is, the string **"love"**.

Example – remove character from a string

Let us write a function **remove** which takes two arguments—a string **s** and a character **ch**—and returns a new string with all instances of **ch** removed from **s**; **s** is unchanged. For example, the call:

> remove("Red, red wine", 'e');

would return the string **"Rd, rd win"**. Here is the first version:

```java
public static String remove(String s, char ch) {
   String snew = "";       // start with an empty string
   for (int j = 0; j < s.length(); j++)
      if (s.charAt(j) != ch) snew = snew + s.charAt(j);
   return snew;
}
```

The function looks at each character of **s**. If it is *not* the same as **ch**, it is added to the new string being formed. If it is the same, it is ignored. Like before, each time a new character is added to **snew**, a new string is created and the old string is left in memory. At the end, **snew** holds (the address of) the final string but all the intermediate strings are left in memory waiting to be 'garbage collected'.

We can write the function more efficiently using a **char** array, as follows:

```java
public static String remove(String s, char ch) {
   char[] hold = s.toCharArray();
   int n = 0;              // used to index hold
   for (int j = 0; j < hold.length; j++)
      if (hold[j] != ch) hold[n++] = hold[j];
   return new String(hold, 0, n);
}
```

First observe that the returned string could never be longer than **s**. If **len** is the length of **s**, the first statement creates a **char** array **hold** of size **len**, containing the characters of **s**. This array will be big enough to hold the string to be returned, since characters can only be removed, not added.

Next, the **for** loop looks at each character **c** of **s**, now stored in **hold**. Note that **hold.length** (no brackets after **length** since **hold** is an array) denotes the number of elements in the array. If **c** is the same as **ch**, it is ignored; if it is different, it is added to the string to be returned.

We use **hold** in two ways; one as the source of characters of **s** and also as the destination of the characters in the string to be returned. The subscript **j** denotes the character being looked at (the source) and the subscript **n** denotes the position in **hold** where the next character from the return string will be stored (the destination).

You may find it easier to follow the logic if you think of the array subscripted by **n** as being different from the one subscripted by **j**. Even though **hold** is both the source and destination, there will be no conflict since **n** can never be greater than **j**. In other words, we cannot overwrite a character from the original string before it is considered.

The value of **n** always indicates the next available destination position which is the same as the number of characters that have already been copied to the destination. For example, suppose that characters have already been tested and stored in **hold[0]** to **hold[3]**, then the value of **n** would be 4, meaning that 4 is the next available position and 4 is the number of characters already stored.

Finally, **new String(hold, 0, n)** creates the return string from the first **n** characters in **hold**. The following shows how the method handles the call:

    remove("review", 'e');

The first step creates the array **hold**:

hold

r	e	v	i	e	w
0	1	2	3	4	5

At this stage, **j = 0** and **n = 0**.

The first character **r** is to be returned so it is copied to position **n** (i.e., **0**). The array looks unchanged but now, **j = 1** and **n = 1**.

The next character looked at is **e**. This is not to be returned so the array is unchanged. Now, **j = 2** and **n = 1**.

The next character looked at is **v** (the one in position **j**). This is to be returned so it is copied to position **1**, denoted by **n**. The array now looks like this:

hold

r	v	v	i	e	w
0	1	2	3	4	5

At this stage, **j = 3** and **n = 2**.

The next character is **i**. This is to be returned so it is copied to position **2**, denoted by **n**. The array now looks like this:

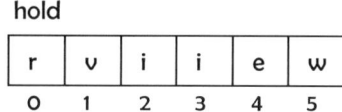

At this stage, **j = 4** and **n = 3**.

The next character is **e** (the one in position **j**). This is not to be returned so the array is unchanged. Now, **j = 5** and **n = 3**.

The next character is **w** (the one in position **j**). This is to be returned so it is copied to position **3**, denoted by **n**. The array now looks like this:

```
hold
 r  v  i  w  e  w
 0  1  2  3  4  5
```

At this stage, the **for** loop terminates; **n** has the value **4** and **j** is undefined. The string to be returned consists of the first 4 characters in **hold**, that is, **"rviw"**.

9.6 A flexible getString function

So far, we have used **next** and **nextLine** from the **Scanner** class to read strings from the input. We use **next** to read a string containing no whitespace characters and we use **nextLine** to read a string up to the end-of-line. However, neither of these allows us to read a string delimited by double quotes, for instance. If we had data in the following format:

```
"Denise Richards" "Clerical Assistant"
```

we would not be able to use **next** or **nextLine** to read this data easily.

We will write a function, **getString**, which lets us read a string enclosed within 'delimiter' characters. For example, we could specify a string as **$John Smith$** or **"John Smith"**. This is a very flexible way of specifying a string. *Each* string can be specified with its own delimiters which could be different for the next string. It is particularly useful for specifying strings which may include special characters such as the double quotes without having to use an escape sequenc like \".

For instance, in order to to specify the string:

```
"Don't move!" he commanded.
```

in Java, we must write:

```
"\"Don't move!\" he commanded."
```

With **getString**, this string could be supplied as

        $"Don't move!" he commanded.$

or

        %"Don't move!" he commanded.%

or using *any* other character as a delimiter, provided it is not one of the characters in the string. We could even use:

        7"Don't move!" he commanded."7

but would normally use special characters like ", $, % or # as delimiters.

Suppose we want to read delimited strings from a file (**input.txt**, say) and we have the declaration:

        FileReader in = new FileReader("input.txt");

We can write **getString** as follows:

```
public static String getString(FileReader in) throws IOException {
//returns the next string found within delimiters
// the first non-whitespace character is the delimiter
   final int MaxLen = 255;
   int c, delim, n = 0;
   char[] str = new char[MaxLen];
   // read over white space
   while (Character.isWhitespace((char) (c = in.read()))) ; //empty body
   if (c == -1) return ""; //no delimiter found
   delim = c;
   while (((c = in.read()) != delim) && (c != -1))
      if (n < MaxLen) str[n++] = (char) c;
   return new String(str, 0, n);
} // end getString
```

The function will find and return the next delimited string (without the delimiters) from the file designated by **in**. The phrase **throws IOException** is necessary since **getString** uses **in.read()** to get the next character.

Comments on **getString**

- The function assumes that the first non-whitespace character met (**delim**, say) is the delimiter. Characters are read and stored in a **char** array, **str**, until **delim** is met again, indicating the end of the string. The delimiter characters are not stored since they are not part of the string.
- The predefined function **Character.isWhitespace** returns **true** if its **char** argument is a space, tab or newline character and **false**, otherwise.
- If **getString** encounters end-of-file before finding a non-whitespace character (the delimiter), the empty string is returned.

- Otherwise, it builds the string by reading one character at a time; the string is terminated by the next occurrence of the delimiter or end-of-file, whichever comes first. The logic for this is expressed by

    while (((c = in.read()) != delim) && (c != -1))

- The function caters for strings of length 255, designated by **MaxLen**. If a string is longer, it is read completely but only the first 255 characters are returned.
- For efficiency in creating the string, a **char** array is used. When the complete string has been read, we use **new String(str, 0, n)** to create a **String**.

We can use **getString** as follows:

```
FileReader in = new FileReader("countries.txt");
String name = getString(in);
while (!name.equals("")) {
  System.out.printf("String read: %s\n", name);
  name = getString(in);
}
```

If **countries.txt** contains the following data:

```
$Trinidad$ @Port of Spain@
&Jamaica& "Kingston"
#Grenada# "St. George's"
```

The above code will print

```
String read: Trinidad
String read: Port of Spain
String read: Jamaica
String read: Kingston
String read: Grenada
String read: St. George's
```

As written, **getString** reads from a file. But what if we wanted to read a string from the keyboard? We will not be able to make the call **getString(System.in)** since **System.in** is not a **FileReader**—it is declared as an **InputStream**. We *could* change the header to

   public static String getString(InputStream in) throws IOException

but, then, we cannot call it with a **FileReader**. However, we *can* call it with **in** if **in** is declared as a **FileInputStream** as in:

   FileInputStream in = new FileInputStream("input.txt");

FileInputStream is what is called a *subclass* of **InputStream** and so is compatible with it. Now we can get the function to read from the file with **getString(in)** and we can get it to read from the keyboard with **getString(System.in)**.

We could also use overloading (page 162) to accomplish the same thing in a different way. We could leave **getString** as it is with the **FileReader** parameter. We could then write *another* version, changing the header to:

```
public static String getString(InputStream in) throws IOException
```

Everything else remains the same. In **main**, say, if we use **getString(System.in)**, *this* version of **getString** will be called. If we use **getString(in)** where **in** is a **FileReader**, the **FileReader** version will be called.

9.7 A Geography quiz program

Let us write a program which quizzes a user on countries and their capitals. The program will illustrate some useful programming concepts like reading from the keyboard *and* a file and being very flexible in terms of user input. The following is a sample run of the program, indicating how we want the finished program to work. The user is given two tries at a question. If she gets it wrong both times, the program tells her the correct answer.

```
What is the capital of Trinidad? Tobago
Wrong. Try again.
What is the capital of Trinidad? Port of Spain
Correct!

What is the capital of Jamaica? Kingston
Correct!

What is the capital of Grenada? Georgetown
Wrong. Try again.
What is the capital of Grenada? Castries
Wrong. Answer is St. George's
```

We will store the names of the countries and their capitals in a file (**quizdata.txt**, say). For each country, we will store its name and its capital. The following shows some sample data:

```
"Trinidad"  "Port of Spain"
"Jamaica"   "Kingston"
"Grenada"   "St. George's"
```

We show 2 strings per line but this is not necessary. The only requirement is that they are supplied in the right *order*. If you wish, you can have 1 string per line or 6 strings per line or different numbers of strings per line. Also, you can use any character to delimit a string, provided it is not a character in the string. And you can use different delimiters for different strings. It is perfectly okay to supply the above data as:

```
$Trinidad$  @Port of Spain@
"Jamaica"   &Kingston&
#Grenada#   "St. George's"
```

We can do this because of the versatility of **getString**. We will use **getString** to read the (delimited) strings from the file and **nextLine** to get the user's answers typed at the keyboard.

Suppose a country's data are read into the variables **country** and **capital**, respectively. The program converts *the letters only* in **capital** to uppercase and stores the result in **CAPITAL**. (Remember that **capital** is a different variable from **CAPITAL**.) For example, **St. George's** is converted to **STGEORGES**.

When the user types an answer (**answer**, say), it must be compared with **capital**. If we use a straightforward comparison like

>   if (answer.equals(capital)) ...

to check if **answer** is the same as **capital**, then answers like **"Portof Spain"**, **"port of spain"**, **" Port ofSpain"** and **"st georges"** would all be considered wrong. If we want these answers to be correct (and we probably should) we must convert all user answers to a common format before comparing.

We take the view that as long as all the letters are there, in the correct order, regardless of case, the answer is considered correct. When the user types an answer, we ignore spaces and punctuation and convert *the letters* to uppercase. This is then compared with **CAPITAL**. For example, the answers above would be converted to **"PORTOFSPAIN"** and **"STGEORGES"** and would elicit a **Correct!** response.

On page 237, we wrote a function **lettersOnlyLower** which kept the letters only from a string and converted them to lowercase. Here, we want the same function but we convert to uppercase instead. We call the function **lettersOnlyUpper**. The code is identical to **lettersOnlyLower** except that **toLowerCase** is replaced by **toUpperCase**. Our test for correctness now becomes:

>   ANSWER = lettersOnlyUpper(in.nextLine());
>   if (ANSWER.equals(CAPITAL)) System.out.printf("Correct!\n");

All the details are captured in Program P9.4 (next page).

You can use the idea of this program to write many similar ones. On the Geography theme, you can ask about mountains and heights, rivers and lengths, countries and population, countries and location, and so on. For a different application, you can use it to drill a user in English-Spanish (or any other combination of languages) vocabulary. Your questions could take the form:

>   What is the Spanish word for water?

or, if you prefer,

>   What is the English word for agua?

Better yet, let the user choose whether she is given English or Spanish words. You can ask about books and authors, songs and performers, movies and stars. As an exercise, think of five other areas in which the idea of this program can be used to quiz a user.

Program P9.4

```java
import java.io.*;
import java.util.*;
public class GeographyQuiz {
  public static void main(String[] args) throws IOException {
    FileReader in = new FileReader("quizdata.txt");
    String country = getString(in);
    while (!country.equals("")) {
      String capital = getString(in);
      askOneQuestion(country, capital);
      country = getString(in);
    }
    in.close();
  } // end main
  public static void askOneQuestion(String country, String capital) {
    Scanner in = new Scanner(System.in);
    String CAPITAL = lettersOnlyUpper(capital);
    System.out.printf("\nWhat is the capital of %s? ", country);
    String ANSWER = lettersOnlyUpper(in.nextLine());
    if (ANSWER.equals(CAPITAL)) System.out.printf("Correct!\n");
    else {
      System.out.printf("Wrong. Try again\n");
      System.out.printf("\nWhat is the capital of %s? ", country);
      ANSWER = lettersOnlyUpper(in.nextLine());
      if (ANSWER.equals(CAPITAL)) System.out.printf("Correct!\n");
      else System.out.printf("Wrong. Answer is %s\n", capital);
    }
  } // end askOneQuestion
  public static String lettersOnlyUpper(String phrase) {
    String word = "";
    for (int j = 0; j < phrase.length(); j++)
      if (Character.isLetter(phrase.charAt(j)))
        word = word + phrase.charAt(j);
    return word.toUpperCase();
  } //end lettersOnlyUpper
  // getString goes here
} //end class GeographyQuiz
```

9.8 Improving Geography quiz

The Geography quiz program P9.4 asks questions in the order that the countries appear in the data file. A more realistic program will choose a country at random. We now show how to do this.

We will use two **String** arrays, **country** and **capital**. The **boolean** array **countryUsed** would indicate if a country has already been used in a question.

Suppose we wish to cater for a maximum of 100 countries. Assuming that the symbolic constant **MaxCountries** is set to 100, we declare **country** and **capital** as:

```
String[] country = new String[MaxCountries];
String[] capital = new String[MaxCountries];
```

The next issue to decide is how the data will be supplied. We will *not* assume a fixed number of countries. We assume that the countries' data are supplied as before—2 strings per country. A sample file with 3 countries looks like this:

```
"Trinidad" "Port of Spain"
"Jamaica" "Kingston"
"Grenada" "St. George's"
```

The program will read the data, counting how many countries are read, until all data have been read or **MaxCountries** countries have been read, whichever comes first. We will code the reading of the data in a method, **getCountriesData**, which takes the arrays **country** and **capital** as arguments. The method returns the number of countries read. The method is shown in Program P9.5.

Program P9.5

```java
import java.io.*;
import java.util.*;
public class GeographyQuiz1 {
   final static int MaxCountries = 100;

   public static void main(String[] args) throws IOException {
      Scanner in = new Scanner(System.in);
      String[] country = new String[MaxCountries];
      String[] capital = new String[MaxCountries];
      int numCountries = getCountriesData(country, capital);
      int numQuestions;
      do {
         System.out.printf("\nI can ask you %d questions\n", numCountries);
         System.out.printf("How many do you want? ");
         numQuestions = in.nextInt();
      } while (numQuestions < 0 || numQuestions > numCountries);

      if (numQuestions == 0)
         System.out.printf("\nNo questions? Well, maybe next time\n");
      else {
         askQuestions(country, capital, numCountries, numQuestions);
         System.out.printf("\nThanks for playing. Until next time...\n");
      }
   } //end main
```

```java
    public static int getCountriesData(String[] country, String[] capital)
                                                throws IOException {
      FileReader in = new FileReader("quizdata.txt");
      String aCountry;
      int n = 0;
      while (!(aCountry = getString(in)).equals("")) {
        country[n] = aCountry;
        capital[n] = getString(in);
        if (++n == MaxCountries) {
          System.out.printf("\nWarning: only first %d countries used\n", n);
          in.close();
          return n; // arrays are full; do not read any more
        }
      }
      in.close();
      return n;
    } //end getCountriesData

    public static void askQuestions(String[] country, String[] capital,
                                                int numC, int numQ) {
      //numC countries, numQ questions
      boolean[] countryUsed = new boolean[numC];
      for (int j = 0; j < numC; j++) countryUsed[j] = false;
      for (int j = 1; j <= numQ; j++){
        int n = rand(numC);
        while (countryUsed[n]) n = (n + 1) % numC;
        // the country in position n is available for use
        askOneQuestion(country[n], capital[n]);
        countryUsed[n] = true;
      }
    } //end askQuestions

    public static int rand(int n) {
    // returns a random integer from 0 to n - 1
      return (int) (n * Math.random());
    } // end rand

    // insert askOneQuestion, lettersOnlyUpper and getString here
} //end class GeographyQuiz1
```

When a country and capital are read, they are stored in the respective arrays at position **n**. If the count reaches **MaxCountries**, no more data is read and the method returns.

Once the data are stored in the arrays, we must decide which questions and how many to ask. For variation, we will ask the user how many questions he wants (rather than asking him if he wants another question after each one). Of course, the number of questions must lie between 1 and the number of countries read. If the user enters 0, the program assumes he has changed his mind about playing.

If the user wants to play, the method **askQuestions** is called; this handles the asking of questions. We use a **for** loop to ask the number of questions requested. But, now, we use a function **rand** to select the next country to ask about. If there are **n** countries, the valid subscripts will range from 0 to **n - 1**. We will want **rand** to return a random number from 0 to **n - 1**. Here is **rand**:

```
public static int rand(int n) {
   // returns a random integer from 0 to n - 1
   return (int) (n * Math.random());
}
```

Math.random is a standard function which returns a random fraction between 0 (inclusive) and 1 (exclusive). Multiplying this fraction by **n** and discarding the fractional part gives us a whole number between 0 and **n - 1**.

We use the array **countryUsed** to keep track of which countries have been used in a question. It is declared as:

```
boolean[] countryUsed = new boolean[numC];
```

and the values are initialized to **false**. When **askQuestions** is called, the value supplied for **numC** (number of countries) is used to declare the size of the array.

Using **rand**, we pick a country for the next question as follows:

```
int n = rand(numC); //numC is the number of countries
while (countryUsed[n]) n = (n + 1) % numC;
// the country in position n is available for use
```

First generate a random number **n**. As long as **countryUsed[n]** is **true**, add 1 to **n**. If **n** becomes **numC**, we must reset it to 0. For example, if **numC** is 10, adding 1 to 9 should bring us back to 0. Note the statement for achieving this:

```
n = (n + 1) % numC;
```

Remember that **a** % **b** returns the remainder when **a** is divided by **b**. As an exercise, if **numC** is **50**, work out the new value of **n** when **n = 0, 25, 49**.

If a country has already been used, the program tries the next one until it finds one that has not been used. Once the country (in position **n**, say) is selected, the method **askOneQuestion** is called to quiz about that country, and **countryUsed[n]** is set to **true**. This is done with:

```
askOneQuestion(country[n], capital[n]);
countryUsed[n] = true;
```

Strings

When the requested number of questions has been asked, the program prints a goodbye message and stops.

Program P9.5 uses **askOneQuestion**, **lettersOnlyUpper** and **getString** that were used in P9.4, the original Geography quiz program. These are not shown in P9.5.

9.9 Passing a String as an argument

We have written many methods in which a **String** value is passed as an argument. We have also seen that a **String** object in Java is immutable; once created, it cannot be changed. A statement which *appears* to change a string only changes the reference to the string, not the string itself. For example, if the statement:

```
str = "Hello";
```

is followed by

```
str = "Hi";
```

then the latter creates a new string **Hi** and sets **str** to point to it. This also means that **str** is no longer pointing to **Hello**. Once we understand this, it is easy to see what happens when a **String** is passed as an argument to a method. Consider:

```
public static void changeGreeting(String s) {
    s = "Hi";
}
```

and suppose another method contains:

```
str = "Hello";
changeGreeting(str);
System.out.printf("%s\n", str);
```

Is **Hi** or **Hello** printed? Suppose **str** is allocated memory location 4545. Then this location contains an address (325, say)—the address of the string **Hello**:

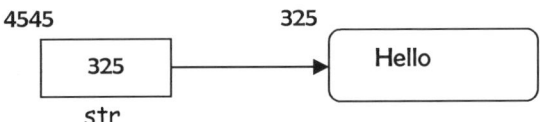

When **changeGreeting** is called, the value of **str** (i.e., 325) is copied into a temporary location (8000, say) and *this* location is passed to the method where it is known as **s**. Since the value of **s** is 325, it is actually pointing to **Hello**. The statement

```
s = "Hi";
```

creates the string **Hi** (at location 450, say) and stores 450 in location 8000 as the value of **s**:

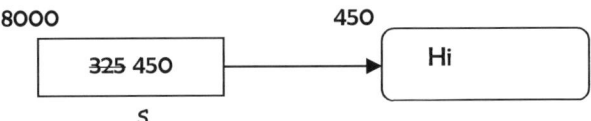

249

Observe that **s** is now pointing at **Hi** and no longer pointing at **Hello**.

Location 4545 (i.e., **str**) was never passed to the method, so the method cannot change the value of **str**. When **changeGreeting** returns, **str** still has the value 325 which still points to the string **Hello**; hence **Hello** is printed.

9.10 Searching a String array

On page 206, we showed how to search an array of strings using sequential search. On page 219, we wrote a function, **binarySearch**, to search an **int** array. We now re-write it to search an array of **String**s using a binary search.

```
public static int binarySearch(String key, String[] list, int lo, int hi) {
//search for key from list[lo] to list[hi]
//if found, return its location; otherwise, return -1
  while (lo <= hi) {
    int mid = (lo + hi) / 2;
    int cmp = key.compareTo(list[mid]);
    if (cmp == 0) return mid; // search succeeds
    if (cmp < 0) hi = mid -1;   // key is 'less than' list[mid]
    else lo = mid + 1;       // key is 'greater than' list[mid]
  }
  return -1; //lo and hi have crossed; key not found
}
```

Recall that in order to use binary search, the list must be sorted. Our function assumes it is sorted in ascending or alphabetical order. The search technique remains the same, but the coding of the function is slightly different since we cannot use the relational operators (== and <) with strings. Since we need to know if one string is equal to, or less than, another, it is best to use the **compareTo** method described on page 229.

Note that we call **compareTo** only once. The value returned (**cmp**) tells us all we need to know. If we are comparing words or names and we want the case of the letters to be ignored in the comparison, we can use **compareToIgnoreCase**.

9.11 Sorting a String array

On page 199, we wrote a function, **getSmallest**, which returns the location of the smallest number in an **int** array. We re-write the function to return the location of the 'smallest' string in a **String** array. For strings, 'smallest' refers to 'first' in alphabetical order or, to be more technical, first in the collating sequence of the underlying character set. The function is shown on the next page.

We use **compareToIgnoreCase**. If case matters, use **compareTo**.

```
public static int getSmallest(String[] list, int lo, int hi) {
  int small = lo;
  for (int j = lo + 1; j <= hi; j++)
    if (list[j].compareToIgnoreCase(list[small]) < 0) small = j;
  return small;
}
```

To swap two elements in a **String** array, use the following:

```
public static void swap(String[] list, int i, int j) {
//swap elements list[i] and list[j]
  String hold = list[i];
  list[i] = list[j];
  list[j] = hold;
}
```

With **getSmallest** and **swap**, we can write **selectionSort** to sort a **String** array.

```
public static void selectionSort(String[] list, int lo, int hi) {
//sort list[lo] to list[hi] in ascending order
  for (int j = lo; j < hi; j++) {
    int s = getSmallest(list, j, hi);
    swap(list, j, s);
  }
}
```

You can test it with:

```
String[] str = {"Such", "that", "The", "first", "six", "Numbers", "are"};
selectionSort(str, 0, str.length - 1);
```

Note, again, that since **str** is an *array*, we use **str.length** (no brackets) for its size.

We also re-write **insertionSort** from page 215 to sort a **String** array.

```
public static void insertionSort(String[] list, int n) {
//sort list[0] to list[n-1] in ascending order
  for (int j = 1; j < n; j++) {
    String key = list[j];
    int k = j - 1; //start comparing with previous item
    while (k >= 0 && key.compareToIgnoreCase(list[k]) < 0) {
      list[k + 1] = list[k];
      --k;
    }
    list[k + 1] = key;
  } //end for
} //end insertionSort
```

The only changes are in the declaration of **list** and how we compare two strings.

9.12 Example – word frequency count

Let us write a program to read an English passage and count the number of times each word appears. Output consists of an alphabetical listing of the words and their frequencies.

We can use the following outline to develop our program:

```
while there is input
  get a word
  search for word
  if word is in the table
    add 1 to its count
  else
    add word to the table
    set its count to 1
  endif
endwhile
print table
```

This is a typical "search and insert" situation. We search for the next word among the words stored so far. If the search succeeds, we need only increment its count. If the search fails, the word is put in the table and its count set to 1.

A major design decision here is how to search the table which, in turn, will depend on where and how a new word is inserted in the table. The following are two possibilities:

1. A new word is inserted in the next free position in the table. This implies that a sequential search must be used to look for an incoming word since the words would not be in any particular order. This method has the advantages of simplicity and easy insertion, but searching takes longer as more words are put in the table.

2. A new word is inserted in the table in such a way that the words are always in alphabetical order. This may entail moving words which have already been stored so that the new word may be slotted in the right place. However, since the table is in order, a binary search can be used to search for an incoming word.

   For this method, searching is faster but insertion is slower than in (1). Since, in general, searching is done more frequently than inserting, (2) might be preferable.

   Another advantage of (2) is that, at the end, the words will already be in alphabetical order and no sorting will be required. If (1) is used, the words will need to be sorted to obtain the alphabetical order.

We will write our program using the approach in (2). The complete program is shown as Program P9.6.

Program P9.6

```java
import java.io.*;
import java.util.*;
public class WordFrequency {
   final static int MaxWords = 50;
   public static void main(String[] args) throws IOException {
      String[] wordList = new String[MaxWords+1];
      int[] frequency = new int[MaxWords+1];
      FileReader in = new FileReader("passage.txt");
      PrintWriter out = new PrintWriter(new FileWriter("output.txt"));

      for (int j = 1; j <= MaxWords; j++) frequency[j] = 0;
      int numWords = 0;
      String word = getWord(in).toLowerCase();
      while (!word.equals("")) {
         int loc = binarySearch(word, wordList, 1, numWords);
         if (loc > 0) ++frequency[loc];
         else //this is a new word
            if (numWords < MaxWords) { //if table is not full
               addToList(word, wordList, frequency, -loc, numWords);
               ++numWords;
            }
            else out.printf("'%s' not added to table\n", word);
         word = getWord(in).toLowerCase();
      }
      printResults(out, wordList, frequency, numWords);
      in.close();
      out.close();
   } // end main

   public static int binarySearch(String key, String[] list, int lo, int hi) {
   //search for key from list[lo] to list[hi]; if found, return its location;
   //otherwise, return -lo if it must be inserted in location lo
      while (lo <= hi) {
         int mid = (lo + hi) / 2;
         int cmp = key.compareToIgnoreCase(list[mid]);
         if (cmp == 0) return mid;        // search succeeds
         if (cmp < 0) hi = mid -1; // key is 'less than' list[mid]
         else lo = mid + 1;        // key is 'greater than' list[mid]
      }
      return -lo; //key must be inserted in location lo
   } //end binarySearch
```

```java
        public static void addToList(String item, String[] list, int[] freq,
                                     int p, int n) {
        //adds item in position list[p]; sets freq[p] to 1
        //shifts list[n] down to list[p] to the right
           for (int j = n; j >= p; j--) {
              list[j + 1] = list[j];
              freq[j + 1] = freq[j];
           }
           list[p] = item;
           freq[p] = 1;
        } //end addToList
        public static void printResults(PrintWriter out, String[] list, int freq[],
                                        int n) {
           out.printf("\nWords      Frequency\n\n");
           for (int j = 1; j <= n; j++)
              out.printf("%-15s %2d\n", list[j], freq[j]);
        } //end printResults
        public static String getWord(FileReader in) throws IOException {
        //returns the next word found
           final int MaxLen = 255;
           int c, n = 0;
           char[] word = new char[MaxLen];
           // read over non-letters
           while (!Character.isLetter((char) (c = in.read()))) && (c != -1)) ;
           //empty while body
           if (c == -1) return ""; //no letter found
           word[n++] = (char) c;
           while (Character.isLetter(c = in.read()))
              if (n < MaxLen) word[n++] = (char) c;
           return new String(word, 0, n);
        } // end getWord

    } //end class WordFrequency
```

When P9.6 was run with the following data in **passage.txt**:

> The quick brown fox jumps over the lazy dog. Congratulations!
> If the quick brown fox jumped over the lazy dog then
> Why did the quick brown fox jump over the lazy dog?
> Why, why, why? To recuperate! Recuperate?

it produced the output shown on the next page.

Comments on Program P9.6

- For our purposes, we assume that a word begins with a letter and consists of letters only. If you wish to include other characters (like a hyphen or apostrophe), you need only change the **getWord** function.

```
Words           Frequency
brown           3
congratulations 1
did             1
dog             3
fox             3
if              1
jump            1
jumped          1
jumps           1
lazy            3
over            3
quick           3
recuperate      2
the             6
then            1
to              1
why             4
```

- **MaxWords** denotes the maximum number of distinct words catered for. For testing the program, we have used 50 for this value. The arrays are declared with a size of **MaxWords + 1**. We store words using **wordList[1]** to **wordList[MaxWords]**. We do not use **wordList[0]**. This makes it slightly more convenient to write a flexible **binarySearch** routine (see comment below).

  If the number of distinct words in the passage exceeds **MaxWords** (50, say), any words after the 50th will be read but not stored and a message to that effect will be printed. However, the count for a word already stored will be incremented if it is encountered again.

- **binarySearch** is written so that if the word is found, its location is returned. If the word is not found, and **n** is the location in which it *should* be inserted, **-n** is returned. It is for this reason that we do not use **wordList[0]**. If we did, we would not be able to easily distinguish between a word *found* in location 0 and a word that *needs to be inserted* in location 0 (since 0 = -0).

- **addToList** is given the location in which to insert a new word. Words to the right of, and including, this location, are shifted one position to make room for the new word. When a word is shifted, its frequency is shifted with it.

Exercises 9

1. Explain what happens when **String m = "Error: file not found";** is executed.

   Explain what happens when **m = m + ". Program aborted";** is executed.

2. Write a function which, given a string of arbitrary characters, returns the number of vowels in the string.

3. Write a function which, given a string of arbitrary characters, returns the number of consonants in the string.

4. Write a program to request the number of a month and print the name of the month. Write an appropriate function and prompt the user until a valid number is entered.

5. Write a function which, given a string, reverses the characters in the string and returns the new string. For example, given **"lived"**, return **"devil"**.

   Using your function, write a simplistic version of **Palindrome**. Which is more efficient, this version or Program P9.1? Why?

6. Write a program to request a month and day and print the corresponding sign of the zodiac. For example, given **Nov 14**, print **Scorpio**. Decide on an appropriate form of input.

7. Write a function **indexOf** which, given a string **s** and a character **c**, returns the *position* of the first occurrence of **c** in **s**. If **c** is not in **s**, return −1. For example, **indexOf("brother", 'r')** returns 1 but **indexOf("brother", 'a')** returns -1.

8. Write a function **substring** which, given two strings **s1** and **s2**, returns the starting position of the first occurrence of **s1** in **s2**. If **s1** is not in **s2**, return −1. For example, **substring("mom", "thermometer")** returns 4 but **substring("dad", "thermometer")** returns −1.

9. Using **charAt** and **length**, write your own version of **compareTo**. The two strings to be compared are given as arguments to the method.

   Similarly, write your own version of **compareToIgnoreCase**.

10. Give an example that shows why a character array might be more efficient than a **String**.

11. Write a program to read English words and their equivalent Spanish words into two arrays. Request the user to type several English words. For each, print the equivalent Spanish word. Choose a suitable end-of-data marker. Modify the program so that the user types Spanish words instead.

12. Write a program which works as follows: the computer 'thinks of' a number from 1 to 100 and the user tries to guess it. After each guess, the user is told whether the guess was too high or too low. If he fails to guess the number in 6 tries, he loses.

13. Write a program to test a user with arithmetic problems. The computer 'thinks of' two numbers and gives them to the user to add (subtract, multiply, divide). When the user enters his answer, the program tells him whether it is right or wrong. Decide how many attempts you want to give the user. Incorporate a scoring system.

14. Write a program to simulate 600 throws of a die and determine the number of 1s, 2s, 3s, 4s, 5s and 6s that show. Write the program (a) without using arrays and (b) using arrays.

15. One-Zero is a game which can be played among several players using a 6-sided die. On her turn, a player can throw the die as many times as she wishes. Her score for that turn is the sum of the numbers she throws *provided* she doesn't throw a 1. If she throws a 1, her score for that turn is 0. Suppose a player decides to adopt the strategy of ending her turn after 7 throws. (Of course, if she throws a 1 before the 7th throw, she must end her turn.) Write a program to play 10 turns using the above strategy. For each turn, print the score obtained. Also print the total score for the 10 turns.

   Generalize the program to request values for **NumberOfTurns** and **MaxThrowsPerTurn** and print the results as above.

16. The game of Hangman is played as follows. The computer 'thinks of' a word and the player tries to guess it. The computer displays a string of *s representing the number of letters in the word. For example, if the word is **secrets** the computer will display 7 *s, like this:

    * * * * * * *

The player must then guess a letter (**ch**, say). If **ch** is not in the word, the player is one step closer to being hanged. If **ch** is in the word, the string of *s is displayed with the letter **ch** replacing a * wherever it occurs in the word. For instance, if the player guesses **e**, the string is displayed as follows:

    * e * * e * *

This procedure is repeated until the player guesses the word or he is hanged, whichever comes first. The player gets hanged if he makes a predetermined number (7, say) of unsuccessful guesses. Each time the player makes a guess, the computer will inform him of the word obtained so far and the number of wrong guesses he can still make before being hanged. A sample run might look like this (the underlined letters are typed by the player):

    Try to guess my secret word
    Countdown to hang: 7
        * * * * * * *
    Guess a letter: s
        s * * * * * s
    Countdown to hang: 7
    Guess a letter: r
        s * * r * * s
    Countdown to hang: 7
    Guess a letter: a
    Sorry, try again
        s * * r * * s
    Countdown to hang: 6
    Guess a letter: e
        s e * r e * s
    Countdown to hang: 6
    Guess a letter: d
    Sorry, try again
        s e * r e * s
    Countdown to hang: 5
    Guess a letter: t
        s e * r e t s
    Countdown to hang: 5
    Guess a letter: c
        s e c r e t s
    Countdown to hang: 5

    You've got it!!

Write the program so that the computer chooses a word at random from a list of words stored in a file.

10 Introduction to objects

In this chapter, we will explain:

- what is a *class*, an *object*, a *field* and a *method*
- that an object variable does not hold an object but, rather, a pointer (or reference) to where the object is actually located
- the distinction between a *class* variable (also called a *static* variable) and an *instance* variable (also called a *non-static* variable)
- the distinction between a *class* method (also called a *static* method) and an *instance* method (also called a *non-static* method)
- what the access modifiers **public**, **private** and **protected** mean
- what is meant by information hiding
- how to refer to class and instance variables
- what is a *constructor* and how to write one
- what is meant by *overloading*
- what is meant by data encapsulation
- how to write *accessor* and *mutator* methods
- how to print an object's data in various ways
- why the **toString()** method is special in Java
- what happens when we assign an object variable to another
- what it means to compare one object variable with another
- how to compare the *contents* of two objects

Java is considered an *object-oriented* programming language. The designers created it such that objects become the centre of attention. Java programs create and manipulate objects in an attempt to model how the real world operates. For our purposes, an object is an entity that has a *state* and *methods* to manipulate that state. The state of an object is determined by its *attributes*.

For example, we can think of a person as an object. A person has attributes such as name, age, gender, height, colour of hair, colour of eyes, etc. Within a program, each attribute is represented by an appropriate variable; for instance, a **String** variable can represent *name*, an **int** variable can represent *age*, a **char** variable can represent *gender*, a **double** variable can represent *height*, and so on.

We normally use the term *field names* (or, simply, *fields*) to refer to these variables. Thus the *state* of an object is defined by the *values* in its *fields*. In addition, we will need methods to set and/or change the values of the fields as well as to retrieve their values. For example, if we are interested in a person's height, we would need a method to 'look into' the object and return the value of the *height* field.

A car is another common example of an object. It has attributes such as manufacturer, model, seating capacity, fuel capacity, actual fuel in the tank, mileage, type of music equipment and speed. A book object has attributes such as author, title, price, number of pages, type of binding (hardcover, paperback, spiral) and if it is in stock. A person, a car and a book are examples of concrete objects. Note, however, that an object could also represent an abstract concept such as a department in a company or a faculty in a university.

Above, we did not speak of a *specific* person. Rather, we spoke of a general category 'person' such that everyone in the category has the attributes mentioned. (Similar remarks apply to car and book.) In Java terminology, 'person' is a *class*. We think of a class as a general category (a template) from which we can create specific objects.

An object, then, is an *instance* of a class; in this example, a 'person' object would refer to a specific person. To work with two persons, we would need to create two objects from the class definition. Each object would have its own copy of the field variables (also called *instance* variables); the values of the variables in one object could be different from the values of the variables in the other object.

10.1 Defining classes and creating objects

So far, our programs have consisted of a single class. Within the class, we have written one or more methods/functions to perform some task. In other words, we have used **class** simply as the framework within which to write our programs. We will now show how to define and use a class to create (we say *instantiate*) objects.

In Java, every object belongs to some class and can only be created from the class definition. Consider the following (partial) definition of the class **Book**:

```
public class Book {
    private static double Discount = 0.25;    //class variable
    private static int MinBooks = 5;          //class variable

    private String author;      // instance variable
    private String title;       // instance variable
    private double price;       // instance variable
    private int pages;          // instance variable
    private char binding;       // instance variable
    private boolean inStock;    // instance variable
    // methods to manipulate book data go here
}
```

The class header (the first line) consists of:

- an optional *access modifier*; **public** is used in the example and will be used for most of our classes. Essentially it means that the class is available for use by any other class; it can also be *extended* to create subclasses. Other access modifiers are **abstract** and **final**; we won't deal with those in this book.
- the keyword **class**;
- a user identifier for the name of the class; **Book** is used in the example.

The braces enclose the *body* of the class. In general, the body will include the declaration of:

- static variables (class variables); there will be one copy for the entire class—all objects will share that one copy. A class variable is declared using the word **static**. If we omit the word **static**, the variable is *instance*.
- non-static variables (instance variables); each object created will have its own copy. It's the instance variables which comprise the data for an object.
- static methods (class methods); these are loaded once when the class is loaded and can be used without creating any objects. It makes no sense for a static method to access non-static variables (which belong to objects) so Java forbids it. All our methods so far have been **static**.
- non-static methods (instance methods); can be used *only* via an object created from the class. It's the non-static methods which manipulate the data (the non-static fields) in objects.

  We have used several instance methods from the **String** class. If **word** is **String** (a **String** object, to be precise) and we write **word.toLowerCase()**, we are asking that the instance method **toLowerCase** of the **String** class be applied to the **String** object, **word**. This method converts uppercase letters to lowercase in the (**String**) object used to invoke it.

  Similarly, if **in** is a **Scanner** object (created when we say **new Scanner...**), the expression **in.nextInt()** applies the instance method **nextInt** to the object **in**; here, it reads the next integer from the input stream associated with **in**.

In the example, we declare 2 class variables (**Discount** and **MinBooks**, declared with **static**) and 6 instance variables; they are instance by default (the word **static** is omitted).

Access to class and instance variables

In addition to **static**, a field can be declared using the optional access modifiers **private**, **public** or **protected**. In the **Book** class, we declared all our instance variables using **private**. The keyword **private** indicates that the variable is 'known' only inside the class and can be manipulated *directly* only by methods within the class. No method from outside the class has direct access to a **private** variable. However, as we will see shortly, we can provide **public** methods which other classes can use to set and access the values of **private** variables. This way we ensure that class data can be changed only by methods within the class.

Declaring a variable **public** means that it can be accessed directly from outside the class. Hence other classes can 'do as they please' with a **public** variable. For example, if **Discount** is declared as **public**, then any other class can access it using **Book.Discount** and change it in any way it pleases. This is not normally encouraged since a class then loses control over its data.

For the most part, we will declare a class' fields using **private**. Doing so is the first step in implementing the concept of *information hiding*, which is part of the philosophy of object-oriented programming. The idea is that users of an object must not be able to deal directly with the object's data; they should do so via the object's methods.

Declaring a variable **protected** means that it can be accessed directly from the class and any of its subclasses, as well as other classes in the same package. We will not use **protected** variables in this brief introduction.

If no access modifier is specified then the variable can be accessed directly by other classes in the same package only.

A method *within* a class can refer to *any* variable (**static** or non-**static**, **public** or **private**) in the class simply by using its name. (An exception is that a *static* method cannot access non-static variables.) If a *static* variable is known outside the class (that is, not **private**), it is referenced by qualifying the variable with the class name, as in **Book.Discount** and **Book.MinBooks**.

From outside the class, a non-private instance variable can only be referenced via the object to which it belongs; this is illustrated below. However, as indicated above, good programming practice dictates that, most of the time, our variables will be declared **private**, so the notion of direct access from outside the class does not arise.

Initializing class and instance variables

When the **Book** class is loaded, storage is immediately allocated to the class variables **Discount** and **MinBooks**; they are then assigned initial values of 0.25 and 5, respectively. The meaning behind these variables is that if 5 or more copies of a book are sold, then a 25% discount is given. Since these values apply to all books, it would be a waste of storage to store them with each book's data, hence their declaration as **static** variables. All book objects will have access to the single copy of these variables. (Note, however, that if we wanted to vary these values from book to book, then they become attributes of a specific book and would have to be declared non-static.)

When the class is first loaded, no storage is allocated to the instance (non-static) variables. At this time, we have only a specification of the instance variables, but none actually exists as yet. They will come into existence when an object is created from the class. The data for an object is determined by the instance variables. When an object is 'created', storage is allocated for all the instance variables defined in the class; each object created has its *own copy* of the instance variables. To create an object, we use the keyword **new** as in:

> Book b;
> b = new Book();

The first statement declares **b** as a variable of type **Book**. From this, we see that a class name is considered to be a type (similar to **int** or **char**) and can be used to declare variables. We say that **b** is an *object variable* of type **Book**.

The declaration of **b** does *not* create an object; it simply creates a variable whose value will eventually be a *pointer* to an object. When declared as above, its value is undefined.

The second statement finds some available memory where a **Book** object can be stored, creates the object and stores the *address* of the object in **b**. (Think of the address as the first memory location occupied by the object. If the object occupies locations 2575 to 2599, its address is 2575). We say that **b** contains a *reference* or pointer to the object. Thus the *value* of an object variable is a *memory address*, not an object. This is illustrated by:

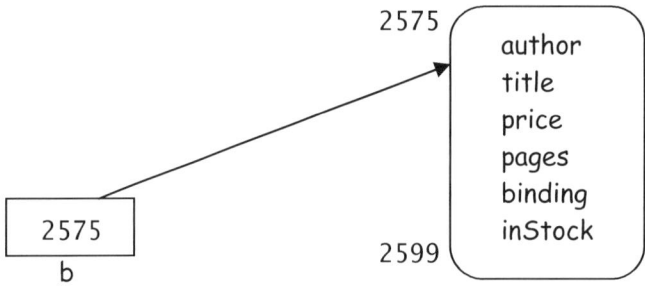

As a shortcut, we can declare **b** and create a book object in one statement, thus:

> Book b = new Book();

We have used similar constructs in many of our programs.

It is a common error to think that the **Book** variable **b** can hold a **Book** object. It cannot; it can only hold a *reference* to a **Book** object. (We are familiar with the idea that a **String** variable does not hold a string but, rather, the address of where the string is stored.) However, where the distinction (between an object and a reference to the object) does not matter, we will speak as if **b** holds a **Book** object.

Once an object **b** is created, we can refer to its instance fields like this:

> b.author   b.title   b.price
> b.pages   b.binding   b.inStock

but we can do so from outside the class only if the fields are declared **public**. We will see later how to access the fields indirectly when they are declared **private**.

When an object is created, unless we say otherwise, its instance fields are initialized as follows:

- numeric fields are set to **0**;
- character fields are set to **'\0'** (Unicode **'\u0000'**, to be precise);
- boolean fields are set to **false**;
- object fields are set to **null** (see page 281). (A variable with the value **null** means that it does not point to anything.)

In our example,

- **b.author** (of type **String**) is set to **null**; remember that **String** is an object type
- **b.title** (of type **String**) is set to **null**
- **b.price** (of type **double**) is set to **0.0**
- **b.pages** (of type **int**) is set to **0**
- **b.binding** (of type **char**) is set to **'\0'**
- **b.inStock** (of type **boolean**) is set to **false**

We could specify an initial value when we declare an instance variable. Consider

```
public class Book {
    private static double Discount = 0.25;
    private static int MinBooks = 5;

    private String author = "No Author";
    private String title;
    private double price;
    private int pages;
    private char binding = 'P'; // for paperback
    private boolean inStock = true;
}
```

When an object is created, **author**, **binding** and **inStock** will be set to the specified values while **title**, **price** and **pages** will assume the default values. A variable is given a default value only if no explicit value is assigned to it. If we create an object **b** with

```
Book b = new Book();
```

the fields will be initialized as follows:

- **author** is set to **"No Author"**;   // specified in the declaration
- **title** is set to **null**;   // default for (**String**) object type
- **price** is set to 0.0; // default for numeric type
- **pages** is set to 0;   // default for numeric type
- **binding** is set to **'P'**;   // specified in the declaration
- **inStock** is set to **true**.   // specified in the declaration

10.2 Constructors

Constructors provide more flexible ways of initializing the state of an object when it is created. In the statement

```
Book b = new Book();
```

Book() is termed a *constructor*. It is similar to a method call. But, you might say, we did not write any such method in our class definition. True, but in such cases, Java provides a *default constructor*—one with no arguments (also called a *no-arg* constructor). The default constructor is quite simplistic—it just sets the values of the instance variables to their default initial values. Later on, we could assign more meaningful values to the object's fields, as in:

```
b.author = "Noel Kalicharan";
b.title = "C by Example";
b.price = 24.95;
b.pages = 362;
b.binding = 'P';  //for paperback
b.inStock = true;  //stock is available
```

Now suppose that when we create a book object, we want Java to assign the author and title automatically. We want to be able to use statements such as:

```
Book b = new Book("Noel Kalicharan", "C by Example");
```

for creating new book objects. We can do this but we must first write an appropriate constructor, one defined with two **String** parameters. The following shows how it can be done:

```
public Book(String a, String t) {
   author = a;
   title = t;
}
```

Important points

- A constructor for a class has the *same name* as the class. Our class is called **Book**, therefore the constructor must be called **Book**. Since a constructor is meant to be used by other classes, it is declared **public**.
- A constructor can have zero or more parameters. When called, the constructor must be given the appropriate number and type of arguments. In our example, the constructor is declared with two **String** parameters, **a** and **t**. When calling the constructor, two **String** arguments must be supplied.
- The body of the constructor contains the code that would be executed when the constructor is called. Our example sets the instance variable **author** to the first argument and **title** to the second argument. In general, we can have statements other than those that set the values of instance variables. We can, for instance, validate a supplied value before assigning it to a field. We will see an example of this in the next section.

Introduction to objects

- A constructor does not have a return type, not even **void**.
- If initial values are provided for instance variables in their declaration, those values are stored *before* the constructor is called.

For example, if the class **Book** is now declared as:

```
public class Book {
   private static double Discount = 0.25;
   private static int MinBooks = 5;

   private String author = "No Author";
   private String title;
   private double price;
   private int pages;
   private char binding = 'P'; // for paperback
   private boolean inStock = true;

   public Book(String a, String t) {
      author = a;
      title = t;
   }
}
```

then the statement

```
Book b = new Book("Noel Kalicharan", "C by Example");
```

will be executed as follows:

- storage is found for a Book object and the address of the storage is stored in **b**;
- the fields are set as follows:

author is set to **"No Author"**;		// specified in the declaration
title is set to **null**;		// default for (String) object type
price is set to **0.0**;		// default for numeric type
pages is set to **0**;		// default for numeric type
binding is set to **'P'**;		// specified in the declaration
inStock is set to **true**.		// specified in the declaration

- the constructor is called with the arguments **"Noel Kalicharan"** and **"C by Example"**; this sets **author** to **"Noel Kalicharan"** and **title** to **"C by Example"**, leaving the other fields untouched. When the constructor is finished, the fields will have the following values:

author	"Noel Kalicharan"
title	"C by Example"
price	0.0
pages	0
binding	'P'
inStock	true

Overloading a constructor

Java allows us to have more than one constructor provided each has a different signature. Suppose we want to be able to use the no-arg constructor as well as the one with author and title arguments. We can include both in the class declaration like this:

```
public class Book {
   private static double Discount = 0.25;
   private static int MinBooks = 5;

   private String author = "No Author";
   private String title;
   private double price;
   private int pages;
   private char binding = 'P'; // for paperback
   private boolean inStock = true;

   public Book() { }

   public Book(String a, String t) {
      author = a;
      title = t;
   }
}
```

Observe that the body of the no-arg constructor consists of an empty block. When the statement

```
Book b = new Book();
```

is executed, the instance variables are set to their initial values (specified or default) and the constructor is executed. In this case, nothing further happens.

Be warned that when we provide a constructor, the *default* no-arg constructor is no longer available. If we want to use a no-arg constructor as well, we must write it explicitly, as in the above example. We are free, of course, to write whatever we want in the body, including nothing.

As a final example, we provide a constructor which lets us set all the fields explicitly when an object is created. Here it is:

```
public Book(String a, String t, double p, int g, char b, boolean s) {
   author = a;
   title = t;
   price = p;
   pages = g;
   binding = b;
   inStock = s;
}
```

If **b** is a variable of type **Book**, a sample call is:

    b = new Book("Noel Kalicharan", "C by Example", 24.95, 362, 'P', true);

The fields will be given the following values:

author	"Noel Kalicharan"
title	"C by Example"
price	24.95
pages	362
binding	'P'
inStock	true

10.3 Data encapsulation, accessor and mutator methods

We will use the term *user class* to denote a class whose methods need to access the fields and methods of another class.

When a class' field is declared **public**, any other class can access the field directly, by name. Consider the class:

```
public class Part {
   public static int NumParts = 0;    // class variable
   public String name;       // instance variable
   public double price;   // instance variable
}
```

Here, we define one static (class) and two instance variables as **public**. *Any* user class can access the static variable using **Part.NumParts** and can include statements such as:

    Part.NumParts = 25;

This may not be desirable. Suppose **NumParts** is meant to count the number of objects created from **Part**. Any outside class can set it to any value it pleases, so the writer of the class **Part** cannot guarantee that it will always reflect the number of objects created.

An instance variable, as always, can only be accessed via an object. When a user class creates an object **p** of type **Part**, it can use **p.price** (or **p.name**) to refer directly to the instance variable and can change it, if desired, with a simple assignment statement. There is nothing to stop the user class from setting the variable to an unreasonable value. For instance, suppose that all prices are in the range 0.00 to 99.99. A user class can contain the statement

    p.price = 199.99;

compromising the integrity of the price data.

To solve these problems, we must make the data fields **private**; we say we must *hide* the data. We then provide **public** methods for others to set and retrieve the values in the fields. Private data and public methods are the essence of *data encapsulation*. Methods which set or change a field's value are called *mutator* methods. Methods which retrieve the value in a field are called *accessor* methods.

Let us show how the two problems mentioned above can be solved. First, we redefine the fields as **private**:

```
public class Part {
   private static int NumParts = 0;    // class variable
   private String name; // instance variable
   private double price; // instance variable
}
```

Now that they are **private**, no other class has access to them. If we want **NumParts** to reflect the number of objects created from the class, we would need to increment it each time a constructor is called. We could, for example, write a no-arg constructor as follows :

```
public Part() {
  name = "NO PART";
  price = -1.0;         // we use -1 since 0 might be a valid price
  NumParts++;
}
```

Whenever a user class executes a statement such as

```
Part p = new Part();
```

a new **Part** object is created *and* 1 is added to **NumParts**. Hence the value of **NumParts** will always be the number of **Part** objects created. Further, this is the *only* way to change its value; the writer of the class **Part** can guarantee that the value of **NumParts** will always be the number of objects created.

Of course, a user class may need to know the value of **NumParts** at any given time. Since it has no access to **NumParts**, we must provide a *public accessor method* (**GetNumParts**, say – uppercase **G** for a static accessor provides a quick way to distinguish between static and non-static) which returns the value:

```
public static int GetNumParts() {
   return NumParts;
}
```

The method is declared **static** since it operates only on a **static** variable and does not need an object to be invoked. It can be called with **Part.GetNumParts()**. If **p** is a **Part** object, Java will allow you to call it with **p.GetNumParts()**. However, this tends to imply that **GetNumParts** is an instance method (called via an object and operates on instance variables), so it could be misleading. We recommend that class (static) methods be called via the class name rather than via an object from the class.

Introduction to objects

As an exercise, add a field to tbe **Book** class from the previous section which counts the number of book objects created and update the constructors to increment this field.

An improved constructor

Instead of a no-arg constructor, we could take a more realistic approach and write a constructor which lets the user assign a name and price when an object is created, as in:

```
Part af = new Part("Air Filter", 8.75);
```

We could write the constructor as:

```
public Part(String n, double p) {
   name = n;
   price = p;
   NumParts++;
}
```

This will work except that a user can still set an invalid price for a part. There is nothing to stop the user from writing:

```
Part af = new Part("Air Filter", 199.99);
```

The constructor will dutifully set **price** to the invalid value 199.99. However, we can do more in a constructor than merely assign values to variables. We can test a value and reject it, if necessary. We will take the view that if an invalid price is supplied, the object will still be created but a message will be printed and the price will be set to −1.0. Here is the new version of the constructor:

```
public Part(String n, double p) {
   name = n;
   if (p < 0.0 || p > 99.99) {
      System.out.printf("Part: %s\n", name);
      System.out.printf("Invalid price: %3.2f. Set to -1.0.\n", p);
      price = -1.0;
   }
   else price = p;
   NumParts++;
}
```

As a matter of good programming style, we should declare the price limits (0.00 and 99.99) and the 'null' price (-1.0) as class constants. We could use:

```
private static final double MinPrice = 0.0;
private static final double MaxPrice = 99.99;
private static final double NullPrice = -1.0;
```

and use these identifiers in the constructor.

269

Accessor methods

Since a user class may need to know the name or price of an item, we must provide public accessor methods for **name** and **price**. An accessor method simply returns the value in a particular field. By convention, we preface the name of these methods with the word 'get'. The methods are:

```
public String getName() {    // accessor
   return name;
}

public double getPrice() {    // accessor
   return price;
}
```

Note that the return type of an accessor is the same as the type of the field. For example, the return type of **getName** is **String** since **name** is of type **String**.

Since an accessor method returns the value in an instance field, it makes sense to call it only in relation to a specific object (since each object has its own instance fields). If **p** is an object of type **Part**, then **p.getName()** returns the value in the **name** field of **p** and **p.getPrice()** returns the value in the **price** field of **p**.

As an exercise, write accessor methods for all the fields of the **Book** class from the previous section.

These accessors are examples of non-static or instance methods (the word **static** is not used in their declaration). We can think of each object as having its own copy of the instance methods in a class. In practice, though, the methods are merely *available* to an object. There will be one copy of a method and the method will be *bound to* a specific object when the method is invoked on the object.

We can picture a **Part** object **p** as follows (assuming the object is stored at location 725):

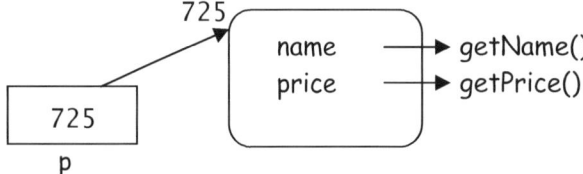

Think of the fields **name** and **price** as locked inside a box and the only way the outside world can see them is via the methods **getName** and **getPrice**.

Mutator methods

As the writer of the class, we have to decide whether we will let a user change the name or price of an object after it has been created. It is reasonable to assume that he may not want to change the name. However, prices change so we should provide a method (or methods) for changing the price. As an example, we write a *public mutator method* (**setPrice**, say) that user classes can call, as in:

```
p.setPrice(24.95);
```

to set the price of **Part** object **p** to 24.95. As before, the method will not allow an invalid price to be set. It will validate the supplied price and print an appropriate message, if necessary. Using the constants declared above, here is **setPrice**:

```
public void setPrice(double p) {
  if (p < MinPrice || p > MaxPrice) {
    System.out.printf("Part: %s\n", name);
    System.out.printf("Invalid price: %3.2f; Set to %3.2f\n", p, NullPrice);
    price = NullPrice;
  }
  else price = p;
}
```

With this addition, we can think of **Part p** like this:

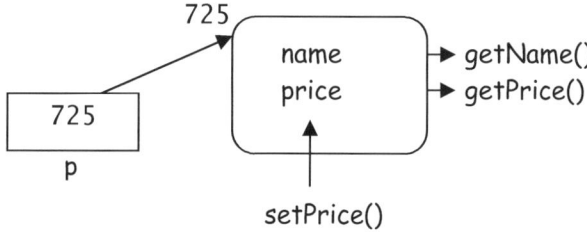

Observe the direction of the arrow for **setPrice**; a value is being sent from the outside world to the private field of the object.

Again, we emphasize the superiority of declaring a field **private** and providing mutator/accessor methods for it as opposed to declaring the field **public** and letting a user class access it directly.

We could also provide methods to increase or decrease the price by a given amount or by a given percentage. These are left as exercises.

As another exercise, write mutator methods for the **price** and **inStock** fields of the **Book** class from the previous section.

10.4 Printing an object's data

In order to verify that our parts are being given the correct values, we would need some way of printing the values in an object's fields.

Using an instance method (the preferred way)

One way of doing this is to write an instance method (**printPart**, say) which, when invoked on an object, will print *that* object's data. To print the data for **Part p**, we will write:

    p.printPart();

The methods follows:

```
public void printPart() {
   System.out.printf("\nName of part: %s\n", name);
   System.out.printf("Price: $%3.2f\n", price);
}
```

If we had created a part with:

    Part af = new Part("Air Filter", 8.75);

then **af.printPart()** would display:

```
Name of part: Air Filter
Price: $8.75
```

When **printPart** is called via **af**, the references in **printPart** to the fields **name** and **price** become references to the fields of **af**. This is illustrated below:

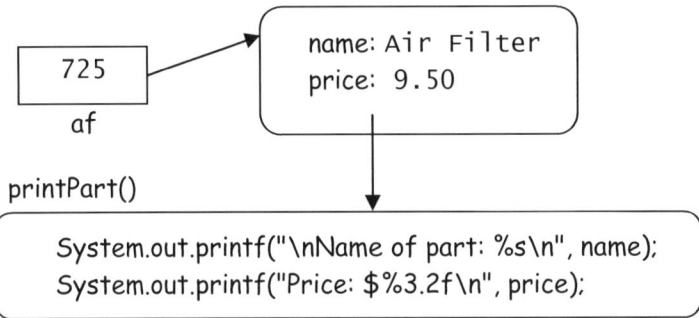

Using a static method

We could, if we wish, write **printPart** as a **static** method which will be called with **p** as an *argument* in order to print its fields. In this case, we will write:

```
public static void printPart(Part p) {
   System.out.printf("\nName of part: %s\n", p.name);
   System.out.printf("Price: $%3.2f\n", p.price);
}
```

The field names have to be qualified with the object variable **p**. Without **p**, we would have the case of a static method referring to a non-static field, which is forbidden by Java.

If **c** is a **Part** object created in a user class, we will have to use:

```
Part.printPart(c);
```

to print its fields. This is slightly more cumbersome than using the instance method, above. By comparison, we have used, for instance, **Character.isDigit(ch)**, to access the static method, **isDigit**, in the standard class, **Character**.

Using the toString() method

The **toString** method returns a **String** and is special in Java. If we use an object variable in a context where a string is needed, then Java will attempt to invoke **toString** from the class to which the object belongs. For example, if we write:

```
System.out.printf(p);
```

where **p** is a **Part** variable. Since it is not clear what it means to print an arbitrary object, Java will look for guidance in the class itself. Presumably, the class will know how to print its objects. If it provides a **toString** method, Java will use it. (If it doesn't, Java will print something generic like the name of the class and the address, in hexadecimal, of the object, for instance: **Part@72e15c32**.) In our example, we could add the following to the class **Part**:

```
public String toString() {
   return "\nName of part: " + name + "\nPrice: $" + price + "\n";
}
```

If **af** is the 'Air Filter' part, then

```
System.out.printf(af);
```

would invoke the call **af.toString()** so, in effect, the **printf** becomes

```
System.out.printf(af.toString());
```

af.toString() will return

```
"\nName of part: Air Filter \nPrice: $8.75\n"
```

and **printf** will print

```
Name of part: Air Filter
Price: $8.75
```

10.5 The class Part

Putting all the changes together, the class **Part** now looks like this:

```java
public class Part {
  // class constants
  private static final double MinPrice = 0.0;
  private static final double MaxPrice = 99.99;
  private static final double NullPrice = -1.0;
  private static int NumParts = 0;    // class variable

  private String name; // instance variable
  private double price; // instance variable

  public Part(String n, double p) {    // constructor
    name = n;
    if (p < MinPrice || p > MaxPrice) {
      System.out.printf("Part: %s\n", name);
      System.out.printf("Invalid price: %3.2f; Set to %3.2f\n", p,
                                  NullPrice);
      price = NullPrice;
    }
    else price = p;
    NumParts++;
  }

  public static int GetNumParts() {   // accessor
    return NumParts;
  }

  public String getName() {  // accessor
    return name;
  }

  public double getPrice() {   // accessor
    return price;
  }

  public void setPrice(double p) {     // mutator
    if (p < MinPrice || p > MaxPrice) {
      System.out.printf("Part: %s\n", name);
      System.out.printf("Invalid price: %3.2f; Set to %3.2f\n", p,
                                  NullPrice);
      price = NullPrice;
    }
    else price = p;
  }
```

```java
    public void printPart() {
      System.out.printf("\nName of part: %s\n", name);
      System.out.printf("Price: $%3.2f\n", price);
    }

    public String toString() {
      return "\nName of part: " + name + "\nPrice: $" + price + "\n";
    }
  } // end of class Part
```

Testing the class Part

When we write a class, we must test it to ensure that it is working as it should. For the class **Part**, we must check that the constructor is working properly, that the accessor methods return the correct values and the mutator method sets the (new) price correctly.

We must also check that the class handles invalid prices properly. In the following, we create 3 part objects (one with an invalid price) and print their name/price information. We then print the number of parts created by calling **GetNumParts**. *Before* we run the test program, we should work out the expected output so we can *predict* what a correct program should output. If the output matches our prediction, fine; if not, there is a problem which must be addressed.

```java
public class TestPart {
  // a program for testing the class Part
  public static void main(String[] args) {
    Part a, b, c; // declare 3 Part variables

    // create 3 Part objects
    a = new Part("Air Filter", 8.75);
    b = new Part("Ball Joint", 29.95);
    c = new Part("Headlamp", 199.99); // invalid price

    a.printPart(); // should print Air Filter, $8.75
    b.printPart(); // should print Ball Joint, $29.95
    c.printPart(); // should print Headlamp, $-1.0

    c.setPrice(36.99);
    c.printPart(); // should print Headlamp, $36.99

    // print the number of parts; should print 3
    System.out.printf("\nNumber of parts: %d\n", Part.GetNumParts());
  }
} // end of class Test
```

When run, the following output is produced:

```
Part: Headlamp
Invalid price: 199.99; Set to -1.0

Name of part: Air Filter
Price: $8.75

Name of part: Ball Joint
Price: $29.95

Name of part: Headlamp
Price: $-1.0

Name of part: Headlamp
Price: $36.99

Number of parts: 3
```

This is the expected output so we are assured that the class is working as it should.

How to name your Java files

Before this chapter, all our programs consisted of a single public class. Java requires you to store such a class in a file called "name of class".java. So if the class is **Palindrome**, we must call the file **Palindrome.java**.

In this example, we must store the **Part** class in a file called **Part.java** and we must store the **TestPart** class in a file called **TestPart.java**. We would compile these classes with commands such as

    javac Part.java
    javac TestPart.java

and run the test with

    java TestPart

Recall that this will execute **main** from the class **TestPart**. Note that it makes no sense to attempt

    java Part

since Java will simply complain that there is no **main** in **Part**.

We could, if we wish, put both classes in one file. However, only one of the classes can be designated as **public**. So, for example, we could leave class **Part** as it is and simply remove the word **public** from **public class TestPart**. We could now put both classes in one file which must be named **Part.java** since **Part** is the **public** class.

When we compile **Part.java** (which contains both classes) Java will produce files **Part.class** and **TestPart.class**. We can then run the test with **java TestPart**.

A final word on the **Part** class. If, for some strange reason, the class **Part** did not provide a **printPart** or a **toString** method, a user class can write its own method to print a part's fields. However, it would have to use the accessor methods of **Part** to get at an object's data since it cannot reference the **private** fields directly. The following shows how to do this:

```
public static void printPart(Part p) {
// a method in a user class
   System.out.printf("\nName of part: %s\n", p.getName());
   System.out.printf("Price: $%3.2f\n", p.getPrice());
}
```

From the user class, we can write:

```
Part af = new Part("Air Filter", 8.75);
printPart(af);
```

to produce:

```
Name of part: Air Filter
Price: $8.75
```

10.6 Working with objects

So far, we have seen how to define a class and create objects from the class using a constructor. We have also seen how to retrieve data from an object using accessor methods and how to change data in an object using mutator methods. We now look at some issues that arise in working with objects.

Assigning an object variable to another

An object variable (**p**, say) is declared using a class name (**Part**, say) as in:

```
Part p;
```

We emphasize again that **p** cannot hold an object but rather a pointer (or reference) to an object. The value of **p** is a memory address—the location at which a **Part** object is stored. Consider the following:

```
Part a = new Part("Air Filter", 8.75);
Part b = new Part("Ball Joint", 29.95);
```

Suppose the 'Air Filter' object is stored at location 3473 and the 'Ball Joint' object is stored at location 5768. Then the value of **a** would be 3473 and the value of **b** would be 5768. After the two objects have been created, we have the following situation:

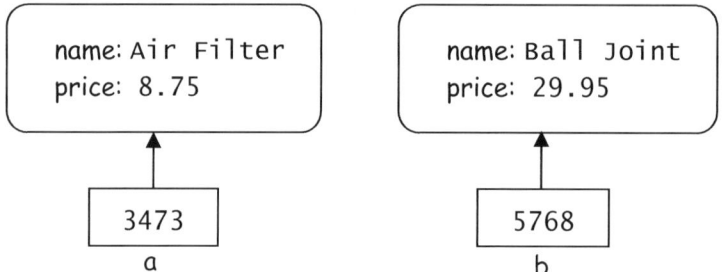

Suppose we then assign **a** to **c**:

    Part c = a; // assign 3473 to c

This assigns the value 3473 to **c**; in effect, **c** (as well as **a**) now points to the 'Air Filter' object. We can use either variable to access the object. For instance,

    c.setPrice(9.50);

sets the price of the 'Air Filter' to 9.50, and we have the following situation:

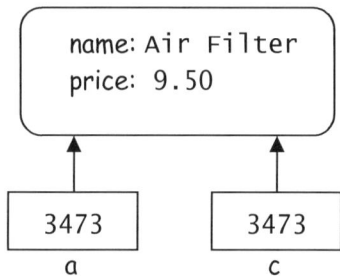

If we now retrieve the price of object **a**:

    a.getPrice(); // returns the price 9.50

the (new) price of 'Air Filter' would be returned.

If we write:

    c = b; // assign 5768 to c

c is assigned 5768 and now points to the 'Ball Joint' object. It no longer points to 'Air Filter'. We can use **b** or **c** to access 'Ball Joint' data. If we have the *address* of an object, we have all the information we need to manipulate the object.

Losing access to an object

Consider:

    Part a = new Part("Air Filter", 8.75);
    Part b = new Part("Ball Joint", 29.95);

Assume these statements create the following situation:

Introduction to objects

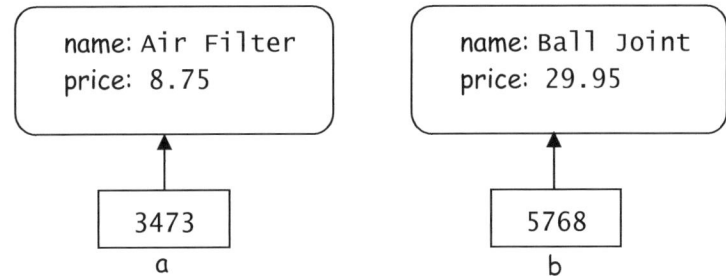

If we now execute:

    a = b;

the situation changes to:

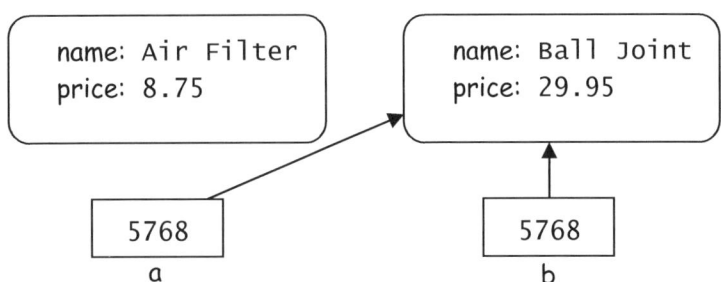

Both **a** and **b** now have the same value, 5768. They both point to the 'Ball Joint' object. In effect, when we change the value of **a**, we lose access to the 'Air Filter' object. When no variable points to an object, the object is inaccessible and cannot be used. The storage occupied by the object will be 'garbage collected' by the system and returned to the pool of available storage. This takes place automatically without any action on the part of the program.

However, if we had written:

    c = a;   // c holds 3473, address of "Air Filter"
    a = b;   // a, b hold 5768, address of "Ball Joint"

we would still have access to 'Air Filter' via **c**.

Comparing object variables

Consider:

    Part a = new Part("Air Filter", 8.75);
    Part b = new Part("Air Filter", 8.75);

Assume these statements create the following situation:

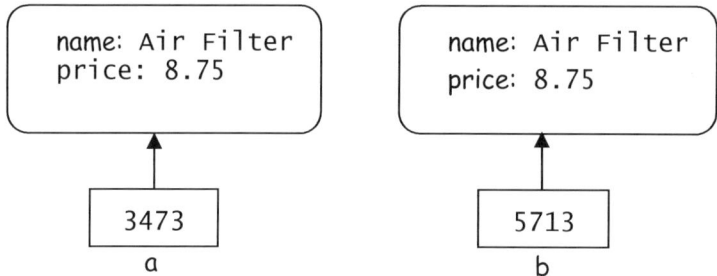

We create two identical, but separate, objects and store their addresses in **a** and **b**. It may come as a surprise that the condition

$$a == b$$

is **false**. However, if you remember that **a** and **b** contain addresses and not objects, then we are comparing the address in **a** (3473) with the address in **b** (5713). Since these are different, the comparison is **false**.

Two object variables would compare equal only when they contain the *same address* (in which case, they point to the same object). This could happen, for instance, when we assign one variable to another.

We would, of course, need to know if two *objects* are the same. That is, if **a** and **b** point to two objects, are the *contents* of these objects the same? To do this, we must write our own method which compares the fields, one by one.

Using the class **Part** as an example, we write a method **equals** which returns **true** if one object is identical to another and **false**, otherwise. The method can be used as follows to compare **Part** objects pointed to by **a** and **b**:

$$if\ (a.equals(b))\ ...$$

The method simply checks if the **name** fields and the **price** fields of the two objects are the same. Since the **name** fields are **String** objects, we call the **equals** method of the **String** class to compare them[1].

```
public boolean equals(Part p) {
   return name.equals(p.name) && (price == p.price);
}
```

In the method, the variables **name** and **price** (without being qualified) refer to the fields of the object via which the method is invoked. Thus if we had used the expression

$$a.equals(b)$$

---

[1] There is no conflict in using the same name **equals** to compare **Part**s and **String**s. If **equals** is invoked via a **Part** object, then the **equals** method from the **Part** class is used. If **equals** is invoked via a **String** object, then the **equals** method from the **String** class is used.

they refer to the fields **a.name** and **a.price**. Of course, **p.name** and **p.price** refer to the fields of the argument to **equals** (**b**, in the example). In effect, the **return** statement becomes:

> return a.name.equals(b.name) && (a.price == b.price);

Now, given the statements:

> Part a = new Part("Air Filter", 8.75);
> Part b = new Part("Air Filter", 8.75);

(a == b) is **false** (since they hold different addresses) but **a.equals(b)** is **true** (since the contents of the objects they point to are the same).

10.7 The null pointer

When an object variable is declared, as in

> Part p;

it is undefined (just like variables of the primitive types). The most common way to give **p** a value is to create a **Part** object and store its address in **p** using the **new** operator, as in

> p = new Part("Air Filter", 8.75);

Java also provides a special pointer value, the keyword **null**, which can be assigned to any object variable. We could say:

> Part p = null;

In effect, this says that **p** has a defined value, but it does not point to anything. If **p** has the value **null**, it is an error to attempt to reference an object pointed to by **p**. Put another way, if **p** is **null**, it makes no sense to talk about **p.name** or **p.price** since **p** is not pointing to anything.

If two object variables **p** and **q** are both **null**, we can compare them with == and the result will be **true**. On the other hand, if **p** points to an object and **q** is **null** then, as expected, the comparison is **false**.

Null pointers are useful when we need to initialize a list of object variables. We also use them when we are creating data structures like linked lists or binary trees and we need a special value to indicate the end of a list. These uses are beyond the scope of this book.

10.8 Passing an object as an argument

An object variable holds an address—the address of an actual object. When we use an object variable as an argument to a method, it's an address that is passed to the method. Since arguments in Java are passed 'by value', a temporary location containing the value of the variable is what is actually passed. On page 273, we met the static method **printPart** in the class **Part** for printing a part:

```
public static void printPart(Part p) {
   System.out.printf("\nName of part: %s\n", p.name);
   System.out.printf("Price: $%3.2f\n", p.price);
}
```

Suppose a user class contains the statements:

```
Part af = new Part("Air Filter", 8.75);
printPart(af);
```

and suppose the first statement assigns the address 4058, say, to **af**. When **printPart** is called, 4058 is copied to a temporary location and this location is passed to **printPart** where is becomes known as **p**, the name of the formal parameter. Since the value of **p** is 4058, in effect it has access to the original object. In this example, the method simply prints the values of the instance variables. But it could also change them, if it wanted.

Consider the following method in the class **Part** which adds **amount** to the price of a part:

```
public static void changePrice(Part p, double amount) {
   p.price += amount;
}
```

The user class can add 1.50 to the price of the 'Air Filter' with the call:

```
Part.changePrice(af, 1.50);
```

As indicated above, the parameter **p** has access to the original object. Any change made to the object pointed to by **p** is, in fact, a change to the original object.

We emphasize that the method *cannot* change the *value* of the actual argument **af** (since it has no access to it) but it *can* change the *object* pointed to by **af**.

In passing, note that we have used this example mainly for illustrative purposes. In practice, it would probably be better to write an instance method to change the price of a **Part** object.

10.9 Array of objects

In Java, a **String** is an object. Therefore, an array of **String**s is, in fact, an array of objects. However, a **String** is a special kind of object in Java and, in some ways, is treated differently from other objects. For one thing, a **String** is immutable; we cannot change its value. For another, we think of a **String** as having one field—the characters in the string— whereas a typical object will have several. For these reasons, we take a look at arrays of objects other than **String**s.

Consider the class **Part** defined on page 274. The class contains two instance variables defined as follows:

```
public class Part {
    private String name; // instance variable
    private double price; // instance variable

    // methods and static variables
}
```

It is helpful to recall what happens when we declare a **Part** variable **p** as in:

```
Part p;
```

First, remember that **p** can hold the *address* of a **Part** object, not an object itself. The declaration simply allocates storage *for* **p** but leaves it undefined. We can assign the **null** value to **p**, as in:

```
p = null;
```

or we can create a **Part** object and assign its address to **p**, as in:

```
p = new Part("Air Filter", 8.75);
```

Now consider the declaration:

```
Part[] part = new Part[5];
```

This declares an array called **part** with 5 elements. Since they are object variables, these elements are set to **null**, by default. As yet, no **Part** objects have been created. We can create objects and assign them individually to each element of **part**, as follows:

```
part[0] = new Part("Air Filter", 8.75);
part[1] = new Part("Ball Joint", 29.95);
part[2] = new Part("Headlamp", 36.99);
part[3] = new Part("Spark Plug", 5.00);
part[4] = new Part("Disc Pads", 24.95);
```

The array **part** can now be pictured as shown on the next page. Each element of **part** contains the address of the corresponding object.

Remember that, in general, each element of an array can be treated in exactly the same way as a simple variable of the array type. For instance, **part[2]** can be treated in the same way as **p**, above. And just as we can write **p.setPrice(40.00)**, we can write **part[2].setPrice(40.00)** to change the price of 'Headlamp' to **40.00**.

How do we refer to the fields of a **Part** object? As usual, it depends on whether the code is being written inside the class **Part** or outside of it. If inside, the code can access the instance variables **name** and **price** directly, for example, **part[2].name**. If outside, it must use the accessor and mutator methods to get and set the values in the fields, for example, **part[2].getName()**.

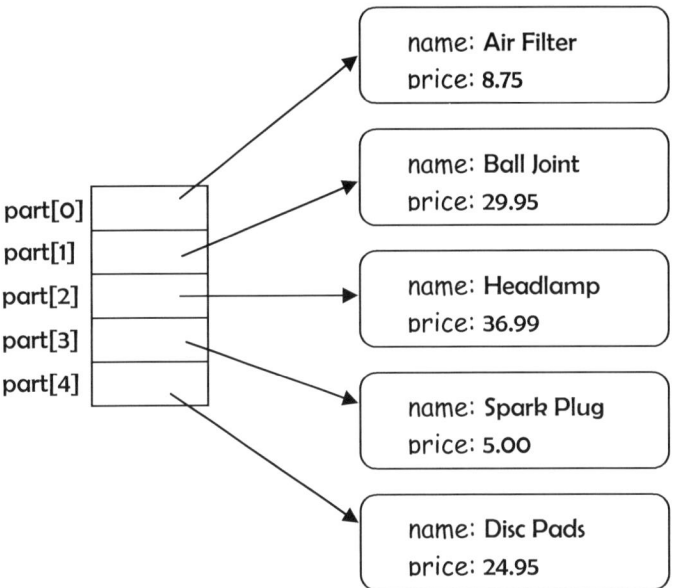

If we have to deal with hundreds of parts, it would be better to store the parts' data in a file (**parts.dat**, say) and read them into the array using a **for** or **while** loop. Suppose the above data were stored in the file like this (we write the part name as one word so it could be read with **next** from the **Scanner** class):

```
AirFilter    8.75
BallJoint   29.95
Headlamp    36.99
Spark Plug   5.00
DiscPads    24.95
```

We could set up the **part** array with the code:

```
Scanner in = new Scanner(new FileReader("parts.dat"));
Part[] part = new Part[5];
for (int j = 0; j < part.length; j++)
   part[j] = new Part(in.next(), in.nextDouble());
```

This code is much better and more flexible. To read 1000 parts, we just need to change the declaration of **part** and supply the data in the file. The above code remains unchanged. As usual, we don't *have* to fill the entire array with parts data. We can read data until some end-of-data marker (**End**, say) is reached.

If we need to print the parts' data, we could use:

```
for (int j = 0; j < part.length; j++) part[j].printPart();
```

If we want to interchange two parts in the array (for example, **part[2]** with **part[4]**), we can do it the same way we swap the values of two variables, thus:

```
Part p = part[2];
part[2] = part[4];
part[4] = p;
```

It is useful to note that the actual objects remain where they were originally stored. All we do here is exchange the addresses stored in **part[2]** and **part[4]**. In the diagram on the previous page, think of the arrows as being interchanged.

Finding the part with the lowest price

Suppose we want to find the part with the lowest price (in some sense, we want to find the 'smallest' object). Assuming we are writing this code outside the class **Part**, we can write **getLowestPrice** to return the position of the part with the lowest price as follows:

```
public static int getLowestPrice(Part[] part, int lo, int hi) {
// return the position of the part with the lowest price
// from part[lo] to part[hi], inclusive
  int small = lo;
  for (int j = lo + 1; j <= hi; j++)
    if ( part[j].getPrice() < part[small].getPrice()) small = j;
  return small;
}
```

If we were writing inside the class **Part**, we could leave the method as it is. But since we now have direct access to the instance variables, we could replace the **if** statement with:

```
if ( part[j].price < part[small].price) small = j;
```

To print the name of the part with the lowest price, we could write:

```
System.out.printf("\nPart with lowest price: %s\n",
    part[getLowestPrice(part, 0, part.length-1)].getName());
```

As an exercise, write a function to return the item with the highest price.

10.10 Searching an array of objects

In Chapters 8 and 9, we saw how to search for an item in an array of primitive types and an array of strings. We now consider how to search an array of objects (more precisely, references to objects) with more than one field. For example, suppose we had a **Person** class defined (partially) by:

```
public class Person {
  String name;
  int age;
  char gender;
  // constructors, static fields and other methods
}
```

and we wish to search an array **person** containing objects of type **Person** for one with a given name, **key**. In the case of searching for a primitive type or string, the type of the search key is the same as the type of elements in the array. In the case of searching an array of objects, the type of the search key is the same as *one of the fields* of the object.

Our search method must compare **key** with the correct field. In this example, we compare **key** with **person[j].name**. The following searches for a given name in an array of **Person**. We use **equalsIgnoreCase** so that case differences in the key and the array would not matter; **Mary** would be the same as **mary**.

```
// search for key in the first n elements of the array person;
// if found, return the position, else return -1
public static int sequentialSearch(String key, Person[] person, int n) {
   for (int j = 0; j < n; j++)
      if (key.equalsIgnoreCase(person[j].name)) return j;
   return -1;
}
```

If we want to search for someone with a given **age**, we just need to declare **key** as **int** and change the **if** statement to:

```
if (key == person[j].age) return j;
```

Note that this would return the first person it finds with the given age.

We write Program P10.1 (next page) to test this function.

The **main** method sets up an array called **person** with data for 7 persons. It then requests the user to enter names. For each name, **sequentialSearch** is called; it returns a value **n**, say. If found (**n >= 0**), the age and gender of the person is printed. If not, the message **Not found** is printed. The following is a sample run:

```
Enter names, one per line, and I'll tell you
their age and gender. To end, press Enter
Olga
36 F
Bart
Not found
bert
32 M
INGA
21 F
```

Note how we define the class **Person**. We omit the word **public** so we can put it in the same file as **SearchTest**. For variety, we use no access modifier (**public** or **private**) on the fields names—**name, age, gender**. When we do this, other classes in the same *file* can refer to the field names directly; for example, in **main**, we refer to **person[n].age** and **person[n].gender**.

Program P10.1

```java
import java.util.*;
public class SearchTest {
  public static void main(String[] args) {
    // set up an array with 7 persons
    Person[] person = new Person[7];
    person[0] = new Person("Gary", 25, 'M');
    person[1] = new Person("Inga", 21, 'F');
    person[2] = new Person("Abel", 30, 'M');
    person[3] = new Person("Olga", 36, 'F');
    person[4] = new Person("Nora", 19, 'F');
    person[5] = new Person("Mary", 27, 'F');
    person[6] = new Person("Bert", 32, 'M');

    Scanner in = new Scanner(System.in);
    String s;
    System.out.printf("Enter names, one per line, and I'll tell you\n");
    System.out.printf("their age and gender. To end, press Enter\n\n");
    while (!(s = in.nextLine()).equals("")) {
      int n = sequentialSearch(s, person, person.length);
      if (n >= 0)
        System.out.printf("%d %c\n\n", person[n].age, person[n].gender);
      else System.out.printf("Not found\n\n");
    }
  } // end of main
  // search for key in the first n elements of the array person ;
  // if found, return the position, else return -1
  public static int sequentialSearch(String key, Person[] person, int n) {
    for (int j = 0; j < n; j++)
      if (key.equalsIgnoreCase(person[j].name)) return j;
    return -1;
  } // end of sequentialSearch
} // end class SearchTest

class Person {
  String name;
  int age;
  char gender;

  Person(String n, int a, char g) {
    name = n;
    age = a;
    gender = g;
  }
} //end class Person
```

We can also use a binary search on an array of objects, provided the objects are sorted based on the field we wish to search. For example, we can binary-search the **person** array for a name provided the objects are arranged in order by name. Here is the function:

```
// search for a person with name key in the first n elements of the
// array person ; if found, return the position, else return -1
public static int binarySearch(String key, Person[] person, int n) {
    int lo = 0;
    int hi = n - 1;
    while (lo <= hi) {       // as long as more elements remain to consider
        int mid = (lo + hi) / 2;
        int cmp = key.compareToIgnoreCase(person[mid].name);
        if (cmp == 0) return mid; // search succeeds
        if (cmp < 0) hi = mid - 1;   // key is 'less than' person[mid].name
        else lo = mid + 1;       // key is 'greater than' person[mid].name
    }
    return -1;                   // key is not in the array
} // end of binarySearch
```

As an exercise, write a program similar to P10.1 to test **binarySearch**.

10.11 Sorting an array of objects

On page 251, we saw how to sort an array of strings using selection and insertion sort. To selection-sort an array of objects, we just need to change the type of **list** (and **hold** in **swap**) to the type of the object and rewrite the **if** statement in **getSmallest** to compare the appropriate field. For example, to sort an array of **Person** in ascending order by **name**, we rewrite the three routines as follows:

```
public static void selectionSort(Person[] list, int lo, int hi) {
// sort list[lo] to list[hi] using selection sort
    for (int j = lo; j <= hi; j++)
        swap(list, j, getSmallest(list, j, hi));
}

public static int getSmallest(Person[] list, int lo, int hi) {
// return the position of the 'smallest' name from list[lo] to list[hi]
    int small = lo;
    for (int j = lo + 1; j <= hi; j++)
        if (list[j].name.compareToIgnoreCase(list[small].name) < 0) small = j;
    return small;
}
```

```
public static void swap(Person[] list, int j, int k) {
// swaps list[j] with list[k]
   Person hold = list[j];
   list[j] = list[k];
   list[k] = hold;
}
```

We could sort the array **person** from Program P10.1 with the call:

selectionSort(person, 0, person.length - 1);

We could then print the array **person** with:

for (int j = 0; j < person.length; j++) person[j].printPerson();

where **printPerson** is defined in class **Person** as:

```
void printPerson() {
   System.out.printf("%s %d %c\n", name, age, gender);
}
```

For the array in P10.1, this will print:

```
Abel 30 M
Bert 32 M
Gary 25 M
Inga 21 F
Mary 27 F
Nora 19 F
Olga 36 F
```

We also re-write **insertionSort** to sort an array of **Person**:

```
public static void insertionSort(Person[] list, int lo, int hi) {
//sort list[lo] to list[hi] in ascending order by name
   for (int j = lo + 1; j <= hi; j++) {
      Person hold = list[j];
      int k = j - 1; //start comparing with previous item
      while (k >= 0 && hold.name.compareToIgnoreCase(list[k].name) < 0) {
         list[k + 1] = list[k];
         --k;
      }
      list[k + 1] = hold;
   } //end for
} //end insertionSort
```

We could sort the array **person** from Program P10.1 with the call:

insertionSort(person, 0, person.length - 1);

10.12 Word frequency count revisited

In Section 9.12, we wrote a program to count the number of times each word appears in an English passage. We used two arrays: a **String** array **wordList** to hold the words and an **int** array **frequency** to hold the counts. We now show how the same problem could be solved in a slightly different way using a class.

We can think of each word in the passage as an object with two attributes—the letters in the word and the number of times it appears. We will define a class, **WordInfo**, from which we will create 'word objects':

```
class WordInfo {
  String word;
  int freq = 0;

  WordInfo(String w, int f) {
    word = w;
    freq = f;
  }
  void incrFreq() {
    freq++;
  }
} //end class WordInfo
```

The class has two fields—**word** and **freq**. It has a constructor to initialize a **WordInfo** object to a given word and frequency. It also has a method to add 1 to the frequency of a word. If **wo** is a **WordInfo** object created, for instance, with

```
WordInfo wo = new WordInfo(aWord, 1); //String aWord
```

wo.word refers to the word and **wo.freq** is its frequency. And we can add 1 to its frequency with **wo.incrFreq()**.

Next, we define a **WordInfo** array; each element holds data for one word.

```
WordInfo[] wordTable = new WordInfo[MaxWords + 1];
```

The array is declared with a size of **MaxWords + 1**. We will store words and their frequencies using **wordTable[1]** to **wordTable[MaxWords]**. We will not use **wordTable[0]**. This will make it slightly more convenient to write a flexible **binarySearch** routine (see page 255).

The program is shown as P10.2 (next page). It is essentially the same as P9.6 on page 253. The major difference is that whereas P9.6 uses two arrays—one for the words and one for their frequencies—this one uses one array to store the words and frequencies. However, if **list[j]** is a **WordInfo** object, we must refer to the word with **list[j].word** and to its frequency with **list[j].freq**. This difference is best illustrated by comparing **printResults** in P9.6 and P10.2. In P9.6, we use

```
out.printf("%-15s %2d\n", list[j], freq[j]);
```

Program P10.2

```java
import java.io.*;
import java.util.*;
public class WordFrequency1 {
  final static int MaxWords = 50;

  public static void main(String[] args) throws IOException {
    WordInfo[] wordTable = new WordInfo[MaxWords+1];

    FileReader in = new FileReader("passage.txt");
    PrintWriter out = new PrintWriter(new FileWriter("output.txt"));

    int numWords = 0;

    String word = getWord(in).toLowerCase();
    while (!word.equals("")) {
      int loc = binarySearch(word, wordTable, 1, numWords);
      if (loc > 0) wordTable[loc].incrFreq();
      else //this is a new word
        if (numWords < MaxWords) { //if table is not full
          addToList(word, wordTable, -loc, numWords);
          ++numWords;
        }
        else out.printf("'%s' not added to table\n", word);
      word = getWord(in).toLowerCase();
    }

    printResults(out, wordTable, numWords);
    in.close();
    out.close();
  } // end main

  public static int binarySearch(String key, WordInfo[] list, int lo, int hi) {
  //search for key from list[lo] to list[hi]
  //if found, return its location; otherwise,
  //return -lo if it must be inserted in location lo
    while (lo <= hi) {
      int mid = (lo + hi) / 2;
      int cmp = key.compareToIgnoreCase(list[mid].word);
      if (cmp == 0) return mid;       // search succeeds
      if (cmp < 0) hi = mid -1; // key is 'less than' list[mid].word
      else lo = mid + 1;        // key is 'greater than' list[mid].word
    }
    return -lo; //key must be inserted in location lo
  } //end binarySearch
```

```java
    public static void addToList(String item, WordInfo[] list, int p, int n) {
    //sets list[p].word to item; sets list[p].freq to 1
    //shifts list[n] down to list[p] to the right
       for (int j = n; j >= p; j--) list[j + 1] = list[j];
       list[p] = new WordInfo(item, 1);
    } //end addToList

    public static void printResults(PrintWriter out, WordInfo[] list, int n) {
       out.printf("\nWords     Frequency\n\n");
       for (int j = 1; j <= n; j++)
          out.printf("%-15s %2d\n", list[j].word, list[j].freq);
    } //end printResults

    //getWord goes here
} //end class WordFrequency1
//the WordInfo class from page 290 goes here
```

whereas, here, we use

```
out.printf("%-15s %2d\n", list[j].word, list[j].freq);
```

In **main**, P9.6 sets the array **frequency** to 0 and adds 1 with **++frequency[loc]**. In P10.2, a word's count is set to 1 when it is first met using **new WordInfo(item, 1)** in **addToList**. And its frequency is incremented with **wordTable[loc].incrFreq()**.

In binarySearch, P9.6 uses key.compareToIgnoreCase(list[mid]). But P10.2 uses key.compareToIgnoreCase(list[mid].word). Everything else remains the same.

In **addToList**, P9.6 requires a **String** array and an **int** array as arguments. P10.2 requires just the **WordInfo** array. When P9.6 moves a word, it must also move its frequency. P10.2 just needs to move the **WordInfo** object; the word and its frequency move together.

Exercises 10

1. What is meant by the *state* of an object? What determines the state of an object?
2. Distinguish between a class and an object.
3. Distinguish between a class variable and an instance variable.
4. Distinguish between a class method and an instance method.
5. Distinguish between a public variable and a private variable.
6. Explain what happens when the statement **String S = new String("Hi")** is executed.
7. To what values are instance fields initialized when an object is created?
8. What is a *no-arg* constructor? How does it become available to a class?
9. You have written a constructor for a class. What do you need to do to use the *no-arg* constructor?
10. What is meant by the term *data encapsulation*?

11. What are *accessor* and *mutator* methods?
12. "An object variable does not hold an object". Explain.
13. Explain why the concept of "private data/public methods" is important in object-oriented programming.
14. Explain the role of the **toString()** method in Java.
15. A bookseller needs to store information about books. For each book, he wants to store the author, title, price and quantity in stock. He also needs to know, at any time, how many book objects have been created. Write Java code for the class **Book** based on the following:
    - Write a no-arg constructor which sets the author to "No Author", title to "No Title", price to 0 and quantity in stock to 0.
    - Write a constructor which, given four arguments—author, title, price and quantity—creates a **Book** object with the given values. The price must be at least $5.00 and the quantity cannot be negative. If any of these conditions is violated, the price and quantity are both set to 0.
    - Write accessor methods for the **author** and **price** fields.
    - Write a method which sets the price of a book to a given value. If the given price is not at least $5.00, the price should remain unchanged.
    - Write a method to reduce the quantity in stock by a given amount. If doing so makes the quantity negative, print a message and leave the quantity unchanged.
    - Write an instance method which prints the data for a book, one field per line.
    - Write a **toString()** method which returns a string which, if printed, will print the data for a book, one field per line.
    - Write an **equals** method which returns **true** if the *contents* of two **Book** objects are the same and **false**, otherwise.
    - Write a **Test** class which creates 3 **Book** objects of your choice, prints their data and the number of **Book** objects created.
16. Solve the voting problem of Section 8.8 using objects. Print the results in alphabetical order by candidate name. Also print the results in descending order by candidate score.
17. Solve problem 23 on page 224 using objects.
18. Write a program to read English words and their equivalent Spanish words into an object array. Request the user to type several English words. For each, print the equivalent Spanish word. Choose a suitable end-of-data marker. Search for the typed words using binary search.
19. A date consists of day, month and year. Write a class to create date objects and manipulate dates. For example, write a function which, given two dates, **d1** and **d2**, returns -1 if **d1** comes before **d2**, 0 if **d1** is the same as **d2** and 1 if **d1** comes after **d2**. Also, write a function which returns the number of days that **d2** is ahead of **d1**. If **d2** comes before **d1**, return a negative value.
20. A time in 24-hour clock format is represented by two numbers: e.g. 16 45 means the time 16:45, that is 4:45 p.m. Using an object to represent a time, write a function which given two time objects, **t1** and **t2**, returns the number of minutes from **t1** to **t2**. For example, if the two given times are 16 45 and 23 25 your function should return 400.

Appendix A - Keywords in Java

The following is a list of Java keywords. You may not use any of these as your own variable. Keywords are always written in lowercase.

abstract	**assert**	**boolean**	**break**
byte	**case**	**catch**	**char**
class	**const**	**continue**	**default**
do	**double**	**else**	**enum**
extends	**final**	**finally**	**float**
for	**goto**	**if**	**implements**
import	**instanceof**	**int**	**interface**
long	**native**	**new**	**package**
private	**protected**	**public**	**return**
short	**static**	**strictfp**	**super**
switch	**synchronized**	**this**	**throw**
throws	**transient**	**try**	**void**
volatile	**while**		

Appendix B - The ASCII character set

The ASCII character set

The following are the character codes used in the ASCII character set. Codes 0 to 31, and 127, are used for control characters. Some common ones are:

```
 0  NULL
 8  backspace (BS)
10  line feed (LF)
12  form feed (FF)
13  carriage return (CR)
```

The characters from codes 32 to 127 are:

Dec	Binary	Char	Dec	Binary	Char	Dec	Binary	Char
32	0100000	space	64	1000000	@	96	1100000	`
33	0100001	!	65	1000001	A	97	1100001	a
34	0100010	"	66	1000010	B	98	1100010	b
35	0100011	#	67	1000011	C	99	1100011	c
36	0100100	$	68	1000100	D	100	1100100	d
37	0100101	%	69	1000101	E	101	1100101	e
38	0100110	&	70	1000110	F	102	1100110	f
39	0100111	'	71	1000111	G	103	1100111	g
40	0101000	(	72	1001000	H	104	1101000	h
41	0101001	)	73	1001001	I	105	1101001	i
42	0101010	*	74	1001010	J	106	1101010	j
43	0101011	+	75	1001011	K	107	1101011	k
44	0101100	,	76	1001100	L	108	1101100	l
45	0101101	-	77	1001101	M	109	1101101	m
46	0101110	.	78	1001110	N	110	1101110	n
47	0101111	/	79	1001111	O	111	1101111	o
48	0110000	0	80	1010000	P	112	1110000	p
49	0110001	1	81	1010001	Q	113	1110001	q
50	0110010	2	82	1010010	R	114	1110010	r
51	0110011	3	83	1010011	S	115	1110011	s
52	0110100	4	84	1010100	T	116	1110100	t
53	0110101	5	85	1010101	U	117	1110101	u
54	0110110	6	86	1010110	V	118	1110110	v
55	0110111	7	87	1010111	W	119	1110111	w
56	0111000	8	88	1011000	X	120	1111000	x
57	0111001	9	89	1011001	Y	121	1111001	y
58	0111010	:	90	1011010	Z	122	1111010	z
59	0111011	;	91	1011011	[	123	1111011	{
60	0111100	<	92	1011100	\	124	1111100	|
61	0111101	=	93	1011101	]	125	1111101	}
62	0111110	>	94	1011110	^	126	1111110	~
63	0111111	?	95	1011111	_	127	1111111	**DEL**

Appendix C - Representation of integers

Conversion of decimal numbers to binary

We know from ordinary arithmetic that the decimal (base 10) number 356 stands for 6 ones, 5 tens and 3 hundreds. As we go left, the value of each digit is increased by 10; we say the number is written in base 10. Also, to *write* a number in base 10, we must use the digits 0 to 9 (1 less than the base).

Similarly, to write a number in binary (base 2), we must use the digits 0 and 1. And, as we go left, the value of each digit is increased by 2. For example, the value of the binary number 10011 is given by (reading from the right)

1 one, 1 two, 0 fours, 0 eights and 1 sixteen
i.e. $1 + 2 + 0 + 0 + 16 = 19$

As another example, consider the binary number 110101. We can work out the decimal equivalent using:

Binary digit	1	1	0	1	0	1
Value	32	16	8	4	2	1

Adding the values where the binary digits are 1's gives us

$32 + 16 + 4 + 1 = 53$

Thus, the decimal equivalent of 110101 is 53.

How do we do the reverse? Given the decimal number, 43, say, what is the binary equivalent?

One method is to write 43 as a sum of powers of 2 (1, 2, 4, 8, etc.), thus:

$43 = 32 + 8 + 2 + 1$

So 43 consists of: 1 one, 1 two, 0 fours, 1 eight, 0 sixteens and 1 thirty-two. Hence the binary equivalent of 43 is 101011.

Note that we must be careful to put a 0 in those positions where a power of 2 is absent. In this example, these are the positions corresponding to 4 and 16.

Another method is to perform repeated divisions by 2 and save the remainders. The remainders, in order, form the binary equivalent from *right to left*. For example,

43/2	=	21	remainder 1
21/2	=	10	remainder 1
10/2	=	5	remainder 0
5/2	=	2	remainder 1
2/2	=	1	remainder 0
1/2	=	0	remainder 1

The remainders, from top to bottom, form the binary equivalent from right to left, thus: **101011**.

Representation of integers

An integer is a whole number—positive, negative or zero—for example, 25, -16, 0, 32767, -1. We have just seen how to convert a positive integer from decimal to binary. Also, the bigger the number, the more bits we need to represent it. For instance, we needed 5 bits for **19** but 6 bits for **43**.

A computer uses a fixed number of *bits* (short for binary digits) for storing integers. So we use terms such as 8-bit integers, 16-bit integers and 32-bit integers. Whatever the size, the principles remain the same; the only difference is that with more bits we can store a wider range of numbers. In order to keep things simple, we will consider 4-bit integers. The problem, therefore, is:

> Using 4 bits, how can we store positive and negative integers?

The most common method for storing integers on a computer is called *two's complement*. Before we look at this method, let us say what is meant by *one's complement*.

The one's complement of a binary number is obtained by changing 1's to 0's and 0's to 1's (this is called *inverting the bits*). For example, the 4-bit one's complement of **0110** is **1001**.

Note that if we were asked for the 4-bit one's complement of **11**, we would need to write **11** as **0011** and *then* invert the bits, giving **1100**.

Also note that it is *wrong* to simply say "the one's complement of **011**"; we *must* specify how many bits are involved by saying, for instance, "the 4-bit one's complement of **011**". As a matter of interest, observe that:

- the 3-bit one's complement of **011** is **100**, and
- the 4-bit one's complement of **011** is **1100**.

Two's complement

The two's complement of a binary number is obtained by adding **1** to its one's complement. Above, we saw that the 4-bit one's complement of **0110** is **1001**. Therefore, the 4-bit two's complement of **0110** is:

$$\begin{array}{r} 1001\ + \\ \underline{1} \\ 1010 \end{array}$$

As another example, the 4-bit two's complement of **011** is **1100 + 1 = 1101**.

Suppose we want to store integers on a computer using 4 bits. With 4 bits, we can have 16 different *bit patterns*—from **0000** to **1111**. Therefore, we can represent

16 different integers using 4 bits. We just need to decide which integer to represent by which bit pattern.

Of the 16 bit patterns, 8 begin with 0 and 8 begin with 1. We will let those which begin with 0 represent the equivalent positive integer; for example, 0101 will represent +5. The full list is:

```
0000    represents    0
0001    represents    1
0010    represents    2
0011    represents    3
0100    represents    4
0101    represents    5
0110    represents    6
0111    represents    7
```

Note that the largest positive integer we can represent using 4 bits is 7. In general, the largest positive integer we can represent using n bits is $2^{n-1} - 1$.

Next, we need to decide which negative integers to represent by the bit patterns beginning with 1. In *two's complement representation*, we represent a negative integer by the two's complement of the bit pattern representing the corresponding positive integer. For example, to represent -5, we take the bit pattern for +5, that is, 0101, and find the two's complement, that is, 1011. So -5 is represented by 1011. Using this procedure, we find that:

```
-1    is represented by    1111
-2    is represented by    1110
-3    is represented by    1101
-4    is represented by    1100
-5    is represented by    1011
-6    is represented by    1010
-7    is represented by    1001
```

There is still one bit pattern, 1000, which has not been used. Since the 4-bit two's complement of 1000 is, indeed, 1000, we can let 1000 represent either +8 or -8. But since, in all other cases, positive numbers begin with 0 and negative numbers begin with 1, we let 1000 represent -8.

Hence, using two's complement, the largest negative number we can represent is 1 more than the largest positive number. In general, the *range* of integers we can store with n bits, using two's complement, is

$$-2^{n-1} \text{ to } +2^{n-1} - 1$$

For example, using 16 bits, the range of integers we can store is

$$-2^{15} \text{ to } +2^{15} - 1, \text{ that is, } -32768 \text{ to } +32767$$

Appendix D – How to get a Java compiler

Java is a programming language originally developed by Sun Microsystems and released in 1995. For everything Java, you can go to

http://java.sun.com

For the latest version of the compiler, click on the link **Java SE** (Standard Edition) under **Popular Downloads** on the right side of the page.

On the next page, click on **Get the JDK download** to get the latest release. (If you are interested in previous releases, click on **Previous Releases**.)

Next, select the **Accept** radio button to accept the license agreement.

Finally, choose the version for your platform (Windows, Unix, etc.). For example, if you are using Windows, you can choose the first option **Windows Offline Installation** to download the compiler kit to your computer.

Once downloaded, double-click on the file to install the Java Development Kit.

Another popular resource is "The GNU Compiler for the Java Programming Language". The homepage is at

http://gcc.gnu.org/java

For other Java resources, you may want to look at

http://www.thefreecountry.com/compilers/java.shtml

Index

abundant number 176
access modifier 260
accessor 267
    methods 270
account number, string 52
address 6, 10
aesthetics 123
algorithm 4
    development 6
    program for 6
alphabet 24
alphabetic character 12
and, && 69
argument 155
    array as 195
arithmetic operators 31
array 184
    declaration 185
    largest in 197
    of objects 282
    search 204
    smallest in 199
    storing values 187
    subscript error 186
    variable 184
ASCII 25
assembler 2
assembly language 2
assignment, double to float 38
    float to double 38
    operator 101
    statement 20, 46
    object variable 277
attribute 258
average 99, 107
average and differences from 190

batch mode 106
binary search 217
    object array 287
block 96
block style 73
boolean 29
    data type 12, 43
Boolean expressions 67
Boole, George 43
bug 81
byte 29
bytecode 8
calculating pay 78, 175

cast 134
Celsius 127
char 29
character 12
    alphabetic 12
    arrays vs strings 236
    constant 12, 133
    count 142
    data type 12
    digit 12
    function isDigit 177
    function isLetter 178
    function isLowerCase 178
    function isUpperCase 177
    in expressions 134
    lowercase 12
    numeric 12
    read and print 135
    read from file 145
    compare 144
    set 24
    special 12
    test for digit 151
    uppercase 12
    value 133
    write to file 147
    vs numbers 150
charAt() 229
char data type 42
children's game 225
classifying a triangle 87
class method 260
    variable 260
closing files 110
COBOL 2
combinations 172
comment 8, 19
compare characters 144
    object variables 279
    strings 115
compareTo() 229
compareToIgnoreCase() 230
compiler 3, 8
compiling a program 8
compound statement 96
concatenate 45
condition 68, 70
    compound 68
    simple 68

Index

constant, boolean 12
   character 12
constant floating point 35
   integer 12
   real 12
   string 12
constructor 264
   default 264
   no-arg 264
   overloading 266
control character 25, 42
convert characters to integer 150
copy file 147
counting 98
   characters 142
crash 9, 54
creating objects 259

data 5
   encapsulation 267
   pointer 56
data type, character 12
   floating-point 11
   integer 11
   numeric 12
   real 11
   string 12
debug 9, 81
declaration 8
declare variables 31
decrement operator, -- 100
defensive programming 100, 127, 192
deficient number 176
defining classes 259
desk checking 6
digit character 12
digit test 151
diskette 107, 111
documenting a program 9
double 29, 35
   printing 36
double/float to integer 41
do..while statement 235
dry running 6

Easter Sunday 90
echo input 147
endfor 117
end-of-data value 92
English-Spanish vocabulary 244
equals 115, 228
equalsIgnoreCase() 229
equilateral triangle 87
Eratosthenes 224

error, execution 100
   run-time 100
escape sequence 18, 43
Euclid's algorithm 96
exact divisors, sum of 175
exception, throw 108
executing a program 10
execution error 100
expression, relational 67
   floating-point 38

factorial 167
Fahrenheit 127
field name 258
field width, integer 33
file, closing 110
   input 106
   of characters 106
   output 110
   path 107, 110
   reading from 106
FileReader 106, 146
float 29, 35
floating-point constant 35
   data type 11
   expressions 38
   printing 36
flush buffer 112
for, body of 117
   construct 117
   control part 118
   expressive power 129
   final value 117
   initial value 117
   loop variable 117
   statement 119
format specification 18, 48
   string 18
FORTRAN 2
function 154
   header 159
   self-contained 181

GCD 96
Geography quiz program 243
getInt() 180
getString() 240
Gitanjali 16
greatest common divisor 96

Hangman 257
HCF 165
   Euclid's algorithm 96
hexadecimal constant 30

highest common factor 96, 165
high-level language 2

identifier 28
if construct 70
    statement 71
if...else construct 76
immutable string 227
import java.io.* 108
import java.util.* 53
increment operator, ++ 100
indent 72
initialize class variable 261
    instance variable 261
input instructions 4
    stream 53
insert in place 216
insertion sort 211
instance method 156, 260
    variable 260
instruction code 2
int 29
    declaration 21
integer constant 12
    data type 11
    expressions 31
    to double/float 40
    types 30
interactive mode 106
invalid numeric format 55
isDigit() 177
isLetter() 178
isLowerCase() 178
isosceles triangle 87
isUpperCase() 177

job charge function 174

keeping a count 98
keyword 27

largest character 145
    finding 102
    in array 197

LCM 167
left-justify 33
length() 229
letter frequency count 192
lettersOnlyLower() 237
lettersOnlyUpper() 244
local variable 169, 170, 181
logical operator 68
logic error 9
long 29
lowercase character 12

lowercase to uppercase 135
low-level language 2

machine code 8
    language 2
MacOS 137
magic numbers 83
main 13
maintaining a program 10
maintenance programmer 10
manifest constant 82
Math.random() 248
max() 159
median 224
memory 10
    address 262
    locations 5
merging ordered lists 220
method 13, 154
    body 155
    definition 155
    header 155, 157
    how it gets data 157
    invoking 155
mixed expressions 39
mode 224
multiple-choice 224
multiplication tables 123
mutator 267
    methods 271

named constant 82
name of day 234
naming Java files 276
newline 16, 137
nextInt() 52
nextLine() 57
next(), read string 58
no-arg constructor 264
not, ! 69
null pointer 281
numeric character 12
    data type 11
object 259
    array 282
    as argument 281
    assignment 277
    variable 262
    variables, compare 279
object code 8
object-oriented language 258
octal constant 30
One-Zero game 256
operator, assignment 101

decrement -- 100
increment ++ 100
logical 68
relational 67
precedence 32
or, || 69
output 7
   design 7
   instructions 5
   to a file 110
overloading 162
   a constructor 266

palindrome 230
   better 232
palindromic numbers 223
parameter 157
Part class 274
pass by value 156
path to file 107
payroll program 112
perfect number 176
playing cards 183
precedence of operators 32
primary storage 10
prime numbers 183, 224
primitive data type 29
printable character 42
printf 16, 47
printing characters 136
print object data 272
print the day 163
PrintWriter 110
private 260
problem, algorithm for 4
   analysis 4
   definition 3
problem-oriented language 2
processing instructions 5
program 1, 7
   body 13
   documenting 9
   executing 10
   header 13
   layout 15
   maintaining 10
   running 11, 15
   testing 81
programming language 7
protected 260
pseudocode 72, 118
public 13, 260
Rabindranath Tagore 16

rand 248
random number 248
read 7
   an integer 180
   characters vs numbers 150
   data from a file 106
reading a string with next() 113
   characters 135
   data, double 55
   data, float 55
   strings 57
read string, next() 58
   nextLine() 57
real constant 12
   data type 11
reference 262
relational expression 67
   operator 67
remainder operator, % 32
repetition logic 91
reserved word 27
right angled triangle 88
right-justify 33
rounding 36
running a program 9, 11, 15
run-time error 100, 108

scalene triangle 87
Scanner class 53, 106
scientific notation 35
searching an array 204, 217
   String array 250
   object array 285
selection logic 67
   sort 207
semicolon 78
sentinel value 92
sequence logic 51
sequential search 204
short 29
side-effect 100
Sieve of Eratosthenes 224
signature of a method 162
simple variable 184
skipLines() 155
smallest, finding 104
   in array 199
solving a problem on a computer 3
sorting an array 207, 211
   String array 250
   object array 287
source code 8
   program 8

spacing 26
Spanish-English vocabulary 244
special character 12
standard input 53, 106
    output 14, 106
state 258
statement, assignment 20
static method 156
string 44
String, as argument 248
    class 226
    methods 228
string constant 12, 44
    data type 11
    reading 57
strings 226
    comparing 115
    creating 227
    vs character arrays 236
subscript 184, 186
sum, finding 93
    of exact divisors 175
    of numbers 91
    of two lengths 73
Sun Microsystems 7
SuperMarbles 131
symbolic constant 29, 82
syntax error 8, 24
    rule 7, 24
System.in 53
System.in.read() 136
System.out 112
System.out.print() 14, 17
System.out.printf() 14

System.out.println() 14, 17

technical documentation 10
temperature conversion 127
test data 81
testing a program 81
text file 106
then part 70
throw an exception 108
throws IOException 109
token 24
toString() 273
triangle, equilateral 87
    isosceles 87
    right-angled 88
    scalene 87

undefined error 47
Unicode 25
Unix 137
uppercase character 12
uppercase to lowercase 135
user documentation 10
user-friendly 127

validating data 126
valid program 47
variable 5, 13, 20
    printing 18
voting problem 200

while 96
    construct 91
whitespace 55
Windows 137
word-frequency count 252, 290

Made in the USA
San Bernardino, CA
27 February 2015